In the Midst of Paradise

Pathways to Hope, Health and Happiness

On a Sustainable Earth

RANDY A. SILTANEN, MD

ISBN: 978-0-578-65617-5

Disclaimer: The ideas presented in this book are general in nature and are not intended for use as individualized medical or financial advice. Please always consult your healthcare professional or financial advisor for personal advice.

Sections of this book are adapted from *In the Midst of Heaven,* 2015.

Cover art: The Red Vineyard, by Vincent Van Gogh

To Christian, Laura Jane, and Elias

I have attempted to remove some of the small stones on the trail I have walked before you, but mostly I will point out the larger obstacles I have stumbled on, and let you make your own way. My father once told me you build the child for the trail, not the trail for the child. I think most parents want their children to deftly traverse their own paths. I hope that some of these words will help you enjoy a life well-lived. The world is better, because of you.

Randy A. Siltanen

"There are two ways to live: you can live as if nothing is a miracle;

or you can live as if everything is a miracle."

- Albert Einstein

Randy A. Siltanen

Acknowledgments

My oldest son and I were once talking about the importance of collaboration. We imagined a scenario where we were somehow transported back in time, a couple hundred years or so ago. Although I am a physician and he is an engineer, we would have difficulty teaching our ancestors how to develop a vaccine or design a jet plane.

Each individual adds a small discovery and, bit by bit, a major invention is born of the work of a thousand men and women. We often only remember the names of a select few – like Wilbur and Orville Wright, who refined and added to the works of others before briefly soaring into the sky.

In the pages to follow, I have borrowed from the minds of many fascinating people; some well-known, and some not. Some of these individuals I have met in person, and others I have known only through their books, lectures, or creative works of art. It is perhaps appropriate to liken me to a museum curator, one who displays in this book the handiwork of a very diverse group of talented artists and scholars. I have synthesized an anthology of their myriad words, thoughts, and actions, and integrated them with my own; hoping to illuminate pathways to sustainable health and happiness for the individual, the collective, and the Earth itself – person, people, and planet.

I greatly appreciate the many outstanding physicians who, through advice and example, have helped me to become a better doctor and person. There are too many names to list individually, but special thanks go to Phil Rose and Erik Stowell.

Mom and Dad, Rick, Robin, Sandy, and Robert: I am grateful for your constant love.

Christian, Laura Jane, and Elias: It is my great privilege to be your father and your friend. You are my inspiration.

I continue to learn from my lovely wife Diana; particularly as I observe her efforts as a nurse and community member. Diana unfailingly offers kindness and a receptive ear to her patients; and to all who suffer the ravages of disease, death, and dying. I love you Di.

To every author of every book, study, essay, and poem that I have read: I appreciate your efforts to crystalize information and ideas into beautiful passages that educate and inspire.

My heartfelt thanks to all.

Contents

Part I: Person

Optimizing Personal Health and Happiness

SECTION ONE: Building a Healthy Body

SECTION TWO: Mental Well-Being and Happiness

Part II: People

Health and Happiness for All Earth Citizens

Part III: Planet

Sustaining a Healthy and Happy Earth

Prologue

NEAR MY HOME is a trail I sometimes walk. An adjacent stream tumbles down a granite mountainside, weaving and whispering its way through a mixed evergreen forest. Along the way it cascades into a succession of small pools, each yielding its own inimitable verse; a song of water falling upon water. It is a place of extraordinary beauty.

In these mountains I reflect on my life as a citizen of our planet. I think of the many talents of humankind – brilliant scientific discoveries, feats of athletic excellence, and magnificent works of art. I contemplate humanity's place in a world where elegant snow leopards grace Himalayan hillsides, and giraffes march across an African savannah. I am awestruck by the enormity of this existence, and the profound beauty and diversity of life on Earth.

In this place of quiet I feel the intricate connectedness of our planet and its creatures. I recognize that the wellness of the individual is inseparably entwined with the wellness of the Earth and all its innumerable inhabitants – past, present, and future.

I have found that this complexity is beautiful. From the interactions of minute subatomic particles to the expansile properties of giant galaxies into limitless space, the immense scope and scale of our universe is astonishing. Between these margins of our existence resides an infinity of elaborate pathways, within and amongst every life form and ecosystem of the universe – a symphony of elegant complexities nested within systems of ever-greater complexities.

It is in this impossible immensity, this wild menagerie of the cosmos, that we create our human experience.

Randy A. Siltanen

ONE

A Letter from Dad

FIRST, KNOW THAT you are much loved. Mom and I will always be with you, until we breathe our last breath – and still after that, in some way or form that I have yet to understand.

You are capable of doing just about whatever you put your mind to; but please never feel compelled to reach for a goal that does not interest you. What matters most is that you are a happy person who creates happiness for others.

Sometimes in our lives we may feel that we are in suspended animation – uncertain of *who* we are, *why* we are, and *where* we are going. This is normal. To move forward, we must find a core foundation of who and why we are. The rest of the details of life will fill in on their own; eventually taking us to where we are going.

I think there are really just three major components to living a happy and meaningful life. They are each of equal importance. Here they are: Have fun. Have hope. Have compassion.

Have Fun:

I believe that the meaning of life is Happiness, and the purpose of life is to find and create it – for yourself, and for all others, too.

That's it. That's the meaning and purpose of life. Happiness. Have fun with everything you do – even if it is just studying for a midterm exam with your friends or doing a project at work. Find joyful moments in every day; creating happiness for yourself and all other

Earth inhabitants. Creating happiness for others creates happiness of self.

Have hope:

Have hope in something that is greater than yourself. Submit to Providence. Meditate, or pray. Offer up your tears and your fears – and then express gratitude. You may wish to choose a specific faith or religion, if that is where your heart leads you. If today you are uncertain, consider simply embracing a greater Presence or noble ideal.

Have compassion:

Show care and concern for yourself, all other humans, and all creatures of our Earth – present and future.

Forgive yourself for not being perfect. Please do this. No person has ever been perfect.

Love and give to others. Remember the saying of theologian and writer Henri Nouwen, "My brother's victory is my victory." Love deeply; love broadly.

Really look around and appreciate the absolute magnificence of our blue planet. Protect all of its creatures. Tread softly. You are in the midst of paradise.

Do not compare yourself to others. Comparison is the thief of joy. There will always be someone smarter, stronger, and faster than each of us. It is a competition of just one…. just you. Be the best "you" possible.

You were born with many gifts. Have faith in yourself. *Free yourself of any limits that you or others have created.* Please read that again. Dream big.

This does not necessarily mean to dream of riches and fame. Dream of big causes; like achieving lasting global happiness. Improve your small corner of the world, and it may create ripple effects around the globe.

Know that you will fail very often in your life. Every great person has failed many times. There is no shame in failure. Fear of failure is much worse than failure itself.

I have failed miserably many times in my life; but I have had my successes, too. In a strange way, I almost enjoy a little bit of failure; because I know that at least I had the courage to enter the ring. Everybody gets knocked down. Champions get back up.

Here are some action points. They take effort. Make the effort and you will see the reward. Please trust me.

1. **Enjoy blissful slumber.** Do not underestimate the incredible rejuvenating effects of sleep on health, happiness and longevity. Aim for eight hours of sleep each night. Commit to a regular sleep schedule, trying to go to bed and to wake up at nearly the same time each day. Our bodies are of this Earth. We are at our best when we follow the natural rhythms of the natural world.

2. **Experience Nature.** Go on a walk in the woods or along the ocean. Be present. Take it all in. Get a space at a community garden and plant some flowers and vegetables (give the flowers away and you will be repaid doubly with a smile). Put your hands in the dirt, the very substrate from which your body was formed. *Feel* the world. You are an integral part of this greater whole.

3. **Meditate or Pray.** Do this every morning when you wake up and every night when you go to bed. Some people do this throughout the day, trying to "never leave their place of meditation." I am still working on this. With each meditation, list a few people or things for whom or which you are grateful.

4. **Bring your own sunny weather.** Author Stephen Covey said that – and I like it. There is also a Chinese proverb that says, "Assume a happiness that you do not have, and soon you will have the happiness that you assume." Putting a smile on your face will actually make you happier (they've done studies!).

Show others your warmth. Like attracts like.

5. **Go a week without making a single negative comment.** This is

really difficult. If you can make it a week you are my hero.

6.   **Laugh every day.** If it is bedtime and you have not yet laughed that day, maybe watch a YouTube video of laughing babies; or anything else that will make you smile.

7.   **Never feel trapped.** It is your life. You get to do whatever you want. Do not tether yourself to the expectations of others, or to your past. Yesterday exists only in our memories. Each morning, when you awaken, you are reborn anew. You can do whatever you choose today, and all days to follow.

Remember that not every decision is a financial decision. Sometimes what makes you happy does not make you rich. Finances are important, to a degree, but don't let financial concerns anchor you to a place where you are not fully happy.

8.   **Say mantras each day.** Your brain listens to the words you speak, and responds appropriately. Try reciting your favorite mantras at least once each day. Here are a few that I like:

Every day I will become happier, wiser, and stronger.

I will run into my fears. Fight, not flight.

Forgiveness brings peace.

The best is yet to come.

Each morning I am reborn anew.

9.   **Make the start, make a choice.** You can always change your mind later. Just begin up the mountain instead of always looking for the best trail. You might have to backtrack a little, but there is adventure in that, too! Write down on paper a few career choices or life paths to consider; and then choose one and go with it, if only for a while. This is better than the paralysis of indecision. Something will

work out.

Two quotes to consider:

"Courage will catch up to us if we continue to walk ahead."
-Robert J. Wicks.

"Make the start, begin, and then the work will be completed."
-German philosopher Johan Goethe.

Make the start.

———————————————

I often like to think in metaphors. Here is one to consider:

Envision a river dividing into smaller streams before returning back to the ocean. You must build a canoe for yourself and enter the river. This canoe is built of the core of what you are: The *who* are you, and the *why* are you.

You are a child of this Earth – on a journey of fun, hope, and compassion; living a life that promotes a lasting global happiness. This is your purpose and meaning. This is you and your canoe. This is your who and why.

You must enter the water's flow, and then let it take you where it will. Your *where* is unknown. This may be a little scary, but there is some intrigue in not knowing what you will discover around the next bend. Embrace the uncertainty.

The landscape and waters will change, but you and your canoe do not. The core of "you" is always the same. Others find hope and courage in your steadfast strength and resolve.

Soon, all the rivulets join back together at the same ocean. And the cycle starts anew.

I love you,

Dad

TWO

Imagine

THE MORNING SUN was already warm on my back. Floating prone on the water, I tasted the salt of the Pacific sea. In the ocean below, small schools of brightly colored fish hurried by; their sleek and muscled forms outlined against the variegated background of the sea floor. Cast forth by ripples on the surface, scattered rays of refracted light bounced across a living canvas, illuminating the coral forest and fish alike.

I worked my way toward a rocky shoreline, near a prominence that separated this small bay from another to the north. In the water below, I spotted a lone fish. I remember it to be of a light bluish-purple color, about a foot and a half in length and rather plumpish, perhaps weighing about a pound or two. I am not sure of the species name, as I could find no such creature matching this description when perusing a chart of native tropical fish. It is still a nice memory.

I am usually conscious of my breathing when snorkeling; perhaps because I hear each breath echoing throughout the tubing. It is easy to imagine that the sea also breathes – rhythmic inhalations draw me slightly out into the depths, and then relax again to carry me back toward the shore.

I continued to follow my purple companion, watching it gently sway in the tidal current amongst splendid coral structures. It noticed my presence, moving slowly away when I drew too near, but allowing me to shadow its movements as long as I kept my distance. It was an honor to intimately share the bay with this magnificent creature, one that had never known anything but these glorious surroundings; this tiny microcosm of life ruled by the inexorable cadence of the tidal sea. Inhale, exhale; repeat.

It is quite fascinating to consider the origins of such exquisite beauty. As a child, an uncle of mine once reminded me that ancient life forms arose out of a sea similar to this – what he liked to call the primordial soup. Each with a purpose, some of these creatures eventually crawled on to the shore to seek a new destiny, while others chose to remain within a watery realm.

Like an immense origami art form, our universe and Earth have unfolded from relatively simple beginnings into unfathomable reaches of beauty and complexity. And the production is not yet complete.

Scientists say the universe began with elementary particles; the almost infinitely small structures with peculiar sounding names like quarks, leptons, hadrons, and Higgs bosons. Although of course nothing is certain, consensus expert opinion has it that these elementary particles first declared their presence with a magnificent explosion; bursting forth from an embryonic vestibule of creativity smaller than a poppy seed, racing violently out into the emptiness, vanguards of an incomprehensibly vast universe.

Humans were once astounded to discover that plants and animals were made up of a multitude of individual cells. Soon after this discovery, elegant double helical strands of DNA molecules were found in the nuclei of these cells. It was eventually learned that this DNA supplied the code for building other molecular structures, each of which are made up of many different elements, such as nitrogen, hydrogen, and carbon. The atoms of these elements are each comprised of varying numbers of protons and neutrons, which in turn are built from the tiny elementary particles introduced above.

And, one may wonder, is it possible that elementary particles are made of structures of even lesser size, which are perhaps comprised of even more minute bits of matter, which could consist of yet even smaller constituent parts yet to be discovered? Maybe infinity can proceed in multiple directions.

And where did elementary particles come from? Could they have arrived from another universe? Was this *the* beginning, or just *a* beginning? Maybe there were, or are, an infinite number of universes and beginnings. Or maybe it is only us and our own observable universe.

We know that atoms are held together by mysterious forces, and each atom possesses intrinsic, abundant energy. Thanks to the genius of Albert Einstein and myriad others, there are intriguing ways of describing energy and forces; and scientists today still seek to unite quantum mechanics and classical physics via a single unifying theory.

But what is energy and what are forces? To note their existence, or describe their properties with a board or screen full of equations, is not to say what they actually are. Maybe these questions will remain unanswered. What is known; however, is that the energy of particles that first arrived at the Big Bang is still present today. The particles that comprise our very bodies have the same energy as at the time of their creation, nearly 14 billion years ago. Energy cannot be created or destroyed. But it can be repurposed.

Humankind appears to be a relatively late-appearing expression of a creative and self-organizing universe. It is interesting, however, to consider that the characteristic of self-organization does not preclude the possibility of a universe that was grandly designed to be self-organizing, rather than one that possesses an innate creativity of its own making.

At the time of the Big Bang, particles of light and matter dashed away from their center of origin, continuing an expansion that continues to the present day. Counteracting this expansion was the force of gravity, which tempered the outward driving forces and kept the rate of expansion at the precise rate necessary for our universe to form. Incredibly, experts note that if the expansion had occurred a fraction of a second more slowly, or more quickly, the universe would simply not exist. A perfect set of conditions and an ideal balance had to be met.

In the early stages of expansion, neutrons and protons joined together to form nuclei; emitting the first bursts of light. Immense clouds of simple atoms soon comprised the essence of creation. Also generated at the birth of the universe, a series of waves then passed through and disrupted these immense clouds into smaller fragments, which then coalesced into individual galaxies such as our own Milky Way. Each galaxy would act as its own center of the expansion of the universe, each destined to follow its own unique creative process.

The stars of each of these galaxies exist in a constant state of dynamic tension. Within each star, a balance is struck by the opposing forces of gravity, which pulls matter inward, and fusion, which pushes matter outward – creating a tenuous middle ground in a high stakes game of tug-of-war.

We can find parallels to the dynamic tension of the stars, where opposing forces are always at play. Observing an irregular wave form on a computer monitor, we can watch as it moves up and down while traveling across the screen. We may note that it is the duration and depth of the troughs that give perspective and meaning to the duration and magnitude of the peaks; and vice versa.

Our world exists in a persistent state of unbalanced yet somewhat predictable rhythmic patterns of opposite extremes. It is the extremes that provide perspective, and there is no meaning without perspective. Without darkness, one could not fully comprehend the experience of light. Without cold, there is no complete perception of warmth.

Similarly, the human condition bounces up and down between opposite extremes. We may travel out on grand adventures, but soon our tribal nature compels us to return to the familiar comforts of home and family. We may observe the stock market reflect the vicissitudes of human sentiment, sending equity values from irrational highs to illogical lows, and then back again. And as many great philosophers have noted, our brightest moments and greatest heights of joy are often discovered only after emerging from the dark and deep redoubts of pain and suffering.

We fight, we forgive; and then we do it all over again. Nothing is static, and the pendulum never stops moving. There are always opposing forces, and there is no absolutism. Reflecting patterns similar to those present throughout the universe, our very lives are nothing if not living manifestations of dynamic tension.

It is the destiny of some stars to end their existence as a supernova explosion. In an event analogous to the beginning of the universe, these stars condense into tiny dots of extreme heat and density, as fusion energy is outmatched by the effects of gravity. But the forces of nuclear fusion eventually overwhelm gravitational forces, and in the resulting explosion bits of stellar dust are blasted into space, forging all of the elements presently known to humankind.

The explosion of a star is therefore really more of a transformation than a death, as a large star is eventually reborn into numerous systems of smaller stars and planets, each with their own remarkable potential for self-organizing complexity.

Nearly 5 billion years ago, in what is called the Orion arm of our Milky Way Galaxy, a cloud of cosmic dust from supernova explosions began a gravitational collapse into numerous smaller systems, each structure containing a central star. Our solar system began as such – scattered elements traveling through space, bumping into each other, eventually coalescing into larger and larger structures. Over millions of years, through accretion, stellar dust became the planets of our solar system, including our very own planet Earth.

And through all of these changes, over a span of 14 billion years, the immense potentiality of the elementary particles was present, waiting to one day create a purple fish, destined to meander slowly through an underwater forest of brightly colored coral.

Our Earth has yet to complete its journey. From early beginnings as molten rock, it has co-evolved with the Sun and the Moon. It has formed a renewable crust through which elements travel via convection currents from the planetary depths up to the surface, and then back again. With the evolution of photosynthesis, the Earth has used the Sun to help create life. And as the Sun has become hotter, the Earth continues to compensate by adjusting its own atmosphere.

In a very braided and collaborative partnership, all creatures – including humans – have also co-evolved with the Sun, Moon and Earth.

Night falls upon a summer evening. The rhythmic hum of crickets welcomes a full moon ascending over the horizon. Rays of sunlight strike the rising orb, and reflected moonbeams balance the darkness of the night sky.

Pale-colored garden flowers are thus illuminated, attracting the interest of nocturnal pollinators in search of nectar. Brushing up against bits of pollen, these nighttime feeders carry their hitchhiking payload from bloom to bloom, inadvertently spreading new flower genes; unwitting collaborators in the plant kingdom version of love and romance.

Out on an evening stroll, two lovers gaze upon the moonlit blossoms – and then into each other's eyes. Romance is in the air. Blissful slumber will wait.

When daylight arrives, sunrays penetrate through glass windows; and sleepy closed eyelids as well. Nerve cells in their retinas are now alerted, sending messages to the pineal gland in their brains. Sleep-inducing melatonin levels begin to wane and, in opposite fashion, mood enhancing serotonin levels start to rise. It is time to wake up; and it looks to be a very good day.

Enjoying breakfast on the porch, the couple feels the warmth of the new morning sun; perhaps unaware that its rays are creating vitamin D in their skin, helping to strengthen their bones for the tasks of each day. They amble back to the garden, responding to visceral yearnings to work the soil. They harvest fruit and a few vegetables to eat later that day. Stopping at the garden perimeter, they observe a bumblebee alight upon a purple coneflower. They are drawn toward a deep primeval closeness with our Earth, the dust from which their very bodies were formed.

If they are lucky to live so long, after nearly a century of adventure their human lives will come to an end – the requisite creative destruction of an evolving universe makes no exception for human immortality. An Earthly journey complete, their bodies are gently returned back into the soil.

The spark of Life, the gift of Providence, the indescribable force that harnesses the energy of coalesced elementary particles to breathe individual consciousness into each human creature, is now gone – back to the realm of the stars, perhaps. Yet the potentiality and energy of elementary particles within their bodies will continue to exist, recapitulating the transformational processes of the exploding supernovae, forever reorganizing themselves into new cycles of life and matter.

Eventually, all life forms disassemble into tiny bits of soil – which may then someday enter the digestive tract of an earthworm or insect.

An attentive meadowlark soon finds its breakfast, repurposing the elements of the Earth to add sustenance to his delicate form. Soaring high into a cloudless sky, the small creature descends upon a leafy sun-drenched branch. Feathered chest expanding, an exquisite melody springs forth to float along a morning breeze.

Once dwelling within myriad inert and living forms, the creativity of elementary particles is now manifest anew; as a love song, echoed across a grassy meadow to a hopeful mate yearning to fulfill her own destiny.

Ever changing, life moves ever forward. Who could dream of anything so fantastic?

I wonder what it would be like to view Earth from the International Space Station, orbiting far above the surface of our planet. I imagine that many of our present concerns would appear rather insignificant to an astronaut.

And what if these Space Station astronauts could travel across the universe in search of a perfect place? What would they look for and hope to find? If they could travel at the speed of light, we could imagine that maybe one day their grandchildren's grandchildren could happen upon a true utopia.

When first glimpsing their new home, the space voyagers may be overcome by awe and wonder at the sight of their planet – a brilliant jewel set amongst the stars.

As the travelers alight upon the planet surface, they see sparkling blue oceans teeming with life, and verdant forests crossed by crystal clear streams. Beyond the woods they find a small grassy expanse, stunningly immersed in the color of a million wildflowers. A doe emerges from across the meadow, accompanied by a newborn fawn attempting its first timid steps.

If only there was such an exquisite paradise.

Throughout the course of evolution, the brains of our ancestors became larger and more advanced, particularly in the frontal lobe regions. Along the way, human beings developed increasing levels of consciousness; evolving from purely instinctual creatures into more sentient forms.

This consciousness has given humankind the potential to counteract our instinctual herd mentality – the remnant subconscious brain circuit of distant ancestors that reacts rather than responds, and that does not always recognize the oft-present lunacy of crowd opinion.

Consciousness allows us to contemplate, to marvel at the immense grandeur of the universe; to be amazed. It gives us the ability to love and to be loved, to fully feel the joys and sorrows of life.

Consciousness allows us to ponder, to question, and to consider. It even endows us with the ability to think about our own thoughts.

Consciousness allows us to recognize beauty, in all of its forms.

Consciousness has also given humanity great power; including the ability to exercise dominion over the Earth and all of its creatures. Regrettably, we are collectively failing to use this power in a consistently just and sustainable fashion.

We are born equal children of a beneficent universe, each a living manifestation of planetary elements forged in the fiery heat of an exploding star. I am of this Earth. How can I not wish to protect and cherish it? How can I not love all of the creatures, mountains, and streams from which my body sprang forth? My personal health, my sense of purpose, and my happiness are all dependent upon this Earth and all of its inhabitants.

It is often quite difficult to clearly see the world around me. I view a distorted image, peering through the flawed lens of social conditioning; seeing the world as I have been taught to see it. The seductive opacities of greed, power, and fear further cloud the sensibilities of my vision.

Today there are a multitude of economic, social, and environmental issues that threaten sustainable global happiness. Some of us may elevate the importance of financial concerns over that of the environment and the rest of humanity, forgetting that our economic well-being and happiness are intimately dependent upon the health and happiness of our Earth and all of its inhabitants.

It is tempting to default to primitive or overly reductive ways of thinking. Like an outmatched chess player, I may be so intent on protecting a single pawn that I do not see an imminent checkmate. It can be difficult to override subconscious brain pathways favoring self and immediacy, with more rational decisions that consider the whole of humanity and creation, present and future. The tasks are great, and the idealist will surely have his or her mettle tested when lofty principles are challenged by the harsh realities of daily life.

Many of us hurry about with blinders on, oblivious to anything but the complete fulfillment of our own desires – so tantalizingly close in front of us, but nearly always just out of reach. Often caught up in immediate indulgences, we cannot see that we are fouling our own nest.

We ignore the fact that each day it becomes increasingly unsafe to consume fish from our oceans, to eat produce from our farms, or to even drink water from our kitchen faucets. We continue to burn coal domestically and sell it internationally, thus adding more mercury to our oceans, as well as increasing oceanic temperatures and acidity – killing the coral reefs that a large percentage of ocean fish and island inhabitants depend upon for survival.

We continue to allow fracking for natural gas, polluting our aquifers, and emitting methane into the atmosphere – a byproduct that is a many times more potent greenhouse gas than is carbon dioxide. We cover our fields and orchards with synthetic pesticides, damaging our soils and waterways; killing beneficial plants, insects and other creatures, while also putting human health at great risk.

We sometimes focus on what we want rather than what we have. We complain that our standard of living is falling, and that we would like a nicer house and a newer automobile. All the while, there are headlines of massive coral reef blanching, melting polar icecaps, and dying bee populations.

We observe images flash across our high definition television screens, displaying frightened displaced citizens and their children, driven from their homes and countries by civil war or hunger. We see the body of a small child refugee who did not survive the ocean journey from his homeland, washed up alone upon a distant shore. Yet we remain passively indifferent. Hand over the remote, the ballgame is on.

Is this not madness?

I do not wish to be – or deserve to be – a moralist. The bright light of scrutiny shines in all directions, and my own imperfections and hypocrisies are thus far too well-illuminated. But I do wish for people to plainly see the truth, to see that we have yet to realize an attainable greater measure of global happiness.

America is extraordinarily prosperous. And our greatest riches lie not within our vaults, rather within our history of inclusivity and generosity, and our preservation of natural resources and beautiful lands. This is what makes our America really special. Filling our coffers with even more money at the expense of other world citizens will not make us any happier, or our country any greater. America first? We already are first. An outstretched hand to fellow global inhabitants will bring far greater happiness and riches than will attempting to widen the chasm between us. That is true leadership.

If I choose to not concern myself with the plight of other world populations, living in relative luxury while others struggle and lack basic necessities, I may unknowingly be complicit in turning a peaceable child into a terrorist; one who may one day blow up a crowded marketplace in my own neighborhood. Likewise, if I choose to support unsustainable methods of agriculture, my actions may in part be responsible for killing essential pollinating insects and poisoning our ecosystem; endangering our future food supply and possibly damaging the health of my children and grandchildren.

I wish to encourage all readers to further develop their sense of awareness. I believe that awareness is the ability of a person to self-observe from a distance, to objectively evaluate whether one's current actions are indeed congruent with their personal values and life goals. Awareness allows us to ask ourselves if we are acting in the interest of the few or of the many, and whether we are elevating our current concerns over those of countless future generations.

It is vital that we widen our circle of friends in the world, to encourage and demonstrate a universal democracy – one not limited to just present, local, or human concerns, but rather one that includes the entirety of our planet and all of its inhabitants, present and future.

There is only one us, one planet that is home to one global body of life. Each individual creature is a unique manifestation of the inventiveness of a common beginning, and each is an essential interwoven part of a greater Earth and universe ecosystem.

On this planet, everyone and everything are inseparably connected. If we hurt but one part, we hurt the whole. And when we improve but one part, we improve the whole. This is the premise, and the promise, of the words on these pages.

Born of the incredible creativity of an exploding star, our Earth continues to unfold from relatively simple beginnings into ever increasing complexity. Every creature plays an integral part in this grand event; however, it is humans that have most fully developed consciousness. We are therefore no longer merely instinctual creatures, helpless protagonists aimlessly adrift in the universe story.

We have the ability to alter the script. Composed of inventive elementary building blocks, we have the power to *imagine*, and the responsibility to create. We must build a tall sail; and chart a destination of sustainable global health and happiness.

The pages to follow offer a message of hope. Hope that every person has the opportunity to find purpose in this extraordinary universe. Hope that every challenge will bring its own strength – and that courage will catch up to us if we continue to walk ahead. Hope that humankind will honor and protect our Earth, this beautiful blue planet suspended in the heavens.

I encourage you to make the most of what you were given; taking great care of your body and your mind, optimizing your potential, attempting to find joyful moments in each day of your life. I also invite you to develop a panoramic view of the world, bringing joy to others by helping to find innovative and integrative solutions for many of today's issues; improving global wellness. In so doing, it is my hope that you will find great happiness through a rich and satisfying life.

Randy A. Siltanen

THREE

Sustainable Global Happiness

ABRAHAM MASLOW WAS an American psychologist of the 20th century, most widely known for creating a hierarchy of human needs. Although he died nearly fifty years ago, his ideas are as valid today as at the time they were written.

Maslow's Hierarchy of Needs is often depicted as a pyramid consisting of five sections, one atop the other, where the fulfillment of each lower level serves as a stepping stone to the next level above it.

Physiological needs – like air, water, food, sleep, shelter, and sex – are placed at the base of the pyramid, because fulfilling these needs is essential for human survival. Everything else is built upon this level.

The next level up is the need for **Safety** – such as personal protection, good health, and financial security.

This is followed by the need for a sense of **Belonging** – which includes friendship, intimacy, and family.

Above this level is the need for **Esteem** – which includes the desire for recognition.

Finally, at the top of the pyramid, is **Self-Actualization**; which is the achievement of one's full potential.

To be **Self-Actualized** means to enthusiastically embrace every moment of our life on Earth. It means run, don't walk; because life is large and time is short. We must read, listen, learn, love, work, and play; all to the fullest of our ability – as we have but one chance to live our best life.

31

"I long to embrace, to include in my own short life, all that is accessible to man."

-Anton Chekhov

Later in life, Abraham Maslow determined that his hierarchy was not yet complete. He realized that the idea of Self-Actualization did not quite reach the highest and most holistic level of human consciousness. So, he added another level: **Transcendence**.

Transcendence is the need to rise through, to give of oneself to something greater than oneself. The other levels of the pyramid, culminating in Self-Actualization, provide a fertile substrate for the seeds of Transcendence.

A tree expresses the life of the Sun and soil from which it arises; offering up its fruit and flowers to the inhabitants of our planet. Transferring the energy of the Sun to other creatures and to the soil, the tree increases the potential of the planet, and thus of itself. In Autumn, its petals and leaves drift to the ground, to be incorporated by the Earth – of which it is but a living extension. In an unending cycle, the enriched Earth now endows the tree with a greater ability to grow even taller and broader; creating yet more leaves to gather sunlight, more blossoms to behold, and more fruit for the creatures of our planet.

And, so it is with the Transcendent human being. Transcendence springs forth from Self-Actualization, and then gives back unto itself. The two are one, as a tree and Earth are one.

Transcendence means knowing that optimal individual happiness is interwoven within the greater fabric of global happiness. It means to love deeply, and to love broadly. Like a mystical cistern of water whose level increases after each sip from passing travelers, love shared with others is multiplied rather than diminished.

Transcendence is an expansion of awareness, spatially and temporally – from inner self to outer other; from me today to you tomorrow. It is a place of wonder and awe; where a sunset and a moonrise become a miracle.

Transcendence regards all present and future global citizens as equals; and all species and ecosystems of our planet as wild and precious.

Happiness

Aristotle suggested that happiness is the ultimate desired endpoint of all human existence. We may wish for good health, close friends, and true love; but the reason we desire these things is that they are each a pathway to the same destination – which is happiness.

A lot of people talk about finding happiness. Sometimes happiness is easy to find. On a forest walk, we may stumble upon a meadow of grasses and wildflowers; easily absorbing a burst of textures and color.

We can certainly *find* happiness, in this literal sense, but happiness is also *created*. We can create a measure of individual happiness by building a strong body to carry us on our way. We can also create personal happiness by cultivating a joyful and robust mind: choosing to be grateful, framing life events in a positive fashion, and seeking happiness in the everyday miracles of life on Earth.

We can create even more happiness, by sharing our talents and riches with all other inhabitants of our planet.

We can even create *future* happiness, by choosing to maintain the beauty and bounty of the Earth for all generations to come. This honors the concept of intergenerational equity – the idea that the lives of future citizens are as important as our own.

It is somewhat difficult to define happiness, as it is in part unique to each individual. The realization of complete happiness will also always be an unfinished work in progress, to be added to throughout the length of our lives.

As children, we first find happiness by seeking immediate pleasure. We eat ice cream cones, laugh or giggle about the slightest thing, and shout with joy as we slide down a snow-covered hillside. This type of happiness has its own reason for existing, and at every age we should continue to seek it – even if at times only for the pure exhilaration of the moment.

As the years pass, many of us find that our definition of happiness begins to broaden. We still of course continue to seek a degree of personal gratification, but the fleeting rewards of individual indulgences gradually lose some of their power of attraction. Desiring a more complete and lasting happiness, we often search for something larger.

It is then that we may begin to expand and reinforce our ideas of happiness; perhaps using words such as contentment, fulfillment, purpose and meaning – to augment the pleasure we obtain from satisfying our personal needs and desires.

There are many pathways to optimal happiness, but all converge through a final common route of Transcendence – the idea of giving of oneself to something beyond oneself; where person, people, and planet are one.

American astronomer Carl Sagan said, *"If we crave some cosmic purpose, then let us find ourselves a worthy goal."*

I believe it is really quite simple. The meaning of life is happiness, and the purpose of life is to find, create and share it. This prime directive holds that each person must endeavor to find and create happiness for themselves, and equally for all present and future inhabitants of a sustainable planet. This overarching ideal can be expressed in just three words: Sustainable Global Happiness.

This notion, Sustainable Global Happiness, can serve as humanity's "worthy goal," the desired ultimate destination of every person, city, state, province, and nation.

Each word is uniquely important: *Happiness*, because happiness is the point of life; *Global* Happiness because individual happiness is inextricably entwined with the happiness of all world citizens; and *Sustainable* Global Happiness, because a sustainable Earth is an absolute prerequisite for humanity's present and future happiness.

The journey to Sustainable Global Happiness is illuminated by a brilliant guiding star – the transcendent idea that person, people, and planet are equal and inseparable, in time and in space.

As we travel along the paths of our lives, creating health and happiness for ourselves, our neighbors, and our Earth, we realize that the journey and the destination have become one and the same.

The connectedness of person, people, and planet can be represented by a triangle, as depicted below. The health and happiness of the individual (person), the collective (people), and the Earth (planet) each comprise a distinct side of the triangle, yet each are essential components of an integrated whole. Each entity is joined to the others. What affects one, affects all.

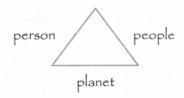

Sustainable Global Happiness

Person: Individual happiness is a vital element of global happiness. And if I am to be fully happy, it is imperative that I keep my body and mind healthy, strong, and resilient.

I must strive to become a self-actualized and transcendent person. I must give my full effort. I must learn all that I can, knowing that imagination springs forth from verdant repositories of knowledge.

I must also understand my place in this world; finding meaning and purpose in my life.

People: Homo sapiens are tribal in nature; and we look to others for love, acceptance and approval. We have learned the value of collaborative interdependence and synergy – noting that together we are greater than the sum of our parts.

We have found that we are most happy and healthy when our brothers and sisters throughout the world are also happy and healthy.

Planet: The base of the triangle is the Planet entity of Sustainable Global Happiness. Without a stable base, the other entities cannot stand. There can be no sustainable happiness without a sustainable planet.

The Earth is our primary source of wealth. Without fresh air, clean water, rich soils and abundant resources, our human bodies cannot survive. Our planet's resources provide materials for the lumber, metals, and energy necessary for modern human existence; and even the overlying paper proxies of currency, stocks, and bonds that engender commerce and investments for our future.

Everything – including the full measure of happiness for humanity – depends upon the health of our Earth.

This book is divided into three sections, one for each of the person/people/planet components of happiness. This is a somewhat contrived distinction, as the health and happiness of each of these entities is intimately intermingled with the others.

With that in mind, we begin with Part I (Person), discussing ideas to increase personal health and happiness through a strong and resilient body and mind.

Part II (People) offers suggestions for achieving health and happiness for all global populations, as the wellness of the individual goes hand in hand with the wellness of the collective.

We conclude with Part III (Planet), discussing ideas to preserve the beauty and bounty of our Earth – the very wellspring of health and happiness for all present and future generations.

Sometimes happiness is on the path right beside us, and we need only recognize magnificent gems that are hidden in plain sight – treasures of extraordinary beauty in our midst. This happiness becomes more manifest if we choose to live with a sense of wonder, in grateful witness to the grandeur of our Earth and our universe. Paradise is all around us. We see what we look for.

PART I: PERSON

Optimizing Personal Health and Happiness

"I saw the angel in the marble and carved until I set him free."

-Michelangelo

Randy A. Siltanen

Section One:

Building a Healthy Body

FOUR

Exercise

Creating Strength, Endurance, and Flexibility

"I believe that a simple and unassuming manner of life is best for everyone, best both for the body and the mind."

-Albert Einstein

OUR BODIES ARE constantly changing organisms, behaving much more like a moving river than the riverbed over which it flows. And similar to an old axe that has been in the family for centuries – with the handle replaced three times and the blade twice – our memories may stay with us but our original physical structure is long gone.

The cells in our bodies are constantly dying and being replaced, making way for fresh cells that can adapt to new circumstances. Each year we are housed in a newly remodeled home: Our intestinal lining cells are replaced every few days, our red blood cells and muscle cells every few months, and our bone cells every few years or more. Interestingly, nerve cells can often live an entire lifetime. Each new cell seamlessly learns its role, allowing the entire body to move gracefully through a new season.

Similar to individual cells, human beings are also destined to live for only relatively short time periods, to be replaced by newer and stronger models, each slightly adapted to improve on the entire organism that we call the human race.

Like many mammals, humans often function most happily and efficiently when organized together as members of a group or pack. Born into a tribe, we are each specifically designed for hunting, foraging, building shelter, and interacting well with other members of our group. When we perform these functions, we strengthen our individual body and mind, and also the entire tribal unit as well.

Human bodies are engaged in a constant tug-of-war between growth and degeneration, a system mediated by very complex chemical pathways. If we fail to make continuous efforts to grow, degeneration mechanisms will predominate, eventually compromising our health, longevity, and happiness.

It is essential for maximal health that we forage, hunt, lift things for shelter, and interact well with others as useful members of the group – or at least have our brain and body think that is what we are doing. The last part, interacting well with others, has no substitute, and it is imperative to successfully interact well with family and friends if we wish to obtain maximal happiness and well-being.

There is a primitive part of our body that acts on a "use it or lose it" concept. This mechanism does not differentiate between foraging vs. walking, sprinting furiously toward prey vs. racing across the court to reach a backhand volley, or lifting a heavy log for shelter vs. doing a push-up. It just knows that our musculoskeletal structures are obviously performing a very important function, and it will do its best to allow that action to continue as long as possible.

If we *act* young and useful, keeping our muscles moving and often strained to the level of fatigue, signals from our body will be sent to the brain, which in turn will churn out chemical messages that stimulate growth, pleasure and continued life. Filled with life-sustaining elements, our bloodstream bathes the tissues of our bodies in a restorative solution of growth. New blood vessels will grow more deeply into our tissues, tendons will anchor down more firmly, and strength and flexibility will be enhanced.

There was once a television show where the host introduced individuals who perform messy tasks so that the rest of us do not have to do them. Similarly, today most of us no longer have to forage, hunt, or lift heavy objects to survive; as we can usually pay someone else to do these chores for us. This has certainly freed up time for many other valuable endeavors; however, our bodies are designed to physically work hard – and it is as if we are programmed with a self-destruct function if we fail to do so.

For maximal well-being we must stress our musculoskeletal structures to the level of fatigue, and frequently elevate our heart and breathing rates significantly above resting levels.

The Bare Minimum

Here is the absolute bare minimum exercise requirement for optimal health and longevity:

Spend at least 20-25 minutes each day doing a physical activity that will noticeably increase your heart rate and breathing rate. The American College of Sports Medicine, The American Heart Association, and the World Health Organization all recommend that adults perform a total of at least 150 minutes of moderate aerobic activity per week.

Find an activity that you enjoy and go for it. Swim, run, fast walk, bike, row, lift weights, play sports, or better yet, all of the above. If necessary, join a gym or find an exercise partner to help keep you motivated.

One example of a good weekly exercise routine could include:

5 days of brisk walking

1 day of upper body strengthening exercises

1 day of lower body strengthening exercises

Your walk can incorporate a warm-up and cool-down leisurely stroll, but most of it should be at a brisk pace. You may wish to include some hills in your route if possible. If you are not the type to join a gym, consider doing upper body exercises at home with a resistance cord, and also push-ups with your knees on the floor. For your leg strength you can perform squats, lunges, hip abduction, and heel raise exercises. Look on YouTube for proper technique. Spend about 20 minutes on each activity, preceded and followed by 5 minutes of stretching.

Combined with a proper diet, an appropriate exercise program can markedly decrease the need for many medications. Hypercholesterolemia, diabetes, and hypertension can often be completely avoided. Depression can be lessened or circumvented in many patients. Chronic pain syndromes can often be prevented by keeping muscles and tendons strong and limber. For most people, a yoga class or a game of tennis can offer more relaxation than that glass of wine or beer you may use to help you unwind each night.

It is best to begin these habits at a young age. If you are older, it is never too late to chart a course of improvement.

There are many reasons used to avoid exercise:

I am already too busy. However, many of our past U.S. Presidents have found time to fit exercise into their schedules – so that pretty much ruins that argument. I should not exchange my health, happiness, and longevity for status or money, which is often what I am doing if I spend too much time at work.

I cannot exercise because I have painful joints and a sore back, and exercise hurts too much. In truth, back problems typically become less troublesome with increased exercise. And strong muscles, tendons, and ligaments can help to protect joints from excessive wear and tear.

Start slowly and be creative. If your knee hurts you when you walk, try swimming, rowing, or bicycling. If that does not work, go to a gym. Here you will find something that you can do; like exercising on the elliptical machine, which is designed to be easy on joints. You will figure it out.

Eye of the Tiger

There are many people who will likely only perform the bare minimum that is required for good health – or perhaps even less. But there are also significant numbers of others who really enjoy being athletes, either at competitive or recreational levels. These people want to push their bodies to near the point of diminishing returns, attempting to maximize their personal health and enjoyment.

Some of these individuals greatly appreciate the upwelling of emotion and esprit de corps associated with engaging in athletic competition. Others do not wish to compete, rather simply find great joy in the very process of exercise for its own sake. What they all share in common is that they want to do more than just the bare minimum necessary for good health – they are interested in achieving *great* health. And they are willing to put in the extra work that will allow them to live life more fully now, as well as in their later years. These are the individuals who want to be able to hike in the mountains someday with their grandchildren, who want to feel fit and full of energy, becoming relatively stronger and more filled with life each year.

These motivated individuals also realize that a fit body helps to build a strong mind; and that many facets of their lives – including mental capacity, mood, and energy level – will benefit from a regimen of daily exercise.

Before introducing more challenging workout suggestions, geared to those who wish to obtain great health, some basic concepts of exercise physiology will be discussed.

There are two major ways that our bodies provide fuel for activity, one is aerobically, and the other is anaerobically. The first utilizes oxygen, the second does not. Aerobic activities tend to utilize slow twitch muscle fibers, while anaerobic activities will recruit fast twitch fibers. Both of these functions are inherently related to our heart rate, a measure that is frequently used in exercise physiology. Our peak heart rate (PHR) is the absolute maximum number of beats per minute that our heart can reach. This number decreases with age, and a rough estimate is 220 minus your age; therefore, if you are 25 years old your PHR is likely in the neighborhood of 195 beats per minute.

Aerobic activities rely on the use of oxygen in energy production, and these mechanisms are in use for activities that require less than around 85% of PHR. Aerobic activities can be further broken down into low-level and higher-level activities.

At low level aerobic activity, one in which our heart rate is less than 65% of PHR, our bodies utilize fat as fuel, and we can continue this relatively low-level activity virtually all day long. This is the mechanism our ancestors used while walking through the forest or plains while foraging for food, and is what we use today when taking a leisurely stroll.

At higher level aerobic activity, one in which our heart rate is between 65%-85% of PHR, our bodies switch to a different fuel, glucose, which it can utilize for relatively high-level activity for periods lasting up to about 2 hours. This is the metabolic pathway that our ancestors used while they were tracking game, and what we now use when going on a mild to moderately strenuous bicycle ride or run.

When we perform low level aerobic activities, where our heart rate is less than 65% of maximal, we gain from the positive effects of gravity on our bone mass, successfully stretching our muscles and tendons as we go. Performing activities that are similar to peaceful foraging, our minds find comfort engaging in the slower rhythms of these movements; somewhat analogous to the natural pull humans have to a campfire. Mesmerized by the glowing red embers, we tap into a primeval sense of ease and well-being that is somehow stored in our DNA, passed down through countless generations. These activities may soothe our soul, while keeping our muscles loose and stretched, and our bones strong.

High level aerobic activity, where our heart rate is about 65-85% of maximal, improves our cardiovascular health. Our heart muscles become stronger, our respiratory processes become more efficient, and we add new blood vessels to more tissue; allowing us to utilize oxygen more efficiently.

The other major type of energy use, anaerobic metabolism, does not require oxygen. This is the mechanism that is utilized for short bursts of intensive activity, lasting up to around a minute or so. In this zone we are pushing the pedal to the metal; with our heart rates rising above 85% of PHR, at or near our maximal level. This is the metabolic pathway that our hunting ancestors used when they had already moved in to position for the kill, but then needed one last quick burst of maximal energy to overtake and subdue their prey – or possibly attempt to escape from a beast that was now chasing them.

Performing aerobic and anaerobic activities are each beneficial for good health, as are strength-training activities. The more energetic athlete will engage in each of these activities, but unlike those performing the bare minimum, they will spend more time doing high aerobic exercise (heart rate at 65-85% of PHR) and relatively less time with low aerobic exercise (heart rate less than 65% of PHR), while also pushing themselves a little harder in the weight room.

Athletes can palpate their pulse and get a pretty good idea of what level of activity they are performing; or if they are looking for more precision, they can buy a heart rate monitor.

In the weight room the motivated athlete will want to utilize full effort, but usually in an activity that he or she can perform for up to about 5-10 repetitions. If you can only lift a heavy weight one or two times, you are risking significant injury while only slightly increasing muscular strength. Except for very high-level athletes, the possible small extra reward may not be worth the risk of an injury that could keep you out of the gym for several months. It could even cost you a visit to an orthopedic surgeon.

One possible regimen for a motivated athlete is this:

3 days per week of 30-60-minute-long aerobic exercise workouts: Include brief episodes of anaerobic near maximal effort at least once a week within this workout. For instance, go for a run or a bike ride than includes a hill or two where near maximal effort is put forth.

3 days per week of 30-60-minute-long strengthening exercises: These can be done as combined upper and lower body exercises at each session, or broken down into specific days for lower or upper body exercises.

Each session includes stretching, balance and a warm-up. This leaves one day a week for a leisurely walk or any other physical activity that you enjoy.

The athlete who is so inclined can certainly do longer workouts, but by going much beyond this level they will begin to realize rapidly diminishing returns on their time investment and will also increase the risk of developing an overuse injury. You can also of course do a little less than these recommendations; or perform an entirely different workout. Invent a routine that works for you.

To help prevent damage to muscles and tendons it is imperative to stretch them each day. Performing balance exercises will also help you to avoid injuries. An injury to your ancestor often meant suffering or death to them and their family. The stakes are now not usually so high, but measures can be taken to reduce your risk of injury as well. Stretch at least 5 minutes every day. Try doing some of your exercises on one leg to improve your balance.

It is also very important that you very slowly build up to the more challenging exercise levels that have just been discussed, even if you are a young person. It is very easy to develop an overuse injury if you attempt to do too much, too soon. Initially, exercise far less than you think you can, and slowly increase your workout level over a period of a month or two. Definitely consider hiring a trainer to get you started.

Consult your medical care provider before starting your workout regimen, particularly if you around 30 years of age or older, or plan to push yourself to near your maximum capability. If something starts to hurt, back off and try something different until it starts to feel better. An occasional bit of minor muscle aching is nothing for concern, but sore joints or tendons are telling you to slow down a little.

Perspective

A word of caution: Although it is uncommon, over-exercising can also be unhealthy, and could possibly even lead to alterations of immune function. What starts off as a good idea may transform into a compulsion, or an obsessive concern over body image or performance. Be careful not to overdo it – exercise should always be fun.

Also, try not to compare your strength and fitness with that of others. It is a competition of one – just you – and winning means to optimize the potential of the body you were given. You do not have to be a home run hitter to be a great player.

An Apple a Day

Many muscle and tendon overuse injuries can be prevented (and rehabilitated) by utilizing eccentric contraction exercises. An eccentric contraction is one where the muscle is lengthening as it works, e.g. when performing a bicep curl, the concentric contraction is when you lift the weight up and the eccentric contraction is when you let gravity *slowly* bring the weight back down.

Eccentric contraction exercises are useful for preventing and rehabilitating rotator cuff shoulder injuries, tennis elbow, patellar tendonitis (jumper's knee), and Achilles tendonitis. Performing exercises slowly will utilize both concentric and eccentric contractions and will maximize total strength and rehabilitation.

Even if you exercise with proper technique, and regularly stretch and practice your balance, you will still likely suffer at least a few injuries during your lifetime. The rehabilitation programs, precision surgeries, and potent medications of modern medicine are truly impressive, but healing is optimized when these treatments are complemented by the power of the mind. Believing that you can get well is an important component of any type of healing. Although the exact mechanism of action may be unknown, meditation, prayer and a positive outlook have all been noted to increase rates of healing and to improve health.

Try to stay warm, as muscles and tendons are more likely to be injured when cold. Also, some bodily processes do not function as well at lower temperatures. If you get a chill after exercising, your body may not be as adept at fighting off pathogens.

Also essential for injury avoidance are proper dietary inputs; to help build musculoskeletal tissues to maximal levels of strength and resilience. A healthy nutrition plan may keep you out of your doctor's office for various other maladies, too. So, go ahead and eat an apple a day – and lots of other organic vegetables and fruits as well.

Randy A. Siltanen

FIVE

Sustainable Nutrition

A Healthy Body and a Healthy Planet

"Human beings, vegetables, or cosmic dust, we all dance to a mysterious tune, intoned in the distance by an invisible piper."

-Albert Einstein

TIMELINE: 50,000 B.C.

THE ACACIA LEAVES hung motionless in the early dawn air. Perched nearly ten feet above the ground, a young hunter peered between tree branches, surveying a grassy expanse near the Great Rift Valley. Two other boys from his tribe had joined him. Suspended high upon limbs of nearby trees, they too waited patiently.

Their quarry would soon be here. They always journeyed this way; enormous herds of gazelles marching through the savannah amongst a canopy of interspersed trees, in a yearly mass exodus toward taller grasses and more dense woodlands.

Across the grassland, Kilimanjaro awakened against a crimson morning sky; its silhouette intersected by a purple grenadier alighting on a nearby limb. Flitting off before it could be captured, the bird startled the young hunter; redirecting his focus and priming his senses for the day. Noting subtle movement in the distance, he signaled to his friends. The herd is coming.

The young hunter examined his spear once again, just like his father had shown him. Drifting off in thought, he imagined how pleased his family would be that evening; eating fresh meat with other members of the tribe, and listening to stories of the hunt.........A soft whistle from one of the others interrupted his daydream. They were here.

Nearly a hundred animals ambled toward him; the quiet of the morning broken by the soft sounds of ungulate feet upon sunbaked soil. A female below called to her fawn. Sweet, musky scent tendrils ascended upward, infusing the young hunter's nostrils with each deep inhalation.

Steadily increasing in cadence and magnitude, his chest wall rose and fell in rhythmic fashion; echoing the force of a heart beating violently within an inescapable thoracic cage. He braced his spear against a branch, so that trembling hands would not betray his presence.

When a second whistle pierced the air, the young hunter leapt out to an animal below. Using the full weight of his body, he plunged his spear deep into the shoulder of his target; scattering the rest of the frightened herd in all directions. Seizing its long black horns, he wrestled the large gazelle to the ground, finishing his task with a quick knife thrust to the throat.

Through the dust, he saw that his fellow tribesmen had also been successful; although one friend had been quite bruised and bloodied by the kicking hooves of a desperate creature. Lifting his quarry upon his back, the weight of the animal accentuated his own injury –an ankle sprained from a hard landing – although he hardly noticed the pain.

On the journey home, the boys practiced the hunting story they would tell others by the evening fire; just like their fathers and grandfathers before them had done, and just like their own great-grandchildren would continue to do for thousands of generations to follow.

THROUGHOUT THE SPAN of humankind's existence, our bodies have been genetically programmed to subsist on scarce amounts of food; often obtained by violent and bloody brawls with clawed and sharp-toothed creatures. If no game was available, our distant ancestors would often wander long distances to gather wild fruits, nuts, vegetables, and insects.

Fast forward about fifty thousand years, from the time of the above hunting story to the present day, and things have obviously changed dramatically. For most of us, food is now abundant, delicious, and not far from the couch. There are thousands of cookbooks with great recipes, lots of treats in the cookie jar, and numerous fast food restaurants that will satiate our hunger within five minutes. Circumstances are vastly different, but our genetic predispositions remain the same – human bodies are still designed for a life of hunting and gathering. It is no wonder that many of us carry at least a few more pounds than necessary.

There are always new diets and theories declaring what is healthiest for us to eat; often promising to help us feel better and get a bit leaner. Some plans advise eating a lot of meat, although many say it is better to consume little or none. Others say to eat fewer carbohydrates, but not all agree. Still others recommend that we eat more fruits, and almost all say to eat more vegetables. With so many different recommendations available, it is often difficult to adhere to a dietary plan that is healthy and sustainable for person, people, and planet.

Throughout history, millions of people have subsisted on very basic diets. In some regions this consisted of eating mostly a simple staple, perhaps a grain or root. In other regions, such as those occupied by Inuit populations, this involved mostly consumption of animal products. Human bodies are quite adaptable and resilient and can often survive on small amounts of very simple fuels.

We now, however, have the luxury of being able to find a diet where we can *thrive*, not just *survive*. We have an advantage over our ancestors, as we can now choose from an enormous variety of readily available healthy and delicious foods.

Many of us diminish this health advantage, by consuming produce grown with synthetic pesticides, or by eating processed non-nutritious convenience foods. Also, the factory-farmed animal products that many of us consume today are quite different than the wild game available to early hunter-gatherers, and even from the meat and milk obtained from the grass-fed free-range domesticated animals tended by our more recent agriculturally-dependent ancestors.

It is a useful life maxim to not unnecessarily intervene in natural systems that have evolved over tremendously long periods of time. Those who adhere to a Paleo-type of diet (the hunter-gatherer diet of our early ancestors) follow this idea, attempting to perpetuate ancient practices by eating foods that human digestive systems and metabolic pathways have learned to efficiently utilize over a period of two to three million years. The followers of this diet avoid grains, beans, and dairy products that were developed only a relatively recent ten to twelve thousand years ago, when the hunter-gatherer method of obtaining food was mostly supplanted by farming.

Many experts think that ten thousand years has been enough time for human bodies to learn how to process these newer food groups. Although most populations have adapted fairly well to humanity's relatively new diet, there are some people who do not absorb or metabolize some of the newcomer foods (wheat, corn, beans, and dairy products) quite as well as they do the meat, fruit and vegetable fare consumed by our far more ancient ancestors.

Each of the above diets has their benefits: The grain-based diet of the last ten thousand years is easy and inexpensive to follow, and is typically more Earth-friendly and sustainable than consuming large quantities of meat – particularly on a planet with nearly 8 billion people. However, at an individual level, a more Paleo hunter-gatherer type of diet may be preferable, or even perhaps necessary, for some people with food sensitivities such as intolerance to lactose, beans, nuts, or certain grains.

In contrast to the dietary changes brought by the introduction of agriculture ten thousand years ago, the eating habits of the last one hundred years have been considerably less tolerated. Many people now consume high fructose corn syrup drinks, processed meats derived from confined and medicated animals, and foods containing large amounts of sugar and preservatives. This diet also often includes pesticide-laden cereals, fruits and vegetables.

The results have been disastrous – skyrocketing rates of obesity, diabetes, hypertension, heart disease, and cancer. Even rising rates of autism could possibly be attributed to a genetic predisposition coupled with an environmental trigger such as pesticide exposure.[1] Human bodies have simply not had enough time to adapt to this new way of food production and eating; and it is unlikely that they ever will.

In a healthy diet, one eats small or moderate amounts of many different food groups; attempting to in some degree mimic the diet of his/her ancestors – while keeping an eye on the total quantity consumed.

Preparing, eating, and sharing food are some of the great pleasures of life. Should you have a big piece of Mom's apple pie on Thanksgiving Day? Absolutely! Any possible minor adverse physical affect would be more than offset by an improvement in your emotional health. Should you have a big piece of apple pie every night to remind you of Mom? Well.... probably not.

So exactly what does constitute a great diet, a plan that is not only healthy for your body, but also easy on our Earth? The answer can be summarized in one extraordinarily simple suggestion that requires no membership or subscription:

Eat a wide variety of locally grown organic plants!

That's it. Eat organic plants. This plan emphasizes eating a wide array of colorful vegetables, along with lesser amounts of whole grains, fruits, seeds, beans and nuts – all organically grown.

For optimal health, every meal should begin with a large serving of various organic vegetables and fruits at the *front* of your plate. Following just this one simple step will put you well on your way to living a long and healthy life.

Beans can also be added as important sources of healthy calories and protein; as can whole grains and eggs, and also relatively small amounts of dairy products. Organic free-range meat and wild seafood provide excellent nutrition, and can be great *adjuncts* to a diet emphasizing large amounts of a wide variety of organic produce. All of these other food groups are great supporting characters, but the true stars of the show are a wide variety of beautiful and colorful organic vegetables and fruits.

This diet is the essential framework of a healthy nutrition plan and, for most people, should make up most of their daily food intake. Each individual can add to and customize this plan to suit his or her own wants, needs, ethical concerns and body type; but eating a large serving of organic vegetables and fruits with every meal is a general core philosophy that can be followed to achieve optimal health.

Plants: Humanity's Best Friends Forever

Using relatively simple substrates, our human bodies are incredibly adept at building the vast majority of the thousands of chemical structures that are necessary for our survival. However, there are some items that our bodies cannot create on their own, instead depending upon plants to supply these life sustaining products. We call these products *essential nutrients*; essential because human life is not possible without attaining them through our diet. These essential nutrients include many elements obtained from the rocks of the Earth, as well as substances created by plants – which includes some fats, carbohydrates, and amino acids; and nearly all of the vitamins necessary for human survival.

You may remember seeing a poster of the periodic table of the elements on the wall of your high school chemistry classroom. The periodic table lists the 98 naturally-occurring elements, each given an atomic number which reflects the number of protons contained in its nucleus. Scientists believe that these elements were formed by the actions of tremendous heat and pressure on the primordial dust of an exploding supernova, some of which eventually coalesced to become part of our Earth.

At least 16 of these elements are essential for human existence, and several more are also likely involved in human functions. Some of these elements – such as carbon and nitrogen – are needed in large amounts, and these are termed *macrominerals*. Others – like copper and zinc – are needed in only small amounts and are called *microminerals* or trace minerals. Luckily for us, we do not need to eat the Earth to get them, as plants do this work for us, by absorbing these nutrients through their root systems.

The chain of nutrition begins with rain falling from the heavens upon the Earth. Aided by bacteria, water begins to weather the rocks of the land, leaching out important minerals. The action of the rain also creates small crevices, which can then be enlarged by the freezing and thawing of water, breaking the rocks down into smaller pieces. Primitive plant forms can survive on this rocky substrate. These plants eventually die and provide a tiny amount of organic material (soil) for more advanced plant forms to grow upon; plants which are sometimes eaten by animal life. These plants and animals in turn will also die and form even more soil.

Eventually, over many thousands of years, three layers of soil will form. The most superficial layer contains mostly organic material from decayed plants and animals, and some insoluble minerals. The middle layer contains relatively little organic material and some soluble minerals; and the deepest layer is essentially bedrock. Plants send out roots into the middle layer, to soak up the essential minerals contained in this region.

While their roots extend into the Earth to accept nutrients from the soil, plant stems and leaves simultaneously reach skyward, obtaining additional carbon from the atmosphere. Using the energy of the sun to combine carbon dioxide (CO_2) and water, they form carbohydrates and oxygen, producing energy for their vital functions and metabolism. Plants use carbon to make simple sugars, which form the building blocks for the synthesis of all organic molecules.

While continuously releasing oxygen into the air for all to breathe, plants also help to cool our Earth – by sequestering CO_2 from the skies above a human civilization that presently produces far too much of this greenhouse gas.

Using inputs from soil and air, plants can create everything that they need to survive. This includes substances that humans are unable to make for themselves (at least not in sufficient quantities); such as Omega-3 and Omega-6 essential fatty acids, and all nine different essential amino acids needed for protein production. This list of plant-made substances also includes *most* of the vitamins necessary for human survival – although vitamin B-12 must typically be obtained from animal sources, and mushrooms are the only good plant source of vitamin D (our bodies also make vitamin D with sunlight exposure).

But it gets better yet, because when we eat plants, we not only get the essential minerals, carbohydrates, fatty acids, amino acids, and vitamins that humans need to survive, we also get additional nutrients that these plants build for their own protection. Plants build up to 25,000 different types of these substances, which they use to defend themselves against viruses, bacteria and harsh climates. These chemicals are called *phytonutrients*, and one of the other properties of some of them is to give color to their host plant.

Research is showing that many phytonutrients are quite beneficial for human health as well. Also referred to as phytochemicals, these substances are not necessarily essential for our daily metabolic processes. However, many are considered to play a *helpful* role in many important human body functions – which may include aiding our immune systems, helping to prevent or treat cancer, and providing cardiovascular protective effects.

What About Anti-nutrients?

Plants certainly contain many beneficial nutrients, but many also contain some *anti-nutrients* as well – which they produce to defend themselves from infections and insects. As their name implies, anti-nutrients can block the intestinal absorption of nutrients in the human digestive tract.

The list of plant anti-nutrient substances includes glucosinolates (in cruciferous vegetables), lectins (present in legumes and whole grains), oxalates (in green leafy vegetables, tea), phytates (found in whole grains), saponins (in legumes, whole grains), and tannins (in tea, coffee, legumes),

Regarding consuming plants that contain anti-nutrients, the general consensus message at this time is that the health benefits of eating these foods outweigh the potential negative nutritional effects.[2]

Many plants that contain anti-nutrients also offer substantial net health benefits; including lowering rates of cardiovascular disease and type 2 diabetes, assisting in weight control, and providing excellent sources of vitamins, protein, healthy fats, fiber, and minerals.

Eating a wide variety of foods is recommended; to avoid loading up on a particular anti-nutrient. Avoiding the consumption of large amounts of a single food at any one meal minimizes the decrease in nutrient absorption that may be associated with the presence of anti-nutrients.

Populations at risk for nutritional deficiencies should work with a Registered Dietician to help monitor their diet for anti-nutrient content.

It may be prudent to sometimes eat fruits and vegetables raw, as some nutrients may be degraded by high temperatures. However, some plant substances become more bioavailable after cooking. For those with digestion problems, it may be necessary to cook some plants to soften them, and peeling will also help. Mix it up – eat some produce raw, and enjoy some cooked as well.

Remember that fresh or frozen fruits and vegetables are more nutritious than canned items. Also, nutrient levels can drop rapidly during transport – one of many reasons to buy from local sources.

Eat a wide variety of predominantly locally grown organic plants.

Eating a **wide variety** of different plants is suggested, because plants produce many essential proteins, fats, and vitamins, and thousands of different types of phytonutrients – just not all in the same organism.

Consumption of **locally grown** food is recommended, as this reduces fuel usage and greenhouse gas emissions, adds a measure of security to our food supply by encouraging biodiversity, and is supportive of local economies and small businesses. It is of course not always possible to buy produce grown in your own region, but usually the closer the better.

Eating **organic** food ensures that you will not be ingesting dangerous synthetic pesticide chemicals along with your healthy nutrients. This is also far better for a regenerative and sustainable Earth environment. Much more information regarding organic food consumption and production is presented later in this chapter.

A plan favoring consumption of mostly **plant** life over animal-based products is recommended for several reasons. Plants often contain a wider variety of nutrients than do animal products, and some studies have shown that a plant-based diet decreases the risk of cardiovascular disease, cancer, and bone fracture.[3]

In addition, the production of meat and animal-based products can be very resource intensive and polluting. It is also at times an inefficient means of providing sufficient calories to large numbers of people.

Livestock systems have been estimated to occupy over thirty percent of the global land surface area. In many regions, carbon-sequestering forests have been cut down to use the land to directly graze animals, or to grow crops to feed to animals in distant markets.[4]

The Union of Concerned Scientists, an alliance of over 400,000 citizens and scientists, argues that beef is ecologically inefficient – as it uses about sixty percent of the world's agricultural land yet produces less than five percent of the world's protein and less than two percent of its calories.[5]

Over-grazing by domesticated animals has resulted in erosion of valuable soil, destruction of native species, and the proliferation of weeds. Cows also belch and pass methane, a potent greenhouse gas that has contributed to climate change.

There are also resource use issues associated with livestock production. Approximately 36% of all U.S. grown corn crops are used to feed animals (another 40% is used to produce ethanol for fuel, and much of the rest is used to make high-fructose corn syrup).[6]

Raising livestock also involves using large amounts of another increasingly valuable resource – water. The average U.S. diet currently requires over one thousand gallons of water per person per day to produce. Cutting consumption of animal products in half would reduce this number by over one-third.[7]

Tightly packed groups of any species of animal (including humans) are also breeding grounds for pandemic illnesses. Approximately 75% of "new" human pathogens reported in the last twenty-five years have originated from animals.[8] An emerging disease is defined as one that is known to newly infect humans, has become virulent, or has recently become drug resistant. In just the last four decades, dozens of these new diseases have appeared.

Presently, the majority of antibiotics used in the U.S. are

administered to livestock and poultry, not people. This policy has contributed to the formation of pathogens resistant to antibiotics that humans depend on to treat infections – creating a public health problem that could get much worse.

Eating meat or other animal products also introduces ethical concerns for some people, particularly if animals are factory-raised and confined in crowded cages, as is often the case with poultry and pigs.

After reading all of this, it may be easy to jump to the conclusion that animal products are the devil. But it is far more complicated than that, and there is certainly not a one-size-fits-all recommendation for meat and dairy consumption. Even though eating meat is not always ecologically efficient, neither is turning on the stove to cook my vegetables instead of eating them raw, or choosing crème brulee and coffee for dessert rather than an apple and a glass of water. It takes over fifty gallons of water to grow the beans for a single cup of coffee.[9]

There will always be some trade-offs between enjoyment and ecologic efficiency. And although many areas could predominantly feed themselves with grains, beans, fruits, nuts, and vegetables, there are also large regions of the world – such as sub-Saharan Africa – that are reliant on utilizing grazing animals as a necessary food source.

Can Cows Save the Planet?

Improper grazing by animal herds is certainly an environmental concern. But, interestingly, it appears that it is also unhealthy for our Earth if its grasslands are not grazed at all.

The concept of holistic land management offers ranchers an intriguing approach to raising cows, goats, and sheep. The general idea is to imitate Nature – by using closely managed domestic herds to replicate the grazing patterns of wild animals.

Holistic land management ranchers acknowledge that Earth's climate has been negatively impacted by the desertification of huge swaths of land in areas of low humidity; in large part due to the effects of poorly managed grazing by domesticated animals. But in an ironic twist, their research indicates that humanity may now actually be dependent on large numbers of domestic herbivores to properly manage native grasslands and help combat climate change.

Native grasslands were once thriving ecosystems, reliant on large herds of wild herbivores – such as buffalo, elk, deer, and antelope – to maintain their normal growing cycles. Many of these herds were decimated by overhunting, and their feeding grounds are now grazed by domesticated animals that do not follow the patterns of their wild predecessors. Presently, most rangeland is usually very heavily grazed, and then often left to rest (or in some locales burned, which damages soil and pollutes air).

Holistic land management ranchers argue that these current practices are not sustainable; noting that native grasses growing in low humidity regions will not decompose appropriately unless they are naturally grazed. These grasses will instead slowly oxidize without adding nutrients to the soil, eventually turning the land into a desert, accelerating climate change. Their research has shown that if large groups of animals are allowed to graze at defined locations and precise intervals – determined by the appearance of the grasses instead of a set calendar schedule – the overall effect is a net improvement of the land.

For millions of years, healthy grasslands co-evolved with grazing ruminants. Following natural rhythms, native plants were eaten by these animals, decomposed by their gut bacteria, and then deposited as nutrient-rich dung and urine in the soil. This promotes a virtuous cycle; one where plants grow more exuberantly, helping soil to better absorb rain water, and ultimately leading to even greater growth of carbon-sequestering plants (offsetting some of the deleterious global warming effects of methane gas produced by ruminants).

Native grasslands, covering vast swaths of land in many continents, require wild or well-managed domesticated animal activity to fully flourish. The lives of grazing animals above the soil surface are entwined with the lives of the multitude of organisms living below the surface. Grassland soil health is only fully optimized if the plants that express its life are grazed, trampled, and fertilized by herbivores and other animals walking over its surface.

As the numbers of wild animals are now markedly attenuated, it may be that holistic ranching ideas are generally correct. Perhaps the best hope to maintain ecological balance in world grasslands – and combat desertification – could now rest on the shoulders of the humble cow and other grazing ruminants, closely replicating the ancient feeding patterns of their displaced wild cousins.

A Few More Details About Grazing and the Environment

The overall effect that grazing animals have on ecology is one of complexity. Over-grazing has certainly been devastating to rangeland, particularly in arid and semi-arid locales. And cows do burp methane gas, to be sure. But grasslands need not be over-grazed; rather *properly* grazed, instead. Also, animal belching is nothing new. Millions of wild herbivores once naturally grazed global grasslands, and methane emissions from animals are no recent phenomenon. However, *too many* animals belching methane, combined with too many humans creating this and other greenhouse gases (GHG's), are indeed a problem.

Deleterious environmental effects related to meat production are undeniable. However, when utilized as part of a comprehensive soil management plan, grazing herds of animals can also have positive ecologic effects. Managed with optimal stock density and frequent moving, animal herds can increase soil vitality. This naturally supercharged soil does not need synthetic fertilizer additions (the overuse of synthetic fertilizer produces increased emissions of nitrous oxide, another very potent greenhouse gas). And this healthier soil supports greater plant life to sequester more CO_2 from the atmosphere, while creating better water absorption and less runoff as well.

Ecologic effects are complicated and do not occur in isolation. Multiple systems in Nature interact with each other in ways that are difficult to predict. Well-managed herds of animals may indeed help to *decrease* atmospheric CO_2 levels. However, the magnitude of change varies by locale – clay soils sequester more CO_2 than do sandy soils, and soil carbon uptake is also influenced by the amount of precipitation in an area. Grazing has also been shown in some locations to be associated with decreased nitrous oxide emissions.

A reduction in CO_2 and nitrous oxide levels may counter, at least in some places, the deleterious atmospheric effects of methane gas produced by cows. To further complicate matters, CO_2, methane, and nitrous oxide each have diverse impacts on weather and climate, and demonstrate their effects at differing time intervals.

Properly managed livestock may in some cases also decrease erosion and run-off; by feeding soil biology, thereby increasing soil health and its water absorptive capacity. However, improperly managed livestock can increase erosion – thus releasing sequestered carbon, and increasing stream sedimentation. Many livestock systems have severely degraded rangeland, and they still do in some places.

What is the overall effect of grazing on ecology? In the last one hundred years, it has likely been a net loss for the environment. That is the short answer. But, slowly, changes are being made. The grass-fed/grass-finished controlled grazing model is certainly an improvement over the far more prevalent grain-fed beef feedlot system, although the degree of benefit is a subject of debate. Choosing to closely replicate the historic numbers and feeding patterns of displaced wild ruminants may indeed turn out to be a good course of action. Following Nature usually works.

Out of necessity or preference, there will always be a large part of the global populace that eats meat. If human population numbers begin to decrease, and if consumers choose to eat only animals that are raised using sustainable methods, an equilibrium can be achieved. But if greater numbers of people continue to demand greater amounts of meat, fattened with soy or corn and/or raised on improperly managed or deforested land, the planet could descend into a spiral of worsening climate change and environmental destruction.

Animals that are grazed on rangeland provide humanity important calories, often derived from soil that may otherwise directly yield very little human nutrition. However, using massive amounts of very fertile farmland to grow crops to feed to animals (rather than for direct human consumption) is not the most efficient use of Earth's resources. Fertile farm soil provides far more calories per acre if its crops are directly consumed by humans.

Rotational grazing of farmland cover crops or post-harvest debris provides a valuable *secondary* soil benefit. However, using millions of acres of rich topsoil for the *primary* purpose of producing corn or soy for animal consumption is not a resourceful or sustainable practice.

It is not necessary that humanity adopts mass veganism, at least not at current population levels. But it is generally healthier for our bodies, and our planet, for most people to eat relatively fewer animal products. Optimally, these animal products should be obtained from locally raised and harvested land and sea animals; preferably wild or free-range creatures eating their native diet.

Producing only ethically raised and sustainably sourced animal products could prove difficult, particularly if the global population increases – as there is a finite amount of land available to raise grass-fed/grass-finished cows, free-range chickens and pastured pork.

With our current population numbers, humanity also certainly cannot completely return to the hunter-gatherer dietary patterns of our distant ancestors. Population growth has burned humanity's boats in that regard.

Presently, humankind is dependent on agricultural systems for survival. Of course, even this is not risk-free. Climate change or plant disease may significantly affect crop yields and nutritive value, and certain geographic regions could easily become imperiled. A close evaluation of optimal global population numbers must be at the center of any discussion of world nutrition and food security concerns. Overpopulation issues are discussed in greater detail in Chapter Twenty.

If the global population expands as predicted to 9 or 10 billion by 2050, individuals will likely, by necessity, consume far less meat than they do today – if they wish to live on a sustainable planet. Primary dietary protein sources would probably have to shift from animal products to nuts and legumes (beans, peas, lentils, etc.). That might not go over very well. A few studies that offer predictions and recommendations for humanity's future are outlined in the Appendix.

For now, *most* people should eat less meat – and try to avoid feedlot and factory-raised options altogether. If you choose to eat fewer animal products, remember to fill the extra space on your plate with vegetables and fruits instead of high-calorie carbohydrates. Many people have heeded some of the dietary recommendations of the last few decades, decreasing their consumption of processed and factory grown meats and dairy products. However, they have often replaced these items with sugary drinks, French fries, and high-calorie processed foods rather than lower-calorie nutritious fruits and vegetables – jumping from the frying pan into the fire.

Today's Menu

Consider starting the day with a breakfast of fresh fruits and vegetables. Making a large smoothie is an easy way to do this. Mixing frozen blueberries, bananas, spinach leaves, ice, and water in a blender is a great start to build on. If you prefer a large breakfast, include oatmeal cereal topped with fruit and nuts. You could also occasionally consider cooking yourself an egg or two (organic, cage-free options).

Lunch is a big organic lettuce salad topped with a colorful variety of fruits, vegetables, nuts, and beans drizzled with olive oil; and a slice of whole grain bread on the side.

For dinner, the main entrée can be a large serving of baked zucchini, tomato, and onion; seasoned with spices. Complementary side entrées include a bean or quinoa dish, and 3-4 ounces of free-range meat or seafood, if desired. A whole grain roll and a small bowl of fresh or frozen mixed berries complete the meal.

An Evolutionary Perspective

Some readers may prefer that the above menu not include any meat or other animal products. It is certainly true that a completely vegan diet can be healthy if properly followed, even in regard to adequate protein intake – but this diet does take far more effort and commitment than do more traditional diets.

A vegan diet requires adequate sun exposure and possible supplements to ensure appropriate levels of vitamin D. Those adhering to a vegan lifestyle must also add vitamin B-12 (via pills or fortified foods) to their diet, as this essential nutrient is not naturally present in plant-based foods. Like it or not, over millions of years, human beings evolved to be at least somewhat reliant on the consumption of animal products for optimal nutrition and health.

But the winds are changing. Humankind has relatively recently become less dependent on our evolutionary predisposition to eat animal products. Wheat, rice, corn, millet, barley and potatoes now provide more than 90% of the total global calories consumed.[10] Collectively, we have adapted at least reasonably well to a predominantly grain-based diet. And, as vitamins and supplements can be added to many of the foods that we eat, it is now possible for most people to meet nutritional requirements without consuming animal products.

This dietary adaptation to grains has generally worked out fairly well for most populations. However, there are some individuals whose bodies may not tolerate the consumption of many grains – particularly wheat products, which may cause or worsen inflammatory conditions in some people. There are others, too, who cannot tolerate beans or nuts in large quantities. Without beans, nuts, and grains to provide adequate daily protein requirements, by default some people may need to consume at least some animal products to achieve optimal health.

All Creatures Great and Small

There are many individuals who are ethically opposed to the idea of killing animals for human food consumption. Some people are also uncomfortable utilizing animals for their milk, eggs, or other products. These sentiments are fair enough.

Each person must answer to an inner voice, maintaining fidelity to personal principles. However, life is often messy, and concessions must sometimes be made. When noble ideals crash headlong into daily life, it is often only compromise that creates a clear path forward.

We are born into a universe that is not of our making; one that follows an unyielding model of creative destruction, where many living forms must consume other living forms to survive. Unsettling as it may be, the fact remains that a lioness must kill a zebra to sustain her own life.

Even a vegan diet often involves some loss of animal life, particularly if mechanized agricultural techniques are employed. Many rodents, birds, reptiles, insects, worms and other living creatures are inadvertently killed during the planting and harvesting of crops. There is perhaps a tendency for humankind to be more protective of some life forms than others.

Humans often appear to rank other creatures (perhaps subconsciously) by perceived degrees of similarity to us; or by using cultural rules based on social conditioning or emotion. The death of a gorilla is met with appropriate outrage. But a mouse? Usually not so much. Even avowed carnivores often employ emotional and inconsistent ranking systems – many citizens of western cultures consider the idea of eating a dog or horse to be abhorrent, yet they have no problem with eating an equally sentient species such as a pig.

Humanity did certainly advance as a hunting species; however, this comes with a responsibility to utilize animal products in an ethical fashion. We evolved hunting animals and eating meat, but at the same time we developed an ever-deepening reservoir of consciousness. With that consciousness comes a realization that humankind is not set above and apart from the rest of the universe – rather we are immersed fully within it.

Although ours is indeed a violent world, this does not diminish the sanctity of each of Earth's creatures. All life is extraordinarily precious and astonishing. It is only by accepting this overarching precept that humanity can exist happily and healthfully within the sphere of Nature.

You may have heard the (perhaps fictional) story that if a frog happens to jump into a pot of very hot water it will immediately jump back out. However, if that same frog jumps into cool water that is slowly heated, it becomes accustomed to the small incremental changes in temperature and will therefore remain in the water until it perishes.

Ten thousand years ago, humans mostly abandoned hunting and gathering in favor of farming and the domestication of animals. This was a logical step undertaken to feed an increasingly large global populace. However, in the last century, humanity has taken an additional *unnecessary* step, slowly altering the conditions in which we treat many of the domesticated animals that we utilize for food.

We have gradually let the water come to a boil, acclimating ourselves to a disquieting new normal, one in which we now raise animals in factories or confined in small cages – because this method allows more meat or other animal products to be produced for less money. Poultry and pigs often endure insufferable existences, spending their entire lives indoors in cramped and crowded conditions.

It is one thing for humankind to obtain physical sustenance from wild or domesticated animals treated with compassion, respect, and dignity. It is quite another to obtain meat, milk or eggs from tightly confined or caged animals subjected to a life of misery.

The "free-range," and "pastured" concepts of animal production are not perfect solutions to a very perplexing and contentious issue. But they offer a compromise. And they do alleviate much of the suffering endured by many creatures that humans use for food.

Eat Your Veggies

The USDA's *MyPlate* plan and the Harvard School of Public Health's *Healthy Eating Plate* each recommend that vegetables and fruits fill up **one-half** of your plate at each meal.[11] Those who struggle with excessive weight should eat even more vegetables relative to the other foods.

Nuts, beans, and relatively small amounts of seafood, meat, or dairy products will provide protein sources and should make up approximately **one-fourth** of the meal.

The remaining **one-fourth** of the plate should be filled with whole grain products such as whole wheat (as tolerated), oats, corn and rice; and foods made with them.

This nutrition plan is a great start. I would add, importantly, that the produce and other foods we consume should all be grown with *organic* methods.

It's in the Genes

It should be acknowledged that weight control is inherently more difficult for some people than others, in part due to differing genetic predispositions. There are possibly even some groups of people who have "thrifty" genes, which in earlier times increased survival, as these individuals could make very efficient use of scarcely available food.

However, food options are now plentiful in the developed world, and this once useful trait has since become more detrimental than helpful. This by no means implies that it is impossible to control obesity if one comes from a family of large people, just that it may definitely be much more challenging for some than it is for others. Some large people certainly do have to work harder to stay fit than smaller people; but those with smaller statures can also have trouble with excess weight.

For most of us, there are no great secrets or diet plans to easily keep excess weight off of our body. The above proposed plan is simple but not easy – eat lots of organic vegetables, a little more fruit as well, and demonstrate portion control with the other food groups while avoiding processed meats and refined grains and sugar.

It may be helpful to use a strategy called crowding, where one fills up first on vegetables, and is therefore not as hungry for other more calorie-laden foods.

Making a major dietary change can be quite difficult, particularly early on. However, this does get significantly easier with time. Taste sensations quickly adapt, and a new diet can often become even more enjoyable than the old.

A Few Tips for Healthy and Sustainable Nutrition

1. **Show discipline while shopping.** Avoid shopping when hungry. Shop mostly in the peripheral aisles, which offer fresh produce. Avoid as much as possible the central aisles, which contain pre-packaged foods.

2. **Choose a wide selection of foods.**

3. **Eat organic produce.** The bulk of one's diet should come from organic whole grains, vegetables, beans, fruits, and nuts.

4. **Eat fewer animal products.** If you eat meat, eggs, or dairy products, choose organic free-range, cage-free, and pastured products.

5. **Eat more slowly.** Chewing food properly aids in good digestion, working on a mechanical basis by breaking food into smaller pieces, as well as on a neurological basis, as the act of chewing sends signals to the brain to begin orchestrating complex sequences involved in gut food absorption. The act of chewing slowly also helps one to more fully enjoy the meal; slowing down enough to mindfully appreciate the very process of eating, increasing overall relaxation and sense of well-being.

6. **Have water make up the vast majority of your fluid intake.** Use a water purifier. Filtering diminishes the amount of chorine, fluoride, pathogens, and other unwanted substances in your drinking water. Avoid the use of plastic bottled water – due to energy intensive production issues, plastic disposal problems, and potential health concerns from materials in the plastic leaching into your drink. A cup or two of coffee per day is probably ok for most people. Juice consumption should be limited. Avoid sodas and sports drinks.

7. **Favor real foods over pills and powders.** Unless one suffers from intestinal malabsorption or other maladies, most people eating a well-balanced diet do not typically require additional vitamins or other supplements. This may change someday, as depleted soils are yielding less-nutritious plants than in years past. Supplements may contain several beneficial substances, but they often do not provide the thousands of phytonutrients and fiber found in whole foods. Supplements are also not well-regulated, and their doses vary. Some experts do recommend occasional supplementation, as a type of insurance policy against inadequate nutrition; however, they also caution that *exceeding* daily recommended levels might cause problems. Should you supplement or not? It depends on your age, your diet, and your health. Consult your Registered Dietician or Healthcare Provider.

8. **Stop eating as soon as you begin to feel satiated,** even if your plate is not empty. Always save rather than discard leftovers. Globally, food waste is a serious problem.

9. **Stop eating 4 hours before bedtime.** Some studies show longevity benefits from restricting eating to a less than 12-hour period each day. Avoiding late evening eating also helps prevent stomach acid reflux and its attendant problems.

10. **Brush after meals.** This of course helps to strengthen teeth and gums. In addition, tooth brushing immediately after a meal often makes snacking a less frequent occurrence.

A Few More Ideas for a Healthy Diet

Use caution when considering eating seafood from lakes, rivers, bays, and estuaries – due to possible high levels of toxins. Check local marine advisories. Do not eat shark or swordfish.

Bread and pasta products should optimally be brown, and state "whole grain" as the first words of the ingredient list.

Brown rice has more nutrients than white rice, but also about eighty percent more inorganic arsenic, negating some of the positive aspects. Consumer Reports recommended that rice consumption be limited to 4½ servings per week for adults, and 2¾ serving per week for children, due to high arsenic levels often found in rice crops.[12]

Choosing organic rice is no guarantee of lower arsenic levels, as there can be naturally occurring arsenic in the soil, or the land may still harbor significant levels of this chemical from pesticides applied decades before a farm had changed to organic methods.

White basmati rice from California, India and Thailand has been shown to have the least amounts of inorganic arsenic; about half that of other types of white rice. Brown basmati rice from these regions has about a third less inorganic arsenic than brown rice from other locales. Arsenic levels can be reduced by boiling rice with twice the usual amount of water and discarding the excess after cooking.

All fruits and vegetables, even organic options, should be rinsed with running water; and when possible scrubbed with a clean brush prior to consumption. Oil-based pesticides may be difficult to remove with just water and a brush. However, the FDA currently recommends against using veggie washes that contain liquid detergents for cleaning, as possible detergent residues could be left behind.

Greatly limit the use of refined sugar or high fructose corn syrup.

Most commercial fruit and vegetable juices should only be consumed in small quantities, as many are often loaded with sugar and contain little or no fiber. Smoothies made from whole organic fruits and vegetables are a better option.

Eat many different types of grains, fruits, and vegetables. Variety is the spice of life! Be aware, however, that some individuals may be intolerant of (or allergic to) foods that their ancestors were not exposed to.

Be cautious of any food that comes in a wrapper. Read the label.

Do not keep lots of sweets and other treats in the house. If it is in your house it is in your mouth.

Drink around 6 to 8 glasses of filtered water per day, adjusting as necessary to your climate and degree of activity. In most circumstances, you do not need to get carried away and drink a lot more than this – you can actually get too much of a good thing. Ideally, urine should be a pale light-yellow color. If a person's urine is always completely clear and they are in the bathroom every hour, they may be overhydrating. Conversely, if a person's urine is often dark, they may be underhydrating.

Carbs, Proteins, and Fats

Regarding Carbohydrates:

Carbohydrates are what our bodies use to fuel daily activities. They are broken down into three classes, which include **sugars**, **starches**, and **fiber** (also called cellulose).

Sugars are simple carbohydrate molecules that our bodies can absorb easily. They taste sweet and are readily found in processed foods like sodas, candy, and ice cream. They are also found in healthier options such as fruit.

Starches are more complex and must first be broken down by intestinal enzymes into simple sugars before absorption. Foods high in starch include corn, rice, bread, and potatoes.

Fiber cannot be absorbed by our intestines; therefore, it provides no energy directly. But fiber serves other important functions, such as normalizing bowel habits, aiding in weight control, and helping to control cholesterol and blood sugar levels. High fiber diets have also been linked to improved heart health. Foods high in fiber include whole grain breads and cereals, brown rice, legumes, vegetables, and fruits.

Many Americans consume up to the equivalent of nearly twenty teaspoons of sugar per day, often in the form of high fructose corn syrup or refined white sugar. As a result, many suffer from diabetes, obesity, metabolic syndrome, and reactive hypoglycemia.

The most commonly ingested sugars are fructose, glucose, and sucrose. Sucrose is a combination of fructose and glucose, and is broken down in the gut lumen prior to absorption. Glucose is easily absorbed in the upper intestine; which is considered a plus if you need quick energy. Fructose is absorbed lower down in the intestine, where it is also utilized by gut bacteria, and therefore excessive consumption can result in gas and bloating.

When ingested in large amounts, glucose can cause a large spike in the release of insulin. This can cause a rapid drop in blood sugar and resultant hunger, with a repeat of the cycle. Insulin also causes the body to store more food calories as fat. For our ancestors, this was often a helpful response, as gorging on fruit in the fall would build up fat stores for a possibly cold and lean winter – a process that is not usually necessary today.

Although glucose can be easily metabolized by all cells in the body, fructose must be metabolized by the liver. Our ancestors consumed less than one-fourth the amount of fructose than we currently do; obtaining all of their fructose from fruits and vegetables. Human livers have not evolved to efficiently process the extra fructose that many people now consume in sugary drinks and processed foods. Excessive fructose consumption results in fatty liver disease, increased storage of fat around our organs (visceral fat), increases in triglycerides and LDL cholesterol levels, and an increase in the production of free radicals (electron-stealing substances that can damage DNA and other cell structures).

For optimal health, one should consider what human bodies have become most adapted to over millions of years. Our ancestors certainly did not consume large amounts of refined sugars. It makes sense to consume sugars in the combinations and amounts already present in fruits and vegetables.

If you satisfy your sweet tooth with cookies and candy, you are consuming sugar along with preservatives and fats. You are also robbing yourself of hundreds of phytonutrients that are already naturally pre-packaged in fruits and vegetables. Eating just empty calories, you will obtain fuel for energy but without any other benefits.

Some acceptable refined white sugar substitutes, when used in small amounts, include raw unprocessed honey, maple syrup, and sugar cane juice. Note that most of our ancestors did not consume these products in large quantities. Children under 1 year of age should not eat honey due to risk of botulism. Sugar cane juice is less processed than refined white sugar and contains a few nutrients. Date sugar may not dissolve well in cooking. Agave nectar is popular but it is also a refined product, containing mostly fructose.

Artificial sweeteners may indeed help restrict caloric intake, but some studies have demonstrated possible troublesome associations with various disease processes.

If you enjoy sweet baked goods, consider replacing refined sugar in the ingredient list with pureed or mashed fruit. Delicious treats can be made without added sugar.

If you decrease your consumption of sugar or sweeteners you can essentially reprogram your taste buds to appreciate much smaller degrees of sweetness. Fruits go from tasting good to tasting great.

Regarding Protein:

Some experts recommend consuming *low but sufficient* amounts of protein (0.31 to 0.36 grams of protein per pound of body weight/day), noting that too high of protein intake has been associated with cancer and increased mortality in humans.[13] Using this formula, a person weighing around 150 pounds should consume between 46 to 54 grams of protein per day (if this same person is ill, older, or exercises very intensely on a routine basis, they may require greater amounts).

On average, American adults consume roughly 50% more protein than the minimum requirement, varying by age group.[14] Sufficient protein is necessary, to be sure, but more is not always better.

A study in the American Journal of Clinical Nutrition noted that in North America only about 30% of protein intake comes from eating plant-derived foods. Globally, about 60% of protein intake is obtained from plant sources.[15] The authors also noted that mixtures of plant proteins can serve as a complete and well-balanced source of amino acids for meeting human physiological requirements.

A diet excluding meat, eggs, and dairy products can provide all of the protein needed for optimal health; however, this takes some discipline to accomplish. Nuts, beans, whole grains – and leafy green vegetables to a lesser extent (one cup cooked spinach provides 5 gm protein) – are all relatively high protein foods.

One may claim that many of our ancestors often ate a very high protein diet, relying heavily on wild game and fish; and therefore, we are genetically designed to do quite well on this diet. This argument does indeed have merit; however, we now live in a different set of circumstances. Some of the seafood species on our planet are quite polluted, and we may not be able to eat large quantities of some of them without concern of toxicity. Also, due to limited availability, relatively few people are sustained on wild game or seafood.

The meat consumed in the U.S. today is most often obtained from confined animal feeding operations (CAFO's). This is not necessarily the health and nutritional equivalent of eating meat obtained from wild game or domesticated animals feeding on natural grasses in open spaces – free from antibiotic and hormone injections, free from pesticides and other toxins in their tissues, and free from the stress of unnatural confined living.

What About Red Meat?

Of note, studies have found that the consumption of red meat is directly related to increased levels of illness, including heart disease and cancer. A report by the Harvard T.H. Chan School of Public Health described a 13% increase in all-cause mortality from eating *non-processed* red meat. This study also found a 20% increase in mortality in those who ate *processed* red meats, including bacon, jerky, sausage, and ham; all of which typically use high levels of sodium and nitrates.[16]

This study took in to consideration variables such as patient age, body mass index, family history of heart disease, and physical activity. However, it did not differentiate between meats obtained from wild vs. domesticated animals; meat obtained from grass-finished vs. feedlot cattle; or beef consumption vs. consumption of other red meat sources such as pork.

The study also did not account for differences in the cuts of meats consumed, or for variations in cooking methods. Well-done or burnt meats cooked at high heat may contain mutagenic substances called HCA's (heterocyclic amines) and PAH's (polycyclic aromatic hydrocarbons).

It would be interesting to determine the effects on morbidity and mortality in a study group that consumed modest amounts of red meat, always prepared at low or medium heat without burning, and obtained only from free-range domesticated or wild animals eating their native organic diet. It would also be interesting to further subdivide this study group into sedentary and non-sedentary individuals, and also those who always consumed their red meat alongside a large serving of organic fruits and vegetables (one study in mice demonstrated that chlorophyll negated the potentially mutagenic effect of red meat heme upon colonic mucosal cells).

The bottom-line is that human bodies can usually fulfill all or most protein needs via plant-based food groups. If necessary or desired, this can be augmented by adding relatively small amounts of seafood, meat, eggs, and dairy products – obtained from wild or free-range animals eating a native organic diet.

Regarding Fats:

Just like carbohydrates and protein, fats are an essential part of a healthy diet. Omega-3 fatty acids (EPA, DHA, and ALA) are a particularly useful type of fat, used by our bodies as an integral part of cell membrane formation and also for hormone synthesis. They have been shown to help prevent heart disease and stroke, they may help control some autoimmune diseases, and they may also possibly play a protective role in cancer prevention.[17]

ALA-type Omega-3 fatty acids can be obtained from a well-balanced vegetarian diet. Walnuts, leafy vegetables, canola oil, chia seeds, and flaxseed are each rich in this beneficial fatty acid. Eating plant-derived Omega-3 fatty acids is not an exact replacement for seafood consumption; but studies show that ALA, similar to DHA and EPA, may also be important for protection against heart disease.[17,85]

DHA and EPA-type Omega-3 fatty acids are obtained by eating fish and other seafood; however, some fish species also contain unsafe levels of various toxins in addition to these beneficial fats.

This presents a bit of a dilemma: Seafood is naturally a superfood; high in Omega-3 fatty acids, protein, and vitamins A, D, and B12. However, it can also be tainted with mercury or other dangerous toxins called persistent organic pollutants – especially PCB's (consumption of PCB's by humans can be lessened by removing the skin and fatty areas of a fish, and grilling on a rack so that fat drippings drop away).

Presently, most health advisories suggest that the health benefits of eating seafood about once or twice a week usually outweigh the risks of toxicity from mercury or persistent organic pollutants. However, this risk/benefit ratio is influenced by the individual's age group, the type and amount of seafood consumed, the location from which it was obtained, and possibly by the presence or absence of healthy lifestyle practices employed by the person who is eating it.

If you choose to consume seafood, mix it up, eat a wide variety – some fatty and some not – and mostly select options with relatively lower mercury levels (e.g. salmon, sardines, tilapia, pollock, shrimp, scallops, clams, and oysters). The National Resources Defense Council (https://www.nrdc.org/sites/default/files/walletcard.pdf)

offers a printable wallet-sized card comparing various mercury levels.

Remember to also emphasize other important healthy lifestyle patterns by practicing dietary modification, exercise, mindfulness via prayer/meditation, and trying to average about 8 hours of sleep each night.

To make sure your seafood choices are also planet-friendly, consider going to the Monterey Bay Seafood Watch website and printing up their wallet-sized card (or download their app) with specific recommendations based on sustainability issues. You can also look for the Marine Stewardship Council label on your seafood purchase, verifying that it was wild-caught from a sustainable source.

Consumption of *unsaturated* fats in plant oils has been shown to be associated with health benefits. Plant oil (olive, avocado, etc.) may not necessarily fit in with our individual ancient ancestral eating predispositions, but many nutrition experts tout its value, particularly if plant oil calories are replacing those from saturated fats.

Unlike other commonly used plant oils, extra virgin olive oil (EVOO) and avocado oil are unrefined. Olive oil consumption is associated with a decreased risk of cardiovascular disease. Olive oil does have a fairly low smoke point, so it should only be used in low or medium-heat cooking (overheating oils can create free radicals). Avocado oil has a high smoke point.

In the last few decades, *saturated* fats (which typically come from animal sources) have been deemed unhealthy when consumed in large amounts. However, there is currently much debate over saturated fats and their effects on cardiovascular health, with some studies suggesting that they may not be as bad as once thought. One point of general agreement seems to be that replacing saturated fats with highly processed carbohydrates may not result in a decrease in heart disease, and may in fact do the opposite.

Coconut oil has traditionally been lumped in with other saturated fat sources as being unhealthy – a categorization that has also been hotly contested by some people. It is possible that coconut oil may have received an undeservedly bad reputation, as it contains much more of the beneficial substance lauric acid when compared to saturated fat from animal products.

Virgin coconut oil contains small amounts of antioxidant compounds that may help diminish inflammation. Whether or not coconut oil is a "health food" is the subject of considerable controversy, so at this point it should probably be used sparingly.

Trans fats are not naturally found in Nature. These are man-made products designed to be solid at room temperature and to have a long shelf life (e.g. vegetable shortening, and some processed snack foods). They have been shown to be very unhealthy, particularly with regard to heart disease, and should be avoided. Trans fats have recently been banned in the U.S.

MORE FOOD FOR THOUGHT: GOING ORGANIC

The USDA defines organic foods as those that are produced without synthetic pesticides or synthetic chemical fertilizers, do not contain genetically modified organisms, and are not processed using irradiation, industrial solvents, or chemical additives.

Organic food is presently more expensive to purchase than food produced with more commonly employed non-organic agricultural methods. However, if a person consumes less meat and processed foods, and drinks mostly water instead of other beverages, their total grocery bill does not change that much – and may even be lowered. And, as more people begin to make healthy choices, economy of scale factors will soon make grocery store organic food options much more affordable.

Many people also have the opportunity to grow organic produce on their own land or in community gardens. With the use of very intensive techniques and fertile soil, it has been demonstrated that a family of four can grow enough food to sustain themselves on as little as a quarter-acre of land.[18] That comes to only about one tennis court-sized area of land per person per year.

If you don't have a lot of free time, or much space for a garden, you may wish to consider planting some fruit trees in your yard – as they provide a lot of food for fairly minimal effort and space. Consider dwarf tree varieties, as they have an even smaller footprint than full-size trees and are easier to harvest. Growing food in your own yard is about as local as it gets; and you also know for sure that synthetic pesticides were not sprayed on your trees. As an added bonus, fruit trees provide beautiful blossoms in the spring and colorful foliage in the fall.

Synthetic Pesticides

Organic food regulations do not allow the use of *synthetic pesticides*, which are chemical products created by humans.

When looking at the big picture, it is absurd to tell our children "Eat your fruits and vegetables," and then negate some or all of the benefit by serving them pesticide-laden produce. Most health authorities say that it is better to ingest fruits and vegetables containing present levels of pesticides than to eat no produce at all – but those are not the only two choices. Organic options are readily available. It is inevitable in modern society that we will be exposed to toxic substances, no matter how careful we are. This makes it even more important to limit this exposure as much as possible, especially when it involves younger age populations.

In toxicology circles they say the dose makes the poison, but one must be very cautious when dismissing the effects of a certain toxin (which by itself may not have been shown to have a definite short-term untoward effect with small dose exposure), especially when tests are performed by the companies who sell the product. The *long-term* effects of the thousands of individual new chemicals that our bodies are presently exposed to are often not known.

It is also quite possible that there can be synergistic harmful effects from these chemicals. The total effect of a combination of chemicals may be greater than the sum of the effects of these substances when taken independently; i.e. the presence of one chemical may possibly enhance or potentiate the effects of a second chemical.

It is also very shortsighted to not consider the deleterious long-term effects that synthetic pesticides are having on the health of our Earth, the consequences of which will be suffered by our young people and future generations. Choosing organic food options helps to build a healthy body and a healthy planet.

A *pesticide* is a generic term for a substance that is used to combat pests. Under the pesticide umbrella are insecticides, herbicides, fungicides, and rodenticides – used to kill insects, weeds, fungus, and animals. Herbicides are the most heavily utilized, accounting for about three-fourths of all pesticides applied in the U.S.

In the world of food or fiber production, a pest is defined as any organism that competes with humans for resources – although Nature does not consider any organism to be a pest any more than it considers a human being to be a pest.

One problem with synthetic pesticides is that they may contain persistent organic pollutants (presently mostly in developing countries). The word organic does not always imply a good thing, and in chemistry this usually refers to a substance containing carbon.

Persistent organic pollutants (e.g. PCB's, DDT, dioxin) are typically lipophilic (fat loving) novel substances that resist environmental degradation. These substances bio-accumulate in fatty tissues and are not easily degraded, because Earth organisms lack previous exposure to them, and therefore have not developed the detoxification and excretion mechanisms necessary to deal with them.

Similar to heavy metals, persistent organic pollutants will also bio-magnify to greater levels as they move up the food chain. A familiar example of bio-magnification is seen with mercury. Mercury gas is a byproduct of coal burning. Winds blow mercury gas over the sea, rain brings it down into the ocean, and then bacteria change it to a more toxic form. Algae are exposed to the mercury and are consumed by plankton. The plankton is then consumed by small fish, which are subsequently eaten in large quantities by predatory fish, effectively magnifying the levels at each step of the way.

When humans consume persistent organic pollutants, obtained from either plant or animal food sources, they put themselves at risk for developing cancer. These substances can also disrupt endocrine, immune, and neurological systems.

Pesticides are designed to kill living organisms. It is important to consider that ingested pesticides may be harmful to beneficial human gut bacteria – which are vital contributors to the health of our digestive tract, our immune system, and the rest of our body. Our gut bacteria are just as much a part of "us" as are the cells of our tissues. Anything that hurts them, hurts "us."

Pesticides are not only dangerous due to relatively immediate effects on humans, but also for the long-term environmental consequences of their use. It has been estimated that over 95% of pesticides ultimately end up reaching a destination other than the intended species.[19] This results in the death of many beneficial insects, birds, and other animals; and pollution of air, water and soil.

It is important to consider the effects of synthetic chemicals on all life forms in the soil. Soil works best when left alone to follow its own natural and interconnected living rhythms, rather than being treated as lifeless dirt that merely acts as a substrate to hold fertilizer and prevent a plant from falling over.

Healthy soil is very much alive. One teaspoon of soil can contain up to a billion bacteria (represented by over 10,000 different species), one million protozoa, twenty nematodes, and several miles of fungal strands called hyphae. Working in concert with each other, as well as with earthworms and insects, the vast majority of these organisms are beneficial to plant life – aiding in nutrient cycling and disease suppression.

Our Earth has settled into a system that works very well when left relatively undisturbed. Synthetic pesticides negatively affect the integrated ecology of the root zone of a plant. These pesticides can bind to minerals such as calcium, boron, and manganese, decreasing bioavailability to the plant – and subsequently delivering less of these essential nutrients to the person who eats the plant.

Pesticide use also reduces biodiversity, which is defined as the degree of variation in life forms. Greater biodiversity is associated with greater health of an ecosystem.

Many farmers continue to spray dangerous pesticides on their crops (our food), to lower their costs and increase their profits. However, as profits increase, so does excessive risk-tolerance.

Some people argue that synthetic pesticide use is necessary to increase yields, to feed the large number of people in the world today. But that argument is simply untrue. There are many currently available – but not commonly implemented – Agroecology methods that can substantially increase yields (more on this in Chapter Twenty-one). At times, these yields may be even greater than those achieved by using synthetic pesticides.

Are Natural Pesticides Any Better than Synthetic Pesticides?

The organic produce that you buy may not have been treated with *synthetic* pesticides – but it may have been treated with one or more *natural* pesticides, so be sure to always wash all of your produce, organic or non-organic.

Choosing a natural pesticide over a synthetic pesticide may not always be better for you and the planet – but it usually is. Although too much of any pesticide can cause problems, using pesticides derived from natural sources (e.g. Spinosad, neem, cedar products, copper, and insect pheromones) may be less dangerous to the health of your body and the environment than using synthetic varieties. But note that "natural" does not always mean safe. One liter of "natural" botulin toxin is probably enough to wipe out every person on the planet.

Natural pesticides are less likely than synthetic products to build up in the environment, and Nature's biological systems may do a better job of breaking them down. But, if possible, it is best not to use any *herbicides*, and to use only very limited amounts of *insecticide* (as a relatively rare last option) whether it is a natural or synthetic product. Integrated Pest Management (IPM) methods, discussed below, should always be used. Currently, small-scale organic farmers are more likely than conventional farmers to employ alternative eco-friendly methods of pest control.

"Natural" and "organic" are not *always* better. They are *usually* better, but it depends on many factors. In fact, it may be healthier for you and the planet to choose a non-organic carrot grown in your backyard (where you may have used only a small amount of carefully applied synthetic fertilizer and no pesticide), instead of choosing an organic carrot sprayed with natural pesticides, and grown and shipped from a thousand miles away. What is "best" for person, people, and planet is often nuanced.

The Bees are Dying

The use of pesticides has contributed to the precipitous decline of many pollinator species, including honeybees. The threats to pollinator species are many, and neonicotinoid type insecticides have been implicated as one of the culprits. And, like insecticides, herbicides are also very dangerous to pollinator species, as they may eliminate crucial flowering food sources that these insects feed on. Other threats to these insects include land use change, pollution, invasive alien species, pathogens and climate change.[20,21,22]

It is not just honeybees (an introduced species from Europe) that are in trouble. A report from the Center for Biological Diversity found that of the 1,400 North American native wild bee species studied, more than half are declining and nearly a quarter are at risk of extinction.[23]

Declining bee populations are cause for immense concern, as 75%

of humanity's food crops and nearly 90% of wild flowering plants depend at least to some extent on animal pollination. A wide diversity of wild pollinators is critical to pollination, even if managed honeybees are present in high numbers.[24]

A complete loss of pollinator services could reduce global fruit supplies by 23%, vegetables by 16%, and nuts and seeds by 22%; resulting in significant reductions in human micronutrient levels and food intakes.[25]   Clover and alfalfa are also very dependent on pollinator species and are extensively utilized to feed livestock.

At the same time that pollinator species are in decline, the population of humans continues to increase.

The Dirty Dozen and Clean 15

The Environmental Working Group's (EWG) Guide to Pesticides contains a comprehensive ranking of produce relative to their pesticide levels. These are listed below and can be downloaded from their website. As per the above discussion, it is by far better for you and the entire planet to eat only organic produce.

If there are times when you do not have the option to eat organic food, such as when dining at restaurants or in the homes of others, you may wish to refrain from eating fruits and vegetables that are included in the "Dirty Dozen" list.

Peeling helps; but remember that pesticides can also be taken up by the plant as a whole and are not always located just on the skin.

If organic foods are not offered or available, you may wish to consider eating from the "Clean 15" list. Consider giving these lists to your local restaurant owners, family members, and friends. Also, recommendations may change each year, so go online for updates. Check out the EWG website; it is full of great information and evaluates 48 different fruits and vegetables for pesticide residues.

Here is the EWG'S 2019 SHOPPER'S GUIDE TO PESTICIDES:

DIRTY DOZEN™ (you should always buy these organic): Ranked in order of most pesticide residues found, starting with the highest – strawberries (USDA tests in 2015 demonstrated an average of 7.7 pesticides per sample), spinach, kale, nectarines, apples, grapes, peaches, cherries, pears, tomatoes, celery, and potatoes.

CLEAN 15™ (lowest in pesticide): Ranked in order of least pesticide residues, starting with the lowest – avocados, sweet corn, pineapple, sweet peas frozen, onion, papaya, eggplant, asparagus, kiwi, cabbage, cauliflower, cantaloupe, broccoli, mushrooms, and honeydew. Note, however, that sweet corn and papaya may be genetically modified.

Remember that it is preferable to eat all organic food; as "Clean 15" foods are not necessarily absent of pesticides; they just have lower levels.

The Making of an Eco-Liberal

You have probably never heard of Robert Van der Bosch. Entomological scientists do not usually make a lot of headlines. A "bug" professor at the University of California Berkeley, Dr. Van der Bosch became one of the early pioneers of the field of Integrated Pest Management (IPM) – and he made quite a few enemies in the process. IPM is an agricultural method that incorporates a multitude of strategies for pest control, of which pesticide use is but one tine of a multi-pronged pitchfork.

The IPM model did not go over well with the pesticide chemical making companies and their salesmen, or even some of the scientists whose labs were supported by their large corporate grants. Dr. Van der Bosch published a scathing exposé and critique of agricultural industry corporations, the public officials responsible to overlook them, and the land grant universities they held sway over. He took an unyielding stance against those who threatened his cherished ideals of the beauty and balance of Nature; undergoing a personal transformation from a quiet scientist to a tenacious fighter.

The professor's adversaries believed that chemical management was the cheapest, fastest, and one-and-only method for pest control. They did not appreciate pesky non-believers throwing dirt at their gospel, and they went to great lengths to discredit him and his reputation.

The fight would not last long. Professor Van der Bosch died of a heart attack shortly after his exposé was published. Like that of Rachel Carson who died before him, the void left by his silenced voice allowed the pesticide agenda to advance much more easily.

Robert Van der Bosch's career was as a combatant against insects that devour or damage human crops. His own particular specialty was the use of natural predation, capitalizing on the idea that bugs are often their own worst enemies, and they will usually keep one another's numbers in check.

The professor's battle cry was essentially one seldom heard in war: "We Cannot Win!"

Here is the matchup of bugs vs. humans:

1.   Estimated Population: 10 quintillion (a 1 followed by 17 zeros) of them vs. 7 billion of us.

2.   Experience: 300 million years on the planet for them vs. 2 million years for us.

3.   Diversity: 1 million species for them vs. one for us.

4.   Reproductive capability: Up to 150 million eggs for them vs. a few children for us.

5.   Generation cycling: Up to one generation/week for them vs. one generation/20 years for us.

Van der Bosch argued that insects have incredible genetic plasticity (as do plants) and can quickly mutate, evolve, and adapt to almost any environmental opportunity or adversity. He noted that they have held their own against cataclysmal geological, climatic and biological changes over a vast expanse of time.

In just a few decades, insects have evolved to become resistant to many of humanity's insecticides and herbicides. If they could, they would probably be laughing out loud at the pure absurdity of our plans to control them (without hurting ourselves in the process). It is extremely difficult to chemically selectively control undesirable insect populations without affecting the intricate food chain that they are a part of — and decreasing the populations of beneficial insects as an unintended consequence. Of concern, the global insect biomass has decreased markedly (70% in some protected regions in Germany) in the last few decades, and pesticide use is one of the culprits.

New insect problems are often created by the use of insecticides, which necessitate the use of even greater amounts of insecticide — a scenario Van der Bosch dubbed "the pesticide treadmill." All the while the damage to Earth ecosystems continues to mount.

Dr. Van Der Bosch was not militantly against the use of all pesticides. To the contrary, he did not believe that modern agriculture could flourish without the prudent measured use of insecticides; if utilized in conjunction with other IPM measures.

Robert Van der Bosch believed that there is a balance in Nature; and he was right. If humanity's goal is that of sustainable global happiness, it is imperative to closely follow patterns that have been developed and honed over the 4-billion-year span of Earth's existence – integrating ourselves as seamlessly as possible into this beautiful and wonderfully complicated planet of ours.

Synthetic Fertilizers

Organic food regulations do not allow the use of *synthetic fertilizers*; which are chemical products created by humans.

You may be thinking "What is the harm in using a little store-bought chemical fertilizer?" Sure, a limited amount selectively applied to small backyard garden areas, where no major runoff occurs, may not necessarily cause easily measurable problems – although collectively it could, and it is probably best practice to use none in most regions. On a larger scale, the increased crop yields brought by synthetic fertilizers are often accompanied by major environmental costs.

Synthetic fertilizer use is often associated with *eutrophication*, which is the addition of unnatural amounts of chemical nutrients to an aquatic system. This includes large quantities of nitrates and phosphates from agricultural fertilizer runoff. These substances are ultimately deposited into our rivers, lakes, and oceans; promoting unnatural plant growth and decay, especially algae and plankton species. This then results in decreased oxygen levels in the water – which can be lethal to fish and shellfish. Nitrates and phosphates have created large dead zones near our coasts; decimating many fisheries, particularly near rivers which contain agricultural runoff.

There are now over 400 major dead zones in the world. The largest U.S. dead zone, at the mouth of the Mississippi, encompasses an area of over 8,500 square miles, which is roughly the size of New Jersey.[26]

Synthetic fertilizer use is also associated with atmospheric problems due to the formation of nitrous oxide – 300 times more potent a greenhouse gas than is CO_2. Any nitrogen that is not taken up by the plant is taken up by soil bacteria, which produce large amounts of nitrous oxide. Adding excessive nitrogen to the soil therefore increases nitrous oxide formation *exponentially*, not linearly.

There are also sustainability issues regarding the use of synthetic fertilizers. Potassium and phosphorus must be obtained by mining, and nitrogen is produced from fossil fuels. Synthetic fertilizer production is also very energy intensive, utilizing large amounts of natural gas.

Another serious problem with adding excessive nitrogen to the soil is acidification. Similar to increasing soil salinity from irrigation, increasing *soil acidification* from synthetic fertilizer use is rendering some farmland less productive.

Ammonium nitrogen-based fertilizer that is not taken up by the plant increases soil acidity. When soil pH drops, aluminum becomes soluble and retards plant root growth, restricting access to water and nutrients. In very acid soils, major plant nutrients (nitrogen, phosphorus, sulfur, calcium, manganese, and molybdenum) may be unavailable to the plant. Acidic soils also negatively affect microbes in the soil – the underpinning of a well-functioning symbiotic ecosystem.

Synthetic nitrogen use creates greater crop yields today, but it is essentially stealing from the yields of future generations. This may someday result in global food insecurity issues – which have historically fueled civil unrest and conflict.

Increased crop yields from synthetic fertilizer have resulted in short term increased profits for the farmer, as well as initially lower prices for the consumer. However, this is a seductive trap – as it is not a sustainable course of action. Collectively, humankind is choosing to consider cost only as it pertains to a monetary price today, deciding to worry about health, social, and environmental costs sometime later in the future.

Genetically Modified Organisms

Genetically modified foods cannot legally be labeled as organic.

A *genetically modified organism* (GMO) is one whose genetic material has been altered using genetic engineering techniques. This results in the creation of modified or new combinations of genes which have not previously existed in nature. In agriculture, these techniques are typically utilized to increase plant resistance to pests and herbicides – not to *intrinsically* increase yields.

The majority of U.S. grown soybean, corn, and cotton crops are now genetically modified. Over one-half of the processed foods on American grocery shelves contain genetically modified organisms.

For millions of years, plant breeding was dominated by natural selection processes that were relatively unaffected by humans. Approximately ten thousand years ago, our ancestors began changing from a society of hunter-gatherers to an agriculturally based species. Grains, fruits, and vegetables were cultivated, and natural selection was altered in a relatively minor degree by human selection of plants for breeding based on desirable characteristics. This type of breeding was limited by natural barriers which do not allow different species to breed with each other, and resulted in relatively modest (albeit very useful) variations over a ten-thousand-year period of time.

This span of ten thousand years is a very small period of time when compared to the age of our Earth, however is quite large when compared to the previous two decades, which has brought an astounding number of new variations of living organisms, due to the intermingling of DNA from completely different species. These new combinations of DNA do not occur naturally and are only made possible by laboratory manipulation.

Unpredictable Outcomes

One of the problems with genetic engineering is that it is very unpredictable. We simply cannot anticipate all of the possible problems that may arise – although many specific concerns have been raised.

Although the FDA has deemed genetically engineered (GE) food crops to be "substantially equivalent" to non-GE crops and therefore safe to eat, many scientists think that there have not been enough long-term feeding trials to assess for possible health problems related to ingesting these new organisms. "Substantial equivalence" is also an imprecise and subjective term, and many crops that have been considered equivalent to their non-GMO counterparts do indeed manifest differences in nutritional profiles, allergen levels, and pesticide residues.

There is also the potential for the evolution of new weeds, pests, bacteria, and viruses, which could mutate in response to genetically modified organisms. Newly created plants could possibly create substances and pollens that are poisonous to beneficial soil microorganisms, insects, and bees.

There is also now genetic pollution carried by wind, birds, and other pollinators that may bring genetically-altered pollen to adjacent organic fields. These nearby fields often contain crops that have been naturally selected over thousands of years to be resistant to disease and weather-related vagaries. Unlike chemical pollution, there is no way to contain genetic pollution, as this type of pollution is an organism that can reproduce and mutate.

The Pesticide Treadmill

Many plants are now genetically modified to be resistant to herbicides. Rather than needing to physically remove or selectively spray weeds, the farmer can now spray his entire acreage without fear of killing his or her crops. The most well-known and ubiquitous varieties are crops that are resistant to glyphosate herbicide.

Of note, researchers at the University of Texas at Austin recently discovered that glyphosate alters the gut microbiome in bees, making them more susceptible to infection and death. This could possibly be a contributing factor in the colony collapse disorder that has plagued honey bees and native bees for decades. It is worth considering that glyphosate (and Bt toxin, discussed below) could also quite possibly interact unfavorably with the human gut microbiome.

Recently introduced, there are now also GMO plants that are engineered to be resistant to two different herbicides, as many weeds have developed resistance to glyphosate alone. Multiple chemicals (2,4-D and glyphosate) can now be sprayed over an entire living field, food crops and weeds alike, without killing the farmer's corn, cotton, or soybean plants. Of note, 2,4-D was a major ingredient of Agent Orange, a defoliant used in the Vietnam War.

This begs the question: When two herbicides in combination are no longer effective in perhaps a decade or so, should a third then be added; and then another each decade or so after that? This is a perfect illustration of Robert Van der Bosch's "pesticide treadmill." At this rate, our grandchildren and their families will be consuming a whole lot of herbicide residues at the kitchen table.

Choosing herbicide-tolerant crops often leads to the increased indiscriminate use of pesticides. This is an indirect, but very harmful consequence of allowing genetically modified food into the market. Indeed, at least presently, this may be the most concerning problem of all regarding GMO's. Many critics find it very disconcerting that the same companies that sell seeds that are genetically engineered to be resistant to herbicides also manufacture and sell these same herbicides. Farmers now use these pesticides on their fields in much greater amounts than they did previously; spraying not just weeds, but food crops – and nearly every inch of soil – as well.

It is true that herbicide use will usually increase crop yields (but only temporarily), because competing weeds are killed. But mechanical and hand-weeding techniques will similarly increase yields – this just costs more money (but only in the short term).

In many places, such as China, there has been a mass exodus of rural populations to cities, attenuating the size of the labor force that is needed to hand-cultivate weeds. Farmers have responded by increasing their use of herbicides. Unfortunately, this not only harms the environment acutely, but also portends a future of diminished yields due to chemical degradation of the soil.

Finding enough manual laborers to work on farms is also a concern in many countries other than China, including the U.S. This may turn out to be a problem that can only be solved with a global major paradigm shift – perhaps including ideas such as raising the minimum wage of farm workers to a more appropriate level, offering food stamps independent of income to manual laborers who work on farms, or even providing a universal guaranteed income. Humanity's present dependency on dangerous herbicides is a solvable problem.

There are also other ways to increase the global food supply besides killing weeds. The vast majority of fertile American Midwest farmland is not used to directly feed humankind. Much of this land is planted in corn crops used to produce unnecessary biofuel (ethanol) for cars and trucks, wasting nutrients obtained from valuable soil. And, as noted earlier in this chapter, many of our nation's corn and soy crops are used for animal feed, which is an inefficient way of providing calories to humans.

Herbicides not only kill weeds; they also disrupt the normal soil microbiome. A sustainable food production model nourishes the soil, allowing it to do its job of supporting plant life. The currently prevalent model weakens the soil; and then keeps crops on life support by adding synthetic inputs.

Corn That Makes Its Own Herbicide

In addition to herbicide-tolerant genes, another gene that has been inserted into genetically modified corn DNA is one that is derived from the bacterium *Bacillus thuringiensis* (Bt). This gene codes for the production of a toxin that kills insects. During its growth period, these new plants manufacture their own toxin – so eating any part of the plant is therefore fatal to an insect. The use of Bt crops has been correlated with lower rates of exogenous insecticide application, as the plant produces its own toxin and therefore it is not necessary to spray additional toxins.

A study from Broderick, et al. found that the degree of mortality induced in some pest species by Bt toxin was dependent on the presence of bacteria located within the intestinal tract of the insect.[27] In some species, Bt acted in concert with enteric gut bacteria to account for the final death of insect larvae.

Of note, a study by Aris and Leblanc found Bt toxin in 93% of human maternal blood samples, and 80% of fetal blood samples – demonstrating that Bt toxin in food is indeed absorbed through the intestinal lining of humans.[28] Also of interest, Vendomois, et al. published a study that demonstrated liver and kidney toxicity to rats fed three different varieties of commercially available genetically modified maize (two of which produced Bt toxin) for a period of ninety days.[29]

Labeling and Transparency

Agribusiness has decided against employing precautionary principles and a policy of transparency. In fact, many large biotech conglomerates are spending enormous sums of money to convince citizens to vote against GMO labeling of food products. Their stated reasons for doing so are dubious at best (e.g. it will cost the consumer more money if a couple extra words are added to a product label).

It is of course much more likely that these companies object to GMO labeling because they believe that profits could be threatened. Many countries already require genetically engineered food products to be labeled. This includes Australia, the European Union, and many other developed countries; but currently the U.S. and Canada do not have this requirement. Powerful lobbying groups have coerced our government officials to tell us that we do not need GMO labeling – because they will do our thinking for us.

Consumers should also be wary of any testing performed by the very companies that stand to greatly profit from their new inventions. There are policy-making government agency officials who review these corporate studies. However, some of these individuals float back and forth between private and public-sector employment in the agriculture industry – a practice that certainly adds to the already large and inappropriate corporate influence on governmental regulatory affairs.

There may be exceptions, but the current motives of many agribusiness conglomerates appear to be primarily profit-driven, often cloaked in a façade of ending world hunger – which in reality is not typically due to low crop yields as much as it is the result of complicated geopolitical forces, inefficient and improper land use, and overpopulation.

Another concern is that Agribusiness has sued farmers for replanting seeds produced from plants that were grown from genetically altered seeds initially purchased from them. From a narrow business perspective this policy is understandable, as companies have invested vast amounts of money to develop and market these seeds, and they want to reap the rewards of their efforts. But from a more general perspective, the specter of a few large private industrial corporations controlling the world's food supply is considered by many to be appalling and dangerous.

As there are so many uncertainties involved with genetically engineered crops, and because the stakes are so high, it would seem quite reasonable to exercise caution regarding their use. However, this is not humankind's present course of action.

Integrated Pest Management

If humanity chooses to discontinue or markedly limit the use of synthetic pesticides, synthetic fertilizers, and genetically modified organisms, where does that leave us? Can high yields, healthy nutrition, financial viability, and environmental sustainability all coexist on the same farm?

It turns out that the answer is yes, most definitely.

Integrated Pest Management (IPM) is a process that includes eco-friendly and profitable methods to safely and sustainably maximize crop yields. These techniques are often as simple as crop rotation or planting a diverse array of crops.

By definition, IPM presently also includes using pesticides if economically necessary. However, *necessary* is a subjective word. At its best, sustainable IPM uses pesticides only as a last resort – but most farms do not presently operate that way. Although many farmers may claim to endorse Integrated Pest Management, synthetic chemical use is often at the top of their list, and other methods of pest control are often relegated to a secondary role.

One majorly successful IPM method is to use cover crops, which increase yields and can also eliminate the need for many herbicides and insecticides. Nature abhors a vacuum, and it also does not like bare ground. The general idea of using cover crops is to avoid any bare soil at any time – *something* is always growing.

Cover crops dampen wide variations in soil temperature and increase water retention, while also providing a home for beneficial insects that will prey on pests. Rather than steal nutrients and water from a cash crop, carefully chosen cover crop combinations can instead improve the growth of adjacent plants or subsequently seeded crops. Nature delights in diversity, and many different types of crops can be seeded together. Every different plant type has something unique to offer the soil biology.

Chemical and mechanical disturbance of soil should be limited. Synthetic pesticides, synthetic fertilizers, and tilling each damage soil organisms and structure. Tillage releases carbon dioxide into the air, and also destroys fungal strands that are important for the health of young plants.

A living root system should be maintained as much as possible throughout the year. Plants transfer carbon from air to soil; exuding it from their roots, feeding a multitude of life forms below the surface.

In turn, well-fed microorganisms will free up nutrients from the soil, and strands of mycorrhizal fungi act as root extensions to bring these nutrients in from a greater distance. It is a mutually beneficial production; a remarkably integrated system of "You scratch my back and I'll scratch yours."

Numerous living creatures can be integrated into agricultural systems: This includes pollinators, predator insects, earthworms, microorganisms – and livestock. Livestock fertilize the soil with their excrement, and the grazing process stimulates plants to pump more carbon into the soil, which feeds beneficial organisms.

Most conventional farming operations do not consistently follow the above principles of soil health. Instead, soil is usually tilled, and then often seeded with a monoculture crop. Its plants are treated with synthetic pesticides and fertilizers. It is often left uncovered after harvest. Livestock do not graze, trample, and fertilize it. And plants that support pollinators and predatory insects are not incorporated into its structure.

Conventional farming operations generally receive a very poor score regarding regenerating and sustaining healthy soil. They often grow crops in a way that creates unhealthy soil, rather than growing healthy soil to sustainably produce healthy crops. Their vision is misdirected – focused on the plant instead of the soil; on money instead of health; on the short-term instead of the future.

Two important measures of soil health are its carbon content and its ability to absorb water. When early Americans first arrived in the Midwest, native prairie land naturally supported grasses as tall as a human, and often even taller. Its organic content was high, and it soaked up water like a sponge. Today, less than two hundred years later, many conventional farms organic content is less than one-half of what it once was. Also, water runs off their compacted soil surfaces, making it unavailable to plants; and carrying topsoil, fertilizer, and pesticides with it into streams and oceans.

IPM proponents encourage woodland regions and flowering plants incorporated between and within fields, to help support pollinators and predators of insects. Biological methods are often recommended, using predators and parasites of pests in a targeted way to suppress their populations. Other essential measures of IPM include choosing the most pest-resistant varieties grown in optimal environments, and using methods such as barriers, traps, physical weed removal and mowing.

New technology may also eventually help with weed abatement. If people cannot (or will not) replace herbicides, maybe robots can. Engineers are building prototype models of robots that can travel alongside rows of carrots, using cameras and image recognition algorithms to identify weeds. Robotic machines then destroy the unwanted plant with electricity or lasers, leaving the adjacent carrot seedling intact.

Very few IPM ideas are presently incorporated into the business model of modern large-scale agricultural systems, which instead narrowly focus on making immediate large profits.

To be sure, many IPM methods of pest control do sometimes involve more easily identifiable costs than more commonly utilized techniques. Spraying glyphosate is presently cheaper (in the short-term) than hand or machine weeding. However, IPM methods also improve the vitality and sustainability of the soil; thereby increasing its long-term value. And many ranchers and farmers have diminished their input costs by eliminating the use of synthetic fertilizers and insecticides.

The real price of pesticides includes many costs that are not immediately apparent. This includes monies spent paying for adverse human health events, environmental impacts, and soil rehabilitation; as well as the cost of losing biodiversity – which cannot be measured in dollars alone.

In the long run, land managed with IPM methods will be far more profitable than land managed with the currently more widely used methods of tillage, monoculture, and chemical inputs.

"A nation that destroys its soils, destroys itself."

-Franklin D. Roosevelt

Bugs Are Us

In her insightful book, *The Ecology of Care*, author Didi Pershouse draws an intriguing parallel; comparing the microorganisms living in the mucous lining our intestines with those living in the soil lining our Earth. Human bodies recapitulate the processes of a greater system. Perhaps this is not all that surprising, considering that we are living extensions of our planet and its ecosystems.

Human DNA relegates many of its functions to the DNA of bacteria located in and on our bodies. These bacteria aid in immunity, nutrient absorption, and many other important functions. Our microbiome also appears to communicate with our brain via chemical cues, affecting our mood and other thought processes.

Similar to the human microbiome, the biome of healthy soil is also very much alive. Like ours, it includes bacteria, viruses, and fungi; but also, nematodes, insects, and much more. A wide menagerie of soil flora is vitally necessary to aid in nutrient absorption in plants, and to provide a sustainable environment within which vegetation can thrive.

Whether living in our human bodies or in our Earth's soil, bacteria and other organisms are not just interlopers along for a free ride; rather they are crucial components of vibrant and interactive systems. Any chemical that we add to our soil, or the food that we eat, may have a profound effect upon this biome – and therefore upon the Earth and its living manifestations that are our human bodies.

Any person eating non-organic food can consider themselves to be a willing test subject in an enormous and unregulated study. This experiment will eventually determine if ingesting pesticides and genetically modified foods is harmful to humans; either via untoward effects on beneficial gut bacteria, or more directly due to intestinal absorption into the bloodstream with subsequent injury or mutation to the cells of various human tissues.

This experiment will also test the limits of our soil, and the overall resiliency of our planet and its creatures.

The question to ask is this: "For what just cause?"

What Else is Going In or On?

As a side note, caution should be employed when considering introducing any type of unnatural substance into the personal ecosystem this is our body. This includes ingested medications, and lotions or soaps that are absorbed through our skin.

Medications alter natural physiologic processes; and it is important to remember that these processes are there for a reason. It is also noteworthy that these pathways are not usually simple or isolated, rather most are remarkably elegant and complex, interrelating with many other intricate pathways. The *intended* effect of a medication is therefore but one of many *side* effects.

For many conditions, the use of pharmacologic treatment is truly necessary. Even so, it must be recognized that all endeavors require the use of precautionary principles, and no exception should be made when it comes to the use of medication.

A person should also be concerned with not only what goes directly *in* their body, but also with what goes *on* their body. In 2004, an Environmental Working Group study tested the umbilical cord blood of 10 random newborns and found that the samples contained an average of **over 200** different industrial chemicals and pollutants.[30] These substances were transferred through the placenta from mothers who were exposed to these toxins via eating contaminated food, breathing polluted air, or by direct skin contact with household cleaning or personal body care products.

Your skin easily absorbs many chemicals which can enter your bloodstream and travel throughout your tissues. Remember this when you buy soaps, shampoos, and skin lotions. Some of these contain several difficult to pronounce chemicals that you probably do not want to have floating around inside of your body.

It's All Connected

It is perhaps both arrogant and absurd to think that humans can intervene in extremely complex natural systems without suffering consequences. It is impossible to touch one part of a mobile in a child's bedroom without making the other parts move. And, of course, our ecosystem is many orders of magnitude more complicated than a toy hanging from a ceiling.

Whatever your belief, via Divine intention or merely chance, our Earth has found a balance that works beautifully. If you think you can improve on it, you had better be exceptionally brilliant, remarkably humble, and uncompromisingly careful. Even then you are likely to gum up the works.

Also, bear in mind that an interrupted established natural pathway gone awry in our human body has an ultimately defined ending, which is our death, premature or otherwise. Interrupting the workings of an entire ecosystem may be much more far reaching, with limitless consequences, possibly extending to unknown thousands of future generations.

The Agricultural Revolution dramatically changed the landscape of the Earth, and there is no turning back the evolutionary clock – barring a catastrophic event to the human population. If every nation chooses to work with Nature, rather than fighting against it, it may be possible that our planet could sustainably provide enough food for an expected population of 10 billion or more people later in this century.

However, that is a very tall order.

It would likely require the continued use of synthetic fertilizer, the judicious use of insecticides, major changes in planetary land use and dietary habits, and the emergence of technological breakthroughs – not to mention the herculean task of garnering international cooperation between all world governments – which to date has yet to be accomplished.

It is perhaps more feasible to suggest that our Earth can indeed sustainably provide enough food for humanity – but only if the planet's current population remains stable or lessens. If we continue with business as usual, even that is a very tall order. Present agricultural production methods result in polluted aquifers, loss of pollinators and other species, and severe soil degradation – problems that are not in line with a sustainable future.

It is certainly possible that technology could save the day. New ways of sustainably producing greater amounts of food, while also decreasing harmful environmental impacts, will likely be discovered.

However, it is also quite possible that technological advances could be overwhelmed by a mad rush of just too many people.

Looking forward into the next century, the sustainable carrying capacity of the Earth is likely much less than the current number of 7.7 billion people – unless there are very major breakthroughs not yet evident on the horizon. The present *sustainable* carrying capacity of the Earth may be closer to 5 billion global citizens (or perhaps less), a point that will be discussed in subsequent chapters.

I hope that I have convinced you to make the extra effort to eat predominantly organic foods. The consequences of maintaining the status quo would likely eventually be quite severe. The problems related to the use of synthetic pesticides, synthetic fertilizers, and currently utilized genetically modified food crops have far too great of a negative impact on personal health and happiness, as well as on the viability of the Earth to sustain future generations of happy and healthy citizens.

Fighting Nature is an unwinnable war. Earth will not allow itself to be controlled indefinitely. It will not acquiesce and bow before humankind. It fights back even now; creating stronger hurricanes, floods, droughts, and resistant pathogens to battle.

The best way forward is to align ourselves with Nature – adjusting our sails rather than cursing the wind.

The Perfect Diet

The perfect diet will come from unrefined and organic local sources, utilizing humane and efficient practices. It will emphasize plant-based foods, predominantly vegetables and fruits, and will be augmented by whole grains, beans, nuts, and seeds. For many people, at least presently, it may be beneficial to include relatively small amounts of seafood, free-range organic meat, and eggs. Adding in minor amounts of organic dairy products in this plan is also acceptable.

The relative amount of each food type consumed is determined by how close one is to his or her desired weight. Those who are overweight will consume relatively greater amounts of vegetables (but not overdoing it with starchy foods such as potatoes).

This diet minimizes the use of added sugars, and limits salt intake. Ingestion of moderate amounts of healthy fats is recommended. The vast majority of what one drinks is clean filtered water.

This meal plan should serve only as a general outline, one designed for the majority of people today. Recommendations will likely change in the future, based on continuing research.

Intensely training athletes may have nutrition requirements that are somewhat different than other people. There are also many people whose illnesses or geographic location require a significantly altered diet, and they must therefore make appropriate personal adjustments for optimal health.

For people with digestive troubles, nutritional imbalances, disease processes, or who are taking medication, it may be necessary to consult with a Registered Dietician to assist with meal planning. Perhaps someday our individual diets be uniquely and effectively tailored to match our ancestral genetic signatures and gut microbiome.

The perfect diet is nuanced, and varies between individuals. There are many factors to consider – ancestral predispositions, geography, disease conditions, gut flora effects, industrial toxin levels in food, greenhouse gas production with food choices, variable nutrient levels in foods, sustainability issues, and age (e.g. older people need more protein and tolerate less lactose).

Presently, the easiest and most planet-friendly start to a lean and healthy body is to eat a large serving of locally-grown organic vegetables and fruits at the beginning of each meal. For breakfast, consider drinking a vegetable and fruit smoothie first, and then eat a small protein source if desired. Start lunch with a big salad and go from there. Dinner begins with a large serving of vegetables at the front of the plate. Your Mom was right: Eat your fruits and vegetables! Just make sure they are organically-grown.

If you follow this sustainable nutrition plan it is almost inevitable that you will lose extra weight, particularly if you faithfully follow a good exercise schedule. As a point more directed to older readers, there is a high likelihood that you will be able to completely eliminate or reduce the dose of many or all of the medications you may be taking. This is particularly true if you use these medications to control diabetes, high blood pressure, or high cholesterol. If you fall into this category, it is imperative that you see your healthcare provider frequently during this transition. These medications are already potentially dangerous, but some can be deadly if taken when they are no longer indicated. You will need to very frequently monitor your blood pressure and blood sugar levels if you take medications for hypertension and diabetes. This point cannot be overemphasized.

You do not need to follow a perfect diet each and every day. But, if you have not already done so, consider making a few changes in your eating habits. Add a few more organic fruits and vegetables to your plate each meal, and then spin it around and eat them first. This is a great start to a healthy body *and* a healthy planet.

You are Not Your Body

The ultimate goal of our sustainable nutrition plan is to minimize any negative influence on our Earth's ecosystems, while also being responsible for the smaller more personal charge that is our body.

You probably cannot get too carried away with attempts to protect the planet for the welfare of others, as well as for its own beauty and intrinsic worth.

You can however be overly concerned regarding your personal appearance. Concern yourself more with the inside health of your body, and less with how you think it looks in a swimsuit. Do the best you can with the body you were given. Find a balance that works for you.

"You" are not your body.

The Connection

Into the dark
A bright star burst
And came together
Virgin Earth

Of this dust
My shape was formed
A sailing craft
To brave the storm

I am not the ship
Nor is it me
But a captain and a vessel
On a shimmering sea

A spark of Life
Creates a bond
A century pact
A connection strong

We travel together
'Cross the ocean deep
Together we laugh
Together we weep

We feel the sun
And, too, the rain
Exuberant joy
Exquisite pain

Through the midst of heaven
Near the dark of hell
Dear old ship
You have carried me well

Dust to dust
Earth fires burn
And to the stars
We shall return

Just one last tear
We near the shore
Farewell good friend
Forever more.

Section Two:

Mental Well-Being and Happiness

SIX

Getting Started

"Weakness of attitude becomes weakness of character."

-Albert Einstein

SOME YEARS BACK, when my older children were still in college, I wanted to share with them a few thoughts about life – you know, the things that really mattered. Even some of the really deep meaning of life type of stuff. We had certainly talked about a few of these ideas over the years, but I wanted to put them in writing. This way they could look at them later if they wished, or maybe pass them along to their own children someday.

Of course, I never really completely solved any of the mysteries of humanity's existence, but I did put together a few pages of thoughts and quotations to give to them. I continue to add to the inventory as the years pass. The words below are not age-specific. Maybe some of them will resonate with you.

_____

Happiness does not always drift in on a gentle breeze – sometimes you must walk toward it. Reach out and create happiness for others, and personal happiness will usually show up along the way.

As Martin Luther King said: "Those who are not looking for happiness are the most likely to find it, because those who are searching forget that the surest way to be happy is to seek happiness for others."

Be generous to the poor, even though you know this may enable a few freeloaders.

Limit your complaints. Complaining can negatively impact our listener – who may fight private battles much more difficult than our own.

Abraham Lincoln once said that a person can be just about as happy as they want to be. There is a lot of truth to that. Savor each day. If you awaken feeling irritable, try starting your day by putting a smile on your face and giving a hearty greeting to your classmates or coworkers. It is amazing how you can markedly improve your mood with just this simple exercise. Try it.

I reminisce fondly on times I spent with my late paternal grandfather Aija, a working-class man who carried himself with a gentle calmness and positive disposition. Aija would sit back in his chair with a contented smile, take a puff of his pipe and say "That's just the way we like it." Acting happy can make you happy. It really works.

Try to laugh every day. Laugh at yourself, too.

Buy yourself a really good mattress and pillow. Go to bed early and get plenty of rest. Try to keep a fairly regular sleep pattern. Read something uplifting, comforting, or fun before drifting off. You are at your finest when well-rested.

Never give up. Always do your best, giving one hundred percent – then let the chips fall where they may. You cannot completely control the outcome of a test or venture, but you have complete control over your amount of effort. Judge your successes by your efforts, not your results.

There is a big difference between concern and worry. Concern means rolling up your sleeves and getting to work. Worry involves wringing your hands and imagining poor outcomes. Stop worrying. My Mom likes to say, "Don't borrow trouble." She is right; worry never helps.

Ralph Waldo Emerson said, "Finish each day and be done with it. You have done what you could. Some blunders and absurdities no doubt crept in; forget them as soon as you can. Tomorrow is a new day. You shall begin it serenely and with too high a spirit to be encumbered with your old nonsense."

Work hard at maintaining your relationships; even if it is one-sided and you are the one who usually has to call or write; or if you are usually the peacemaker. Plan adventures with your friends and family. You will rarely regret any of them.

Forgive others and be forgiven. This means accepting some blame. Do not hold grudges. Distancing yourself from a good friend or family member because they hurt you will only add to your pain. You may be sacrificing love and friendship for pride, which is a very poor trade. Write a letter of reconciliation to a friend or loved one. Call up an old friend you have not spoken with in years. Take that chance; you can live with the possible rejection.

Cherish your family. Stay close to your siblings. When you get older, treat your spouse as if you just started to date and still want to impress him/her. Bring home a bouquet of flowers; go to the movies; write love notes. Be thankful you have been with this person long enough to observe a few wrinkles, many of which are laughter lines. Appreciate the greatest gift you will ever receive, which is your children. Listen to them. Talk with them. Tell them you love them every chance you get. If they sometimes wake up frightened at night and want to sleep in between you and your spouse, by all means let them. There will be plenty of nights for just Mom and Dad.

Do not pollute your mind with trash from books or movies that glorify violence. We each have a finite number of brain cells. Do not waste a circuit on garbage. It is unwise to purposefully imprint a violent or evil image in your brain forever.

Have the courage to try new things. Elbert Hubbard tells us, "To escape criticism – do nothing, say nothing, be nothing."

Remember that a word said cannot be unspoken. The greatest regrets in my life are the times I allowed myself to utter crass, insensitive, or disrespectful words. A momentary lapse in judgment can create untold consequences and inflict great pain upon others. One can receive forgiveness, but it is far better to not say words that need forgiving.

Form meaningful connections with as many different types of

people as possible – including those who may look, think, and act different than you. You can never have too many friends.

Embrace change. Accept new challenges with anticipation, courage, and a smile. Be the one other people look to for leadership. Make your mark, make a difference, do the best with what you have.

Choose a vocation that you enjoy. I heard someone once say to find something that you like; and then don't do too much of it. That is probably good advice. Do not seek a job to obtain prestige, or because you think that is what people expect of you; even if it is your parents that you are trying to please. As Margaret Mitchell said, "Once we lose our reputation, we become truly free." There may be some truth to that.

I once had the good fortune of listening to a commencement speech given by former First Lady Michelle Obama at our daughter Laura's college graduation ceremony. Mrs. Obama implored the students to "Strive to be inspired rather than to be impressive." That is great advice.

Not all of us find a dream job, but it is far better to follow your interest than to chase after a high salary. Most careers will provide you with enough income to meet your needs. Many lower paying jobs provide great benefits and a pension. Follow your passion, not your pocketbook.

It was Albert Einstein who said, "Strive not to be a success, but rather to be of value." The income we receive for our labor should only be considered as a part of our pay; the rest is the satisfaction we obtain from providing a valuable service. We usually focus too much on the first part. I was chatting with a fellow one day and asked him what he did for a living. A grocery truck driver, he responded by saying "I am the guy that brings your food to you." His job was not glamorous, but he enjoyed his valuable role in helping to bring food from farm to table.

Albert Einstein also said, "The ideals which have lighted my way, and time after time have given me new courage to face life cheerfully, have been Kindness, Beauty, and Truth."

The nineteenth century author John Ruskin chastised the merchants of his day, for valuing profit over honor. In an essay, *The Roots of Honour*, he writes the following: "And as the captain of a ship is   bound to be the last man to leave his ship in the case of a wreck, and to share his last crust with the sailors in case of famine, so the manufacturer, in any commercial crisis or distress, is bound to take the suffering of it with his men, and even to take more of it for himself than he allows his men to feel; as a father would in a famine, shipwreck, or battle, sacrifice himself for his son. All which sounds very strange: the only real strangeness in the matter being, nevertheless, that it should so sound."

Ruskin even suggested that it is the responsibility of those of many professions, on due occasion, to die in the line of duty: The soldier rather than abandon his post at battle, the physician rather than depart his clinic in plague, the pastor rather than teach falsehood, and the lawyer rather than accept injustice.

Ruskin also argued that the merchant class, those involved in commerce, should also consider themselves as similar to these other professionals. He proposed that they apply all of their wisdom and energy to produce a product in its perfect state, and distribute it at the lowest possible price, where it is most needed. He posited that although our fee or pay is a necessary adjunct for our efforts, it should not be the driving force in our life and should not be traded for honor.

Always take advantage of your privilege to vote. Be wary of leaders who value profit, convenience and dominance over regard for international neighbors and the environment. Have the courage to cross political party lines when necessary. Do not march in lockstep with other party constituents, rather thoughtfully evaluate all issues and be open to fresh ideas. Consider John Ruskin's criteria for honor when choosing a leader: Would they be the last person to leave the ship in case of a wreck? Would they share their last crust of bread with their crew?

Remain acutely aware of the power of social conditioning. Have the courage to think differently. Always ask: "Why?"

Be financially responsible with what you have, whether this is a lot or a little. This will spare you much grief. Live within your means. Avoid most forms of debt. Exercise caution when listening to financial advisors, even if they have your best interest at heart. Sincerity does not always equate with good advice. Do not take big chances with large parts of your nest egg. For many people, losing one half of your money has a far greater impact on your life than doubling your money does. Diversify your investments.

If you find an automobile that you want, strongly consider saving the money first, and then buying the car. Other than securing funds for purchasing a home, or for pursuing a very carefully considered goal that offers a likely healthy return on your investment (e.g. education or a well-researched business venture), it is best to minimize debt – and most accumulated debt should be repaid as quickly as possible.

Promote peace. I found this quote: "Through the monstrous gap between those fighting the war and those leading cheers march the words of General William Tecumseh Sherman: It is only those who have neither fired a shot nor heard the shrieks and groans of the wounded who cry aloud for blood, more vengeance, more desolation. War is hell."

Live with courage. Edmund Burke said: "All that is necessary for the triumph of evil is that good men do nothing."

Read! Learn from the mistakes and successes of those who came before you.

Listen more than you speak. Listen with the idea to learn, not with the plan to reply.

Consider playing at least one sport, either a team activity or an individual endeavor. This can create a lot of joy. It is alright to play to win. Many sports psychology books can be summarized by the following: Maximize your skill by mentally visualizing the desired outcome. Do not wish poor play upon your opponent. You want to beat them at their best or have them beat you at your best. Be a gracious winner, and even more gracious in defeat.

Do not judge yourself or others by physical attributes or social status. Delve deeper and find what is inside. Befriend all people.

The past exists only in your memories. Every morning you are reborn anew.

Take some chances. Helen Keller wrote: "Security is mostly a superstition. It does not exist in nature. Life is either a daring adventure or nothing."

Respect our Earth and all life forms. Pick up trash that is not yours. Avoid the use of chemicals on the land. Make the world a better place because of you. Leave behind a poem, a piece of art, a garden, or merely a kind word to one in sorrow.

Enjoy the simple elegance of our world. Marvel at how a cloud forms over the ocean, is blown by the wind over land, and then drops nourishing rain to the Earth and its inhabitants before returning again to the sea. Look at a flower up close, examine its exquisite simple beauty. Observe a honeybee as it goes about its day. Cherish the four seasons, the ever-changing variety that enhances the beauty of the world.

Love your yourself, love your neighbor, love your Earth – person, people, planet.

SEVEN

I See You

"Few people are capable of expressing with equanimity opinions which differ from the prejudices of their social environment. Most people are even incapable of forming such opinions."

-Albert Einstein

FRANK NETTER WAS a very accomplished artist, known by most students of the health sciences for his exemplary display of expert anatomical drawings. His beautiful illustrations have graced the pages of countless textbooks, as well as the projector screens of many hallowed lecture halls at prestigious universities throughout the world. Netter's subjects were typically drawn devoid of skin, with various layers of fascia and muscle removed or pulled back to reveal the secret depths of human tissues.

A well-worn textbook lay on the table in front of me. I like to think that this was an anatomy book – as anatomy was one of my favorite subjects – but the truth is that I cannot recall what I was reading that evening. I do know that I had spent so much time studying that I could often close my eyes, think of a page number, and envision the image or text on that particular page. I was a second-year medical student at the time, spending yet another evening in the library at

Oregon Health Sciences University. Each day was pretty much like the one before it: Attend classes all day in lecture hall, run home to grab a quick dinner, return to the library to study for a few more hours, and then head back to the apartment to get some sleep – only to awaken and repeat it all over again the next day.

It is interesting how seemingly small moments can set off a series of events that will forever change your life. Maybe it was fate, or maybe I was just tired, but for some reason I pulled my eyes away from my textbook. Glancing upward, my gaze instantly fell upon a young woman across the library hall. I had seen her once before; at which time she had piqued my interest. I had only managed a brief "Hello" as she walked by, and could only hope for another chance encounter. I did however soon learn her name – Diana.

But now, on this occasion, time was on my side; allowing me to look at her much longer than I should have. I could do so without her noticing, as she was turned obliquely away from me, leaning upon a table, engaged in whispered conversation with a fellow classmate from the School of Nursing. Noting that she was preparing to go home for the evening, I managed to cross her path as she exited into the foyer. Diana wore an emerald green sweater that evening. It nearly perfectly matched the color of her eyes.

I was hooked. I never stood a chance. Sure, it took me a few months to muster up my courage, but one day I picked up the phone, stammered a few well-rehearsed lines, and arranged a tennis date for the following day. Three years later I asked her to marry me, and off we went to Wisconsin, where my new bride worked as a nurse, while I struggled through a medical Internship in my first year as a real doctor. Within another two years we celebrated the birth of our first son, to eventually be followed by a daughter, and then finally another son. The rest, as they say, is history. One chance glance; and three new lives!

I wonder just what it is that draws humans so strongly to our visual perceptions. We stand rapt in awe over a morning sunrise or a meadow of wildflowers. From the shores of Maui, I once viewed a rainbow painted over the skies above Molokai; an image still etched in my mind.

Other mammals do not appear to share the same degree of interest in beauty. Females do look for the strongest mate possible, and males look for fecundity in a female, but it seems to usually end there. The lion's mane actually makes it appear larger and more formidable to its enemies, and also allows some degree of protection of his neck. It may be valuable for form as well as function, but who knows if that matters much to the lioness.

Avian species may be somewhat different. It is postulated that a peacock's plume is designed to attract a mate, and male Bower birds do vie for female attention by building intricate nests; decorating them with different colored objects found on the forest floor. Although the concept of beauty may not belong exclusively to the human realm, we definitely take it to the highest level.

What first captivated me about my wife were her eyes – exotic almond shaped structures, with speckled green irises surrounding windows to a place I found intriguing. Although I would not have continued to pursue her if she did not have many other more important attributes – an easy laugh, a kind heart, and an adventurous spirit – it was her eyes that caught my attention.

I am not quite sure how I garnered Diana's favor. Perhaps the first time that she gazed upon me with deep admiration was when I triumphantly returned from the garden, sweat dripping from my brow, and a recently slain zucchini slung magnificently over my shoulder.

I was able to make Diana laugh, and we shared easy conversation and similar ideals. Luckily for me, this seemed to be enough to pique her interest.

Seeing is Believing?

I saw an interesting experiment on television the other day where a woman was filmed repeating a certain sound several times, but the filmmakers actually dubbed in a different yet somewhat similar sound. The listener would actually "hear" what it looked like her lips were saying, rather than the true sound coming through the television speakers. The actual word spoken could only be heard correctly if the listener's eyes were closed. We all know the saying "Seeing is believing," but our eyes can sometimes fool us into believing something that is not always true.

The unknown biblical author of Hebrews 13 wrote: "Do not neglect to show hospitality to strangers, for thereby some have entertained angels unawares."

Consider getting to know a stranger or someone who may need a friend, someone you may have subconsciously erroneously considered to be too different than you. Continue to probe deeper, beyond the first layer. The renowned anatomical artist Frank Netter certainly found beauty and complexity below the skin surface. Evaluate with your eyes closed, to see the treasures that lay below. You may find an angel.

In a scene from the movie *Avatar*, the female lead locks eyes with her mate, gazing into a much deeper realm, and says "*I see you.*" True beauty may take a while to really see. If you trust just your eyes, you may find yourself accidentally betrayed by a hastily rendered faulty appraisal.

Befriend all people. Ignore ill-conceived boundaries of social stratification that deceive and tell us that some people are of more value than others. Every life is of great importance. You see what you look for. Look for the real lasting beauty, through the visible outer mist that will soon vanish.

I am not sure if this is true, but I have heard that traditional Persian rugs are purposefully designed with a flaw in the weaving, because the weaver is signifying that life is not always perfect. Try not to look for the flaw. If you are lucky, you will probably never see it.

EIGHT

Perception

"Reality is merely an illusion, albeit a very persistent one."

-Albert Einstein

OUR CONSCIOUS MIND cannot will our hand to regrow an amputated digit. And it cannot regenerate a pancreas that no longer produces insulin. But it is possible for us to create new neurologic brain pathways, by mindfully altering present thought processes. Remarkably, the physical structure of the brain can be modified by conscious efforts of the will.

When we see something frightening, our brain mediates the release of epinephrine from our adrenal glands, giving us the additional strength that we may need to run or fight. And when a nursing mother hears an infant cry, she secretes the chemical oxytocin from her pituitary gland, stimulating the release of milk from her breasts. These are reflexive phenomena.

Interestingly, breast milk will also let down in some women who just think about nursing their child. And immunoglobulin levels in our bloodstream can be altered by merely recalling a previous occurrence that made us angry. A pianist can simply mentally rehearse a certain piece – visualizing each finger placement on the keys without actually moving her fingers – and cause a measurable increase in the amount of real estate her brain apportions to performing the fine hand movements necessary to play the composition. Our thoughts influence and create our biology.

Thoughts, sights, and sounds can cause the release of molecules that can be visualized under an advanced microscope – and these stimuli may create or enhance neurologic pathways that can be visualized with functional imaging techniques.

Intangible thoughts and messages become a tangible reality. And because there are differences in the way each individual processes the same information, the reality I create will be very different from yours. These neurologic pathways can store information of an event, and later retrieve it when memory of the event is needed or wanted. These same pathways could also possibly influence the expression of our DNA through epigenetic processes. Thoughts are transformed into physiology.

The really intriguing part of this process is that we have a significant amount of control over these thoughts. Humans have the ability to shape the interpretation of any action or stimulus that we experience, i.e. we can control the way we think about the various events that we encounter each day. We can create our own meaning, and ultimately change our body chemistry and cellular connections.

An event has no meaning except the meaning that we choose to assign to it. We can choose to label an event in any way that best suits our individual needs. We can choose to alter our perception of the stimuli that enter our consciousness. Altered perceptions can alter physiology and improve our physical and mental well-being. Healthy thoughts truly create healthy bodies and minds.

Many researchers have studied the phenomenon of neuroplasticity, which is the ability of the brain to form new or reorganized neural connections. Using functional neurologic imaging, they have shown that through conscious focused efforts of the will, pathologic brain circuits can literally be weakened and replaced by new healthy circuits, using a slightly different part of the brain.[31] Willful effort can change the physical structure of the brain.

We can choose to change our interpretations of events from something harmful into something useful. Numerous studies have shown that negative emotions, such as grief or stress, can lead to illness and early death. There is a greater than tenfold higher risk of a heart attack in the first day after the loss of a loved one. And although correlation does not equate with causation, some studies have indicated that chronic stress is linked to shorter telomeres, the caps on our DNA that help to protect it from injury and aging.

Merely thinking about troubling events can also elevate levels of the stress hormone cortisol in our bloodstream, subsequently impairing our immune system – the body's surveillance system against unwelcome intruders such as infectious agents and cancer cells. If negative emotions can cause heart attacks and also weaken our immune system, it follows that positive emotions or thoughts will relatively enhance and strengthen our body.

We can block stress at its source; which is the improper perception of the events around us. Human beings often do not realize that increased happiness, and improved health, can be obtained by simply changing our perceptions of our surroundings. We often operate under the assumption that if we are dealt a poor hand, a negative outcome is usually predetermined and we will come out a loser that day. In short, we feel that a bad situation equals a bad outcome. We forget that we can often choose to control our reaction to an unpleasant or difficult stimulus, and therefore ultimately change the outcome.

The equation is not Stimulus = Outcome; rather Stimulus + **Perception** = Outcome.

With willful mental effort, we can perceive events in any manner that we choose. We can positively influence our body chemistry and build neural connections that are beneficial to us.

Stimulus + Perception = Outcome. This simple equation indicates that there are only two ways to influence an outcome: we can change the Stimulus that we are faced with, or we can change our Perception of the stimulus.

Changing the stimulus is often difficult, as we cannot control everything that is said to us or that happens to us. But it is sometimes possible to avoid an unpleasant stimulus. We can also try to mitigate its effect by creating a competing more useful stimulus.

Changing the perception of the stimulus can also be difficult, but this is something that is under our control. We have the ability to choose to reject negative interpretations that bring us stress and unhappiness, which ultimately lead to poor health.

There are three major negative unhealthy interpretations of events, and these are: fear, anger, and sadness. If we are at any time unhappy it is usually do to one of these emotions. We can learn to recognize these emotions early on, rejecting or reframing them into a more positive and healthy interpretation.

Before discussing how to change our perceptions, we can first examine how to influence the first part of the equation, which is to filter the stream of stimuli that constantly bombard our senses.

Influencing the Stimulus

There are two ways to positively influence the stimuli to our brains. One is to try to avoid those situations or stimuli that we know are not good for us, or that are known to often cause us stress. The other is to seek out or create positive stimuli that are beneficial to us.

The simplest way to achieve a positive outcome and subsequent good health is to avoid noxious stimuli. We have all had people in our lives that can make our spirit feel diminished after each encounter. Gossips, constant complainers, and overly competitive people fall in this category. Avoid them! Listening to them may adversely influence our own actions, perhaps drawing us into a similar undesirable behavior. Negative words, either spoken by others or ourselves, reach our brain and create unhealthy chemical imbalances and neurologic connections. If you sleep with dogs you get fleas.

Other noxious stimuli to avoid include images or passages of violence and hatred in movies and books. Observing disturbing scenes will create new and unwanted neural connections. Each brain has a finite number of neural pathways. It is imprudent to waste connections on trash that is marketed as entertainment, and it is senseless to unnecessarily cause the release of toxic stress hormones into our bloodstream. There is enough grief in real life to handle.

Another negative stimulus may be our occupation. Occasionally our options in this arena can be limited due to financial considerations, as we have bills to pay and obligations to our families to fulfill. There will always be some pressure in our lives; and often we must simply live with it, finding ways to attenuate our stress by changing our perceptions. However, there may be times where the burden is simply too great to allow an optimally happy life; and the best course of action is to change course and move on to a new adventure. This decision can take great courage, but can often lead to a healthier and more productive life. Money, status, or fear can keep a person tied to a career that does not lead to a full measure of happiness.

One should attempt to avoid negative stimuli; but it is also important to search for or create positive stimuli.

One way to find positive stimuli is to seek out joyful and outstanding individuals. These are the people who have an easy smile and a twinkle in their eye. These are the individuals who laugh frequently, look for the good in any person or situation, and are quick with a compliment. Seek these people out. Birds of a feather flock together.

Be mindful of the countless positive stimuli that are available each day. Most of us are blessed with five fantastic senses: sight, hearing, smell, taste, and touch. Watch the sunset tonight or observe the moon and stars. Listen to the crickets outside or put on some soothing music. Enjoy the fragrance of a rose in your garden and the food on your stove. Close your eyes while you eat your supper and relish each bite of the feast that we enjoy each night. Stroke the fur of your pet, or exchange massages with your partner. Exercise, but do not exceed the point of pleasure. All of these positive stimuli help to create healthy brain and body chemistry.

We can also create positive stimuli by improving our body language and by reciting mantras – which are verbal affirmations of our true capabilities.

Our body and mind are obviously extremely intimately connected, and communication between the two goes both directions. We are accustomed to thinking that the body does what the mind tells it, but the mind also listens to the body. As we purposefully alter our body language, our mind receives these new signals from our body and positively reacts to the new us.

An example of this phenomenon can be demonstrated by purposefully smiling. Studies have shown that the simple act of smiling, even if it is forced, will actually make us happier. This is thought to be a chemically mediated response. Holding ourselves with good posture, standing tall with our shoulders back and chin up, tells our brain that we are a happy and confident person.

Another recent study showed that spending a couple of minutes holding a power pose, with chin up and arms out, results in a significant surge in testosterone levels. This can help our performance in athletic competition, and also improve our verbal presentation skills and interpersonal communications by increasing our level of confidence. All of these are examples of how our mind listens to our body, and then responds with improved performance.

Reciting a mantra is also an excellent way of creating a new positive stimulus to our brain. This verbal reinforcement cements in a new story of how we can feel about ourselves or any situation. Yes, it is ok to talk to yourself. Pump yourself up! You truly can talk yourself into better physiology. If you say out loud, "I know I can do this!" you have just dramatically increased your odds of doing just that. Others do not have to hear you. You can say your mantras softly or privately, and nobody is the wiser.

Altering Perceptions

Human beings have the ability to shape the interpretation our brains create from incoming stimuli. There are certainly some reflexes that happen so quickly that there is not enough time to ponder the various possible responses. If a snowball is coming at our head, we immediately duck, rather than consider an appropriate response and then react. But, in most circumstances, there is time for introspection and self-analysis of our interpretation of events.

It is important to focus on the particular outcome that we desire. For most of us the outcome we desire is to live a happy life – and we do have a significant amount of control over our individual level of happiness.

It was stated earlier that a bad situation does not have to equal a bad outcome. The equation is not Stimulus = Outcome; rather Stimulus + Perception = Outcome. We can exercise our free will and modify our perception of the painful stimulus to improve our outcome. We already have two parts of the equation figured out. We know that the desired outcome is happiness, and that the stimulus has already happened (and we have already done our best to modify or augment it). The next part – which is not easy – is to positively shape our interpretation of the occurrence to achieve our desired outcome.

An event has no meaning other than the meaning we assign to it. When something happens to us, a meaning is immediately ascribed to this event. But in many instances the meaning we give to a situation is simply a learned response, often born of social conditioning, and also often quite unhealthy. Although we may think of it as a somewhat intangible and ethereal entity, the meaning that we create is actually a very real construct – stored via physical connections at the cellular level. If we choose to do so, we can reframe our interpretation of an event to a healthier meaning, and subsequently change our physiology.

Briefly discussed were three major unhealthy perceptions of events that lead to unhappiness and stress. These are fear (anxiety), anger, and sadness. One can learn to recognize these perceptions in the early stages; then reframe or exchange them with a healthier interpretation.

You may argue that our first response, for example anger or fear, is the natural response and that we are just fooling ourselves to think otherwise. This may possibly be true, however if our desired destination is happiness, we want to get there whether or not it takes a little mental massage. Besides, our "natural" or first response is not necessarily always the best response.

A lot of our responses are also not really natural, as they are actually learned responses that we have practiced our entire lives. These may be responses to stimuli or events that fall outside of the boundaries that we ourselves have constructed. These boundaries circumscribe what we think is a field of correctness, e.g. that which we perceive – often erroneously – to be right or true. We often become defensive or angry if events do not fall neatly within the borders of our field. These borders are self-created, and are often irrelevant and influenced by nonsensical social conditioning and our subsequent interpretation.

Be willing to move or take down your self-made fences. Sometimes we are fearful, angry or sad simply because we have programmed ourselves to think that certain situations always make us feel that way.

Even some natural responses can sometimes go awry, as hunter-gatherer physiology has not necessarily kept pace with modern societal stressors. My natural response to danger is to send out epinephrine to my body, increasing my heart rate and strength. I can now run away from the mountain lion that is stalking me; or attempt to fight it if it catches me. The helpful response in one situation however can at times be detrimental in another. A bomb detonation expert must overcome this response, calming her heart rate and hands to accomplish her task. She cannot run away, and the extra strength in her hands can make fine motor movements more difficult to perform. She will use mental manipulation to shape her perception of a dangerous stimulus, to achieve her desired outcome.

When we are feeling unhappy or ill at ease, it is important to recognize and manage our perceptions early on. It is easier to put out a match than a wildfire. If an event has made us fearful, angry, or sad, we can mitigate the unhealthy effects of these emotions. We can acknowledge that these feelings may be normal, but we must also realize that humans often misread events or magnify their significance. This is not to say that we should deny that an event has actually happened, or that the feeling of fear, anger, or sadness is not justified. It is the extent and duration of the emotional response that must be managed.

We can acknowledge that we have been hit with a painful stimulus, and that we are reacting with normal human behavior. But we must recognize that these emotions are not meant to be saved or amplified by constantly replaying them in our minds, cementing in unhealthy memories; which, again, are real physical structures at the cellular level. We can rationally and gradually change our perceptions and exchange these emotions for healthier ideas.

So now let us say that I have recognized my unhappiness, and I have identified that my fear, anger, or sadness is the cause. I can now change my perception, to not let this emotion consume me. Although somewhat simply stated, I can exchange unhealthy emotions for more healthy responses.

Fear can be acknowledged, but it can be welcomed rather than hidden from. And the energy that accompanies fear can be re-channeled toward a useful goal. I can recognize my anger and exchange it for forgiveness. I can feel sadness, but I can then gradually replace it with hope. You may be thinking, "If it was only that easy." It is not easy.

Fear

Robert Louis Stevenson said, "Keep your fears to yourself, but share your courage with others." It is alright to acknowledge fear. However, we should not dwell on our fears, or frequently discuss them with others; as this will shore up unhealthy brain pathways of dread and despair. Instead we must welcome the unleashed wild energy that is our fear, attempting to direct that energy into something beneficial; like the cowboy hero who tames the fierce black stallion, simply redirecting the raw power of the horse to a more useful form. This is admittedly much easier said than done, but this is what great people do.

The American Heritage Dictionary defines fear as: "A feeling of alarm or disquiet caused by the expectation of danger, pain, disaster, or the like; terror; dread; apprehension." I think that the word expectation is a crucial component of the definition. We have all felt fear. And it is alright to acknowledge our fear. Courage is not the absence of fear, rather it is the overcoming of fear.

But how do we get the courage to overcome our fear? One answer is that we can get courage by changing our perceptions and our expectations. Fear is amplified by putting too much emphasis on ourselves and our futures.

Try to not worry about yesterday or tomorrow. Yesterday is over and done. Let it go. Concerning tomorrow, we may be expecting an event that will never happen. Our ability to handle true future problems will likely exceed our expectations. Accept the uncertainty of tomorrow and forget about it – there is some intrigue in not knowing what is around the next bend.

Embrace today. Focus on this very moment. Forget about your personal triumphs and tragedies, and instead consider how to improve the happiness of someone else. You can deflect fear by taking the focus off of yourself.

Author Maxwell Maltz wrote: "Every crisis or difficulty brings its own strength." Welcome the energy that accompanies fear. Use this energy to run into your fears – choosing fight not flight. Choose to be optimistic and confident. Step into this role, as an actor does in a play.

Fear can also be exchanged for love. Concern for the happiness of others defines love. The biblical author John writes: "There is no fear in love, but perfect love casts out fear." Love conquers fear. Love what you are doing for others. Have pure motives and intentions. Your endeavors are meant to enrich the lives of those around you. If you mess up and look like a fool, who cares? You are concerned with the welfare of others. It is not about you.

Here is a good mantra to start your day: "Perfect love casts out fear."

The new emotion – love – will also create neural connections that can be retrieved as pleasant memories as we desire, increasing our happiness and improving our health.

Anger

Albert Einstein wrote: "Anger dwells only in the bosom of fools."

We have of course all felt anger, and sometimes it is obviously a justifiable reaction. However, anger becomes problematic when it becomes a frequent emotion or reflexive response. It is also very detrimental to hang on to our anger, allowing it to "dwell in our bosom." Repeatedly mentally replaying an event that made us angry will physically damage our health, eating away at us like acid.

We can recognize our anger, and then replace it with forgiveness. The anger that we feel may occasionally be justified, however it is often magnified or created by a faulty perception. We may often incorrectly assume that we are the victim of a personal attack. However, that is not always so. Many who speak carelessly of others are not purposefully trying to inflict pain; rather they are unaware of the consequences of their words.

At one time or another, each of us has been the recipient of unfair words or actions. Admittedly, it may be that a few of the people who deliver these blows can be a little mean-spirited. It is most prudent to try to avoid them and forgive them anyway. Maybe someday our efforts will pay off and they will change their ways. Today it will definitely make us healthier if we forgive them and move on.

There are also of course people who may wish to cause us great harm. Perhaps one of them has already severely hurt you; or someone dear to you. Some experts say it is best for your own well-being to forgive them, too. Although I believe they are correct, this is not so easy, and it is my deep regret to say that I have no keen insight or soothing words to offer those upon whom such tragedy may have befallen. I can merely acknowledge your immense pain; and admire your fortitude and willingness to forgive.

Most of those who hurt us are not doing so intentionally, at least not to the degree that we have allowed ourselves to perceive. The person who angered me may be hurting from anger, self-doubt, or low self-esteem. They may be overwhelmed by their own daily tribulations. It may be that this person is subconsciously trying to lessen their own pain by looking for faults in others.

All humans occasionally wallow in self-absorption; ignorant of the impact of their words and actions on others. Each of us has shown weakness through this lack of awareness. The occasional faults of our friends and loved ones can be forgiven. And we can hope that they will respond in kind when we exhibit a lack of awareness and cause them pain. Forgiveness can replace anger.

Here is a good way to start your day: breathe in serenity and peace; breathe out any troubles or anger you may hold. Let your shoulders rest down. Now recite the mantra "Forgiveness brings peace."

Our bodies can become healthier and stronger when fear and anger are sent away. Stress chemicals are no longer being formed, and neural circuits are not wasted on useless memories or concerns.

Sadness

"Into each life a little rain must fall." I am not sure of the author of this quote, but no truer words have ever been spoken. No matter whom we are, what we have done, or however far we run, sadness will eventually find us.

We lose pets, we lose touch with friends or relatives, we lose jobs, and we lose purpose. We lose opportunities because of chances we did not take. We lose a parent, spouse or other beloved family member.

So much loss! So much pain! We may be overwhelmed by the grief and loneliness brought on by our great losses. We may even allow a long-lasting pervasive sadness to settle in. It is certainly alright to feel sadness. We must be true to ourselves and acknowledge that this emotion is a normal and necessary process.

When a forest burns down, the landscape is barren and exposed. The horizon at first reveals only a lonely wasteland.

But then small changes begin to happen. Early the next year a small flower emerges, and later a full lush landscape appears. It is different, certainly; but beautiful, nonetheless. Charred trunks stand as silent sentinels over the new landscape. Witnesses to the past, they are incorporated as essential elements into this new canvas of life.

All humans will suffer great losses. There may also be many things taken from us. It may sound trite, but there is one thing that cannot be taken from us, and that is our hope. Hope will remain with us for as long as we wish. We must choose to never, ever let it go. Do not ever give up!

Hope secures us to the craft even as the waves break the bow.

Hope keeps us alive until the storm passes, which it always will. Hope will still be there when the next dark cloud looms, which again will be followed by calm and blue.

Like the forest, we can mourn for a season. Cloaked in a mantle of snow, we may hide from the elements, with hope as our only companion. But as the snow melts away, our new life must emerge. As in the forest, the charred sentinels are still present as reminders of past sadness, but we welcome the new life that joins us, as it becomes entwined with the old. We will realize that life is a long and passionate adventure. And that the best is yet to come. We will be tough, and embrace the challenge of our new life.

We will choose to always be hopeful. We will thus avoid building unhelpful neural circuitry, and also decrease levels of stress hormones that may accompany prolonged sadness and depression.

Here is another good mantra to start each day: "The best is yet to come!"

Putting It All Together

We have discussed how somewhat intangible information delivered to our senses is transformed into real molecules and neural connections. These are actual physical structures present at the cellular level, which can be augmented and altered by conscious mental effort. For maximal health, it is imperative to mindfully build positive neural connections, which will help to create healthy chemistry throughout our bodies.

We can influence a stimulus that is presented to us. We can also alter our perceptions of this event to achieve a desired outcome.

Helpful ways to influence the stimuli or events that are presented to us include the following:

Although it is not always possible, try to avoid noxious stimuli such as negative personalities, violent images, and occupations that you find too stressful.

Create beneficial stimuli by doing the following: Surround yourself with positive individuals. Take the time to appreciate and enjoy the things that bring pleasure to your five senses. Recite mantras which are verbal affirmations of your true capabilities. Instruct your body to assume a confident, serene pose with appropriate posture and a smile.

Appropriate ways to help us alter perceptions of stimuli that are uncomfortable or painful include the following:

When we are anxious or afraid, we can embrace the energy that accompanies fear. We can channel this energy to run into our fears, and toward actions that place concern for others over self. Fear itself can be banished and replaced with love. "Perfect love casts out fear."

When we feel anger or hurt, we can replace these feelings with forgiveness. Most affronts to us are the result of a lack of awareness in others, rather than personal attacks due to mean-spiritedness. Do not take anything personally. Forgiveness will help me and you as much as it will help those that we forgive. "Forgiveness brings peace."

When an inevitable sadness comes our way, we can replace this sadness with hope. We will choose to be tough and hopeful. "The best is yet to come!"

Thinking Makes It So

You can improve your future by the way you think. But here is something else to consider: *You can also improve your past.* It is your decision how you choose to remember it.

The physical structure of our brain is shaped by the way that we choose to think. We have the ability to alter and create many of our own neural pathways.

Similar to an orchardist who cuts away the diseased branches of a tree, there are cells in our brain that have the ability to prune away unnecessary neural pathways. There is only so much real estate to go around, therefore non-utilized circuits are disassembled to make room for something new or more important.

Just like everything else in the human body, you use it or you lose it. If we choose to dredge up unpleasant memories, we breathe new life into unhealthy brain pathways – dying limbs that would otherwise soon be clipped away.

William Shakespeare wrote, "There is nothing either good or bad, but thinking makes it so."

When recalling your past, consider that you are writing a historical novel about your life – with a few well-placed edits – telling a compelling story of fun times and interesting adventures. It need not be a documentary that meticulously catalogues every unfortunate event that has ever happened to you. There is no outside agency interested in checking your story for accuracy.

Consider two friends, each of whom had a difficult upbringing. One chooses to often recall the bad times of the past; the anger, tension and shouting that she endured as a child. Her memory is indeed accurate, as there were many difficult days in her younger life. However, by constantly recalling painful experiences, old wounds are reopened; and thus, she now suffers.

There is a teaching in the Buddhist tradition that says, "Pain is inevitable; suffering is optional." It suggests that after being pierced by a first arrow of pain, it is quite possible to avoid a second arrow of suffering.

The other friend does not deny being struck by the first arrow; the past moments of pain and anguish that she, too, experienced as a child. But she decides to accept that she is the composite of her life experiences, both good and bad. And she decides to love what is.

When thinking of her past, she chooses to recall mostly the good times – her mother singing melodies at the piano, and her father helping to build projects for show-and-tell at school. She understands that her parents were at times imperfect; revealing the signature characteristic of all humanity. She realizes that they had their own private demons to battle, and old wounds of their own to nurse.

So, she chooses not to suffer, but rather to forgive. She discovers that grace heals. Reflecting on the sunny days of her youth, she often finds herself smiling and laughing. She creates her own happiness.

Memories of negative experiences need not be completely whitewashed away; but they can be reframed in a more positive light. Here is a mental exercise:

Build a box in your mind, and now place within this box all of the bad days you have ever had. Include all of your failures and mistakes; all of the unkind words spoken by you or others; all of the unfairness of a life exposed to the vicissitudes of fortune. Now put the box up in the attic.

The box will always be there; a dusty relic containing the difficult moments of your past. But the painful experiences within the box soon begin to partly fade away, as they exist only in your memory. The actual events have long vanished. It is okay to acknowledge the contents of the box; but you need not often reach into it, dragging out old demons to resuscitate back to life.

Consider the box and its contents as just one single entity, rather than mulling over the particularities of each individual item. It is just one box. Realize that its contents are an essential part of what made you who you are today. As noted by author Stephen Covey, "Character is often forged in crucibles of pain."

For those who choose to find some usefulness and purpose in a painful past, the composite of challenging times may even be transformed into a treasure – perhaps manifesting as greater insight into the pain and suffering endured by their brothers and sisters throughout the world.

Archbishop Desmond Tutu has noted that we have the choice to allow our travails to either embitter us or ennoble us. What a beautiful idea, to suggest that we can be ennobled by our struggles. Knowing firsthand the piercing sting of the first arrow, we can ascribe meaning to our pain; and perhaps then help others to escape similar arrows of pain and suffering.

Time does indeed assuage the pain of all wounds; if only we choose to allow it. Our neural circuits have been designed to discard the dead wood of many of our prior pains and misadventures; but we must decide to let them go.

Choose to remember the happy moments of your life. Recall the pleasant days of your childhood, your successes in life, and the grand adventures that you have had. Visualize many more great days to come.

Improve your future; improve your past. Thinking makes it so.

NINE

See It and Be It

"Imagination encircles the world."

-Albert Einstein

ALTHOUGH A NEURO-ANATOMIST may furrow his brow at the notion, it can be imagined that the human brain contains two distinct yet very integrated structures – like a two-story flat comprised of an older lower unit and a newer upper add-on.

The downstairs apartment represents the remnants of an ancient mammalian brain; the home of our subconscious mind – the constantly evolving entity that reacts to events quickly, without a whole lot of conscious "thinking" involved.

Climb the stairway to the upper add-on, and you will find a unit representing additional frontal lobe real estate; showcasing the advanced electronic circuitry of a relatively newer, more conscious mind. Our conscious mind processes and prioritizes information rather thoroughly, before responding in a more deliberate manner.

Some philosophers have intuited that our minds are connected to an Infinite Intelligence – imagine small ocean harbors opening to a great sea. Others ascribe a unifying consciousness to the universe, noting that our bodies and brains are derived from elements of the cosmos, and therefore we humans are living manifestations of a universe that has learned to contemplate its own existence.

Whether our conscious minds are truly linked to a greater force via undiscovered processes, or if humans are contained in consciousness, rather than vice versa, is for others to say. I do, however, believe that it is useful for all sentient beings to expand their ideas of the possible.

At the level of the individual, the subconscious and conscious mind each have important roles to play, each balancing the other.

Primitive emotions, emanating from subconscious centers, can be overridden by newer cognitive circuits. Left unchecked, caveman physiology and instincts are not always well-suited for a modern world. If you hit a bothersome neighbor on the head with a stick tonight, you may awaken with a cell mate staring you in the face tomorrow morning.

Conscious minds can indeed soften the edges of subconscious actions, but newer forebrain circuits can also sometimes get in their own way; complicating tasks that older hunter-gatherer brain pathways can most easily accomplish on their own.

Consider a jockey and a racehorse at the starting gate of the Kentucky Derby. One creature atop the other, each nervously fidgets as they await the sound of the starting bell. In a surge of power, they are off; and the two now act as one. The rider does indeed guide the steed, urging it on, but he ultimately relinquishes some control; allowing the magnificent animal to do what it can do quite well on its own – which is to run very, very fast.

And, so it is with a human being. It is as if our conscious thoughts ride atop the wild beast that is our subconscious mind and body. We form a deep oneness with this creature. We see through its eyes; we hear through its ears. We feel its pain, its pleasure, and its power. We allow it to experience its innate need to eat, drink, and run; and to fulfill its desire to find a mate and a community. And, in turn, the wild animal allows us to come along for a fantastic ride.

Like the jockey with his racehorse, we have the ability to guide the creature that we inhabit; attempting to imbue a thin mantle of civility to its wildness. Taming the beast is often necessary in polite society, and it has certainly been an essential factor in the ascension of humankind. But there are also times that it is best for our conscious minds to simply let go. We can surrender control to the remarkable manifestation of the universe that is our subconscious mind and body; entrusting it to charge steadfastly to our common goal.

Subconscious Glory

It is game point at Wimbledon. After three hours of athletic combat on the court, a competitor must break her opponent's serve to continue the match. She cannot think of failure. Her conscious mind visualizes a successful return of serve; painting a picture for her subconscious mind to achieve.

Her subconscious mind then jumps into action; watching and listening to the tennis ball come off the opponent's racquet, quickly judging the ball's velocity and spin, and calculating the anticipated trajectory of the bounce. Her subconscious mind then sends messages to nearly every muscle in her body, allowing each to engage in synchronous fashion, shifting her quickly in the proper direction. It simultaneously decides when to intercept the bounce of the incoming ball, and where to deliver it back in to her opponent's court. Firing her muscles in a then different fashion, she delivers a stunning return to extend the match.

Meanwhile, the wristwatch in her locker registers about one second of elapsed time. She is reacting, not responding.

Now imagine this same tennis player, attempting to incorporate and respond to all of this information in a logical and methodical fashion, using conscious decision making. She would need a mathematician to help with the velocity, trajectory, and angle of the incoming ball; a physiologist to help her decide which muscle groups to deploy; and a tennis coach to tell her where best to place the return volley – all of which would take at least a few minutes at best.

If You Think, You Miss

We have all heard the stories of baseball catchers who can no longer throw the ball back to the pitcher, the golfer who suddenly develops the yips and cannot sink a putt, or the usually sure-handed wide receiver who unexpectedly drops the ball when the game is on the line. Some call it "trying too hard" or "over-thinking it".

Like a fox pouncing on a rabbit, our hunter-gatherer ancestors could not afford to often "over-think" it. They just threw the spear at their prey and watched it fall to the ground. Dinner is served. Getting the "yips" meant going hungry and making your mate very unhappy.

Similar to the jockey and his horse, our conscious mind can guide our subconscious mind. However, the conscious mind must not attempt to perform the task alone, rather instead provide a mental picture or verbal statement of what it wants the subconscious mind to do. The conscious mind provides the blueprint, but it then trusts the subconscious mind to build the house.

The successful athlete uses this form of imagery to excel in his sport. He has learned to "See it and be it." The golfer imagines the exact flight of the ball on the way to the green, the basketball player visualizes the ball going through the hoop, and the baseball player sees the pitch careening off his bat and over the center field wall. The conscious mind delivers the work order to the subconscious mind and trusts it to complete the task.

The picture you draw for your subconscious mind must be very simple and specific, indicating what you want – not what you don't want. The directions must say "go one mile and turn left at the big tree" rather than "do not take the first road by the hill or the bridge across the river." When it is time to perform, the subconscious mind needs to be uncluttered, focusing on one image of success, not multiple images of failure.

There is no guarantee of success every time. The subconscious mind is not foolproof – sometimes a fox will leap and miss her quarry. There is, however, a guarantee that success will come *more often* when one utilizes appropriate imagery.

Although it certainly does not have quite the same ring to it, we can also "Hear it and be it." Our subconscious minds do indeed listen to what our conscious minds have to say. That is why mantras have such a positive effect. Say each day that "The best is yet to come!" and it is quite likely that your subconscious mind will lead you to this outcome.

It is not just in athletic competition that one can benefit from a "See it and be it" mentality. We can visualize ourselves being successful in our jobs, in our relationships with others, in our fitness and health, or in any other realm of our lives.

Ralph Waldo Emerson said,

"Live the life you have dreamed for yourself. Go forward and make your dreams come true."

There are two important parts to this advice. First you must dream, and then you must go forward and begin the task. There are many dreamers who forget about the second part, never taking the steps necessary to accomplish their dreams. You have to take that first step.

There are also many who ignore the first part of Emerson's advice, never allowing themselves to dream of a remarkable life. Caught up in the daily grind of living, they merely exist, never realizing that there is much more within their reach.

Dream big. You may fail. In fact, you most probably will – at least initially. Dream big anyways. As Thomas J. Watson, former CEO of IBM, once said:

"Success is on the far end of failure."

Do not be afraid to fail. Fear of failure is far worse than failure itself.

Read almost any business book and you will be regaled with stories of successful athletes, politicians, business leaders, and scientists whose failures far outnumbered their successes; yet through perseverance they emerged triumphant. Never give up.

Dream big. Tear down make-believe fences that you or others have invented for yourself, and that keep you from achieving your goals.

Dream big. Expand your ideas of your own capabilities. Most of us live far within our limits. Never allow yourself to think that you are not good enough or important enough or strong enough. Do not underestimate the treasures that are within you.

Dream big. This does not mean that you must dream of personal riches or recognition. Dream of big causes, and how you can be a part of something important. Dream of a planet comprised of clean oceans, fresh air, and rich soils. Dream of a world of peaceful and healthy citizens. Dream of liberty and justice for all.

You do not necessarily have to have your name in the newspapers or be known to all people. Whether it is a large or small part, play your role magnificently. My wife Diana showed me this quote from Helen Keller:

"I long to accomplish a great and noble task, but it is my chief duty to accomplish humble tasks as though they were great and noble. The world is moved along, not only by the mighty shoves of its heroes, but also by the aggregate of the tiny pushes of each honest worker."

Dream often. Start when you wake up, and then repeat your goal several times throughout the day. Create a video of yourself in your mind. Watch yourself realizing your ambitions.

In your mind's eye, see yourself accomplishing your goals. Be very specific. Observe yourself succeeding brilliantly. Notice the clothes you are wearing, the feel of the ground beneath your feet, the presence of others nearby, the sounds that surround you. Imagine unexpected problems that may come up and watch as you masterfully handle them with equanimity and grace. The subconscious mind does not care if this is real or imagined. It will help bring you to your goal either way.

At night, as you drift off to sleep, think once again of great and noble goals. And then hand them over to your subconscious mind, which will often be fast at work while you sleep – helping to solve problems and guide you to your objective.

You may awaken out of a deep slumber with an inspiration or brilliant new plan. Keep a pen and paper near the bedside to write it down. Sometimes in the early morning hours, in that misty space between sleep and awakening, you may come up with your best ideas.

Gautama, the Buddha said: "The mind is everything; what you think you become."

Sometimes it is necessary for our conscious mind to problem solve. It can devise a rudder and a compass, to help guide us on our way. But we can also tap in to the power of our subconscious mind, the constantly evolving entity born of Providence. We can create for it an image of our intended destination – and then just let go, allowing the current of a self-organizing universe to carry us forward. We may be pleasantly surprised where it takes us.

TEN

Passionate in the Middle

"The only thing that interferes with my learning is my education."

-Albert Einstein

IT HAS BEEN said that the only absolute in life is that there are no absolutes. But it seems that our analytical human minds wish to neatly categorize that which is presented to us. We often prefer to see things as good or bad, all or none, and black and white – even though everyone knows that human existence is a nuanced and multi-colored phenomenon.

Although humankind sometimes tends to favor a mindset of absolutism, a lack of it can be noted when observing many functions of the human body.

If I sustain a laceration, a very elegant clotting mechanism is put into motion. This involves a series of incredibly complex steps that culminate in the rapid cessation of bleeding – provided, of course, that the initial injury is not too great.

However, this impressive clotting response can sometimes go awry. If I have injured a lower extremity, or have remained immobile for a long period of time, the coagulation process can cause a deep vein thrombosis (DVT) to form within a blood vessel. This clot can break loose, travel within the venous system up to my chest, and finally become lodged in one or more of the pulmonary arteries which bring blood to my lungs. If the clot is large, this can cause significant morbidity and possibly result in my death.

As with the coagulation cascade, complex pathways also exist to dissolve pulmonary emboli, and any other clot in our bloodstream. This system, too, can sometimes go awry; causing hemorrhaging into vital structures.

Our bodies continuously fine-tune these opposing mechanisms; seeking a sweet spot between excessive coagulation and excessive bleeding.

Human physiology does not function in rigid absolutes. Engaging in many intricate balancing acts, our bodies typically avoid the extremes at the margins, finding instead a comfortable middle range.

Social Conditioning

We are often conditioned to categorize other people at one extreme or the other. The kicker on a football team is often considered either hero or villain, depending on whether the ball happened to travel perfectly between the uprights at the end of the game.

Of course, he really is the same person that he was before kickoff that day – just an average guy who is not fully a hero or a villain but, like the rest of us, probably a small measure of each.

We are often quick to assign the label of hero; and are therefore perhaps taken aback when our idols succumb to temptation. Conversely, hardened criminals occasionally surprise us with glimmers of benevolence.

The truth is that few if any people are either all good or all bad, rather differing combinations of the two. There are no absolutes. Malice and virtue engage in daily combat. One may win the war, but each claim smaller victories.

In the political realm, we often see irritating efforts at polarization by leaders of the major parties. Many of these attempts to sway our thinking are successful. We therefore sometimes demonstrate unwavering loyalty to our team – even if logic or circumstances suggest that we do otherwise. We may even tend to view those in other parties uniformly as the enemy.

However, in truth, most of the constituents of each party share a mutual goal, which is a safe and comfortable environment for themselves, their loved ones, and all world citizens.

An Initially Valid Concern

Those on each side of an issue or argument typically form their belief system and subsequent actions based on an initially valid reason. The corporate executive correctly realizes that we all need an income to survive, and that her company will provide jobs for many people. The environmentalist understandably recoils when he sees a business owner show apparent disregard for the safety and beauty of our natural resources. Initially, each has a valid cause.

The danger comes later, when originally valid concepts are subsequently adulterated by the proclivities of those who stray beyond the margins of reason or morality – the greedy merchant who is no longer content to provide a necessary product with little environmental impact; and the obstructionist environmental advocate who will unfailingly challenge every move of industry.

A Toxic Mess

One summer, between semesters as a college student, I worked for a sawmill located in the Pacific Northwest. In the first few weeks of my employment I was assigned a variety of undesirable tasks, mostly related to cleaning up various parts of the mill.

Adjacent to a small river was a concrete deck where loads of lumber were routinely dipped into a large container of a purple colored oily solution, which was used to help prevent wood rot. When the mill foreman brought me over to this area, I could see that the purple liquid had dripped all over the deck and had made quite a mess. He then showed me a high-pressure hose and directed me to rinse the chemical solution off of the deck and into the river. I protested that this action would likely kill fish and other aquatic life, and that this was not a task that I was willing to perform.

I had enough backbone to refuse to do his bidding, and luckily was not fired from a much-needed job. But ultimately, I failed in my duty as a global citizen, as at that time I lacked the maturity and confidence to demand that the mill find a responsible way to clean up its toxic messes. I am sure that the foreman simply found another lackey to do his dirty work, and the river was polluted despite my protest.

I was personally confronted with a basic dilemma of seemingly opposing needs. I needed a paycheck, yet I also understood the need to maintain a clean and sustainable environment. This is the very dilemma that plagues each of us today, played out on a much larger stage throughout the world.

Compromise

The world often derives some benefit from the outrageous individuals who operate near the fringes, the intrepid souls whose ideas are often located just barely within the borders of reason.

The entrepreneur, who addresses a need and bravely begins a new venture, creates jobs and often delivers a product that makes all of our lives better. The equally brave environmentalist realizes the importance of preserving our world for future generations. He therefore protests damage to the Earth, unafraid to sound a clarion call for all to hear. Each has a valid cause – often with seemingly cross purposes – but each is ultimately dependent on the other.

Without the use of materials from the Earth, and without manufacturers to produce steel, lumber, and copper wiring, environmentalists (like me) would have no running water, no electricity, and no place to live. Nearly eight billion people cannot all live in teepees. However, it is equally true that humanity requires a clean and sustainable environment if it is to survive.

Left unchecked, big business has tended to emphasize short term profits over environmental responsibility, and it is often the loud voice of the environmentalist who has forced them back on to a proper course. The corporate executive and the environmentalist each serve a vital purpose, and each is dependent upon the other.

Sometimes outliers will stray too far from reason. The corporate executive becomes greedy. Motivated purely by profit, she demonstrates a reckless disregard for the world around her. No longer her cohort, the environmentalist is now her opponent and becomes an eco-terrorist. He drives iron spikes into trees that can harm the logger, destroys property that is not his own, and files a lawsuit each time forest timber is scheduled to be logged.

In his interesting book *Collapse*, author Jared Diamond describes how, in previous years, mining companies would plunder resources in Montana, make a tremendous profit, and then declare bankruptcy, leaving billions of dollars in cleanup costs to be shouldered by the taxpayer.[32]

However, Diamond also made a point to applaud industries and individual companies that do currently engage in responsible activities. The Forest Stewardship Council, an international non-profit organization funded by business, government, and environmental groups, is a successful venture that certifies forests that are managed in an ecologically sound manner.

Many companies are run by people who do have true environmental concerns, and many others are learning that it is much cheaper to employ clean practices today than to pay for the cleanup of an environmental disaster tomorrow. It has been the environmentalist, whose loud protest has alerted the consumer to prior misdeeds of industry, who has been largely responsible for the change of practice shown by many of these companies. A bad reputation is bad for business, and many companies cannot risk a public relations nightmare.

Some businesses have blended environmentalism with business – utilizing natural resources to create jobs and services, but doing so in a sustainable fashion. Founded in 1991, Ecotrust is a non-profit organization whose goal is to help communities meet their social and economic needs while also preserving the environment.

The many programs of Ecotrust include Climate-Smart Forestry, connecting working waterfronts directly to markets, and creating a regional hub for the local food economy. Ecotrust also arranges investment capital for private and public institutions in low-income communities, by issuing New Market Tax Credits to generate economic growth, community revitalization, and environmental restoration.

Ecotrust considers cultural and economic issues when developing plans for restoring and saving pristine forests and waterways; weaving together solutions that serve person, people, and planet – showing that environmental stewardship, community, and financial prosperity can often happily coexist.

Sometimes if you sit in the middle you run the risk of being labeled as wishy-washy. Both sides feel that if you are not with them, you are against them. But such a mindset of absolutism is unproductive, and at times dangerous. A person can be passionate in the middle; intelligent enough to know that we live in a multi-colored world and only a fool sees just in black and white.

In a Buddhist cookbook I read the following advice: "Do not be too rich, as that is like the feeling of having had too much to eat; do not be too poor, as that is like the feeling of being too hungry; the middle is the place to be." I think this outlook works well in a lot of different facets of life; the middle is the place to be.

Try listening carefully to voices beyond both ends of reason, and then seek a place somewhere between the two, where practicality and compromise reside. The middle road is a wide road, with plenty of room for all sorts of dreamers.

ELEVEN

The Power of the Collective

"The high destiny of the individual is to serve rather than to rule."

-Albert Einstein

I REMEMBER WATCHING a nature special on television a few years ago. A part of the show featured a yearling bison being attacked by a couple of wolves. Much smaller than even this very young bison, one of the wolves was stepped on and wounded in the attack, possibly eventually fatally. But in the end, it was the young bison that lost the battle. The rest of the bison herd stood helplessly nearby, witnessing firsthand the brutality of their existence.

This scene was difficult to watch, not only because it brought to mind the unanswerable question of why nature can at times appear to be so cruel, but also because it became apparent that the herd was not really helpless at all.

Together and united, the herd could have easily charged the wolves and killed them, simply by virtue of their mass and brute strength. However, the group lacked the intelligence of the wolf pack – a species that utilizes the power gained by collaborative concerted effort – and therefore the bison suffered the loss of one of their own.

A few centuries ago, a group of about two hundred Spanish soldiers, led by Francisco Pizarro, conquered a nation of approximately ten million Inca natives. Immensely outnumbered, a handful of men exploited two of the major weaknesses of the Inca. One weakness was the failure of the natives to appreciate and harness the power they possessed in sheer numbers alone. The Spaniards also seized upon the Inca's fear, awing the natives with their advanced weaponry.

Leo Tolstoy tells a story of a powerful Russian official who rounded up a group of village men, brought them to a barn and locked the door behind him. Emboldened by the power of his office, the official intimidated the men into submission, pitting one against the other. But then one of the villagers had the insight and courage to perceive the situation in a different light. Realizing the power of their great numbers, he convinced the others to unite together. It was the villagers who soon held the advantage in that locked barn.

Human beings today are not really all that different from the bison, the Inca natives, or the Russian villagers when first brought into the barn. Immense populations are controlled by a relatively few individuals in power; puppeteers who control their dolls by pulling strings of base emotion. These people exploit the fact that the masses are often oblivious to the great power of their numbers, and that they are often unaware that their emotions are being carefully manipulated.

Now Playing

We may be played by unscrupulous government leaders who try to exploit our fears; mesmerizing us with their speeches, spinning hypnotic tales of power and economic dominance, delivering divisive messages that set one country against and above all others.

We must be wary of those who wish to direct our attention away from humanity's most worthy dream – that of Sustainable Global Happiness. It is essential that we fiercely protect our Earth and its ecosystems from harm; and that we honor the dignity and concerns of all world citizens, present and future.

The power of the collective is much greater than the seductive and misleading narrative of relatively few numbers of people in control. Unscrupulous leaders are far outnumbered by intelligent citizens of good character.

Ultimately, it is citizens who wield the most clout – we hold the advantage in the locked barn. Those who wish to play us depend on our ballots as the lifeblood for their very existence. They cannot survive unless we willingly hand them our vote.

TWELVE

Peace is in the Garden

"The difference between the past, present and future is only a
stubbornly persistent illusion."

-Albert Einstein

THE MIND CAN be considered to exist within an extraordinary array of electrical connections located within the structure of the brain. It is interested in preservation of self, and preservation of the body in which it is intimately associated.

The relationship of the mind to the brain is similar to that of a pitcher and the water it carries. The water in the pitcher is dependent on the structural integrity of the container in which it resides. If the pitcher fails, the water is useless.

Similarly, the mind is dependent upon the vessel in which it resides. Injury to the brain will affect the contents that it carries. Damage to the mind due to injury of the brain structure can come from trauma, degenerative disease, or the ingestion of excessive alcohol or other substances that harm the cells of our brain.

Similar to adding poison to the water in a pitcher, the mind can also be directly affected by societal toxins – such as when we observe recurrent images of violence, or hear words of hatred.

As a metaphorical exercise, one can consider the mind, brain, and body to be enclosed within a circle. If we so choose, we may live our lives sequestered within this space; going about our daily lives, feeling both pain and pleasure. However, in this space within the circle we remain focused inward – perhaps fearful of the future and regretful of the past. From this encapsulated vantage point it is often difficult to view the enormity of the present moment.

Now imagine that the circle walls contain unlocked doors; portals to a place outside. If we allow a part of our mind to open these doors, to step outside the circle, we can observe our own lives from a distance. We can mindfully and impartially evaluate the frequent absurdity of our individual actions, as well as that of the collective actions of the societies in which we function. We can expand our awareness.

In the space outside the circle, there are no clocks or calendars. There is no yesterday or tomorrow – it is always just today, this present moment. In this space is a non-judging peace. It is guileless, selfless, and calm. It is a place to come to for rest.

In the space outside the circle one finds increased clarity of purpose and vision. This is a place of realization that our bodies and minds are of this Earth. There is awareness that the very atoms within our bodies once resided in the water, rocks, plants, and animals of our planet; and before that in the primordial dust of a newly forming universe. We realize we are therefore intimately connected to everything else on this planet, and ultimately the entirety of creation – past, present, and future.

In this space we consider ourselves as stewards of our body, considering our physical structures as gifts on loan. We know to enjoy the benefits that our body bestows upon us. We know to strive to maintain it as well as possible, realizing that we will one day return it to the dust from which it came.

Although the space outside the circle is a place of awareness of self, it is also a place of selfless awareness. It is within this space that we realize that all matter is interconnected. No action is without consequence, and the subtle nuance of individual activity may have significant effect on the whole. In this place we question the wisdom of applying short term solutions to meet humanity's wants and needs.

In this space we question everything – to assure ourselves that our motives are noble, that our decisions will first consider the fate of the

Earth and all of its people and creatures, present and future. In this place we know that it is only with great care that mankind should consider altering the balance of a system that has been in place for billions of years, a system that has functioned beautifully without human intervention.

Zen masters, religious leaders, and wise philosophers through the ages have offered great wisdom, recommending useful techniques to help us find the portals of connection to the space outside the circle.

Give yourself time to contemplate. Prayer and/or meditation can be helpful for many. Others use breathing exercises to find a place of peace and rest.

Stand in a gentle breeze, close your eyes, and let the wind blow your cares away. Consciously smile, and then get an image of a garden or any place of comfort; finding your own unique place of mindfulness.

Perhaps within our existence there really is a timeless place of peace, rest, and awareness. Hope prevails.

Randy A. Siltanen

THIRTEEN

Providence

"He who can no longer pause to wonder and stand rapt in awe, is as good as dead; his eyes are closed."

-Albert Einstein

IN THE STREETS of Athens, about twenty-four hundred years ago, a stonemason could be heard discussing philosophy with a group of followers. He was quite well versed in many subjects, including logic and politics. Known as Socrates, he spoke extensively about the merits of virtue – proclaiming that an unexamined life is not a life worth living.

His protégé Plato documented much of the dialogue they shared; allowing subsequent generations to also know of his ideas. In turn, Plato's star pupil was Aristotle; who would later go on to tutor Alexander the Great.

Here is one of Socrates' most profound quotes; a modest admission that underscores the limits of understanding in even the most brilliant of minds:

"I know one thing, and that is I know nothing."

It is likely that Socrates' ideas echoed through time and space across the Ionian Sea – about five hundred years and a thousand miles away – to the tent of Roman emperor Marcus Aurelius, who penned what could be considered a fitting corollary to the words above:

"Everything we hear is an opinion, not a fact. Everything we see is a perspective, not the truth."

On balance, it could be argued that organized religion has indeed been a positive driver of humanity. A young agnostic friend of mine recently acknowledged, "I would hate to live in a world without religion."

Individuals of myriad religious denominations have often come together to create global happiness. World Vision, a faith-based organization, delivers clean water and sanitation to more people worldwide than any government institution. There are countless other religious groups that have also promoted peace, education, and sustainable agriculture throughout the world.

Religion has been noted to be one of the great unifiers of humanity.[33] However, the unifying and cohesive tendencies of religions have often tended to be within members of particular faiths, rather than between different religious denominations.

Over the last millennia, Muslims have killed Christians and Christians have killed Muslims – by the millions. Further down the ranks of division, Protestant Christians have engaged in numerous deadly clashes with Catholic Christians, and Shiite Muslims continue to battle Sunni Muslims. There have also been conflicts amongst and between adherents of Hinduism, Buddhism, and Judaism; and every other major religious faction scattered across the globe.

Many of the followers of these religions possess a unique and personal interpretation of their particular creed. Some Catholics believe in Purgatory, some favor same-sex marriage, and others may not eat meat on Fridays.

Protestants also hold ideas that differ from one group to the next; often identifying themselves with titles such as Baptist, Lutheran or Methodist.

These groups often further subdivide themselves into various splinter sects or synods, each containing individual members that usually do not precisely agree with each other on all matters of church doctrine. It is the same with those who call themselves Jewish, Hindu,

Buddhist, or Muslim; or any individual who identifies with any other religious assembly.

If you get down to exact details, you would probably find that there are nearly eight billion different beliefs regarding the precise nature of Spirituality and human existence – one for each person on the planet.

Maybe it is not so much shared commonalities of belief that connect us to a particular religion, rather instead the tribal instinct of wanting to belong to a group or gathering; to know that there will always be someone with whom we can share our sorrows and our joys.

However, this sense of belonging is only fully optimized if the group maintains fidelity to a central guiding philosophy of inclusivity – one that strives to create sustainable global happiness for all world citizens; no exceptions.

Of course, this is not always the case. Oftentimes religion, like nationalism, implores us to love one singular group – ours – above all others.

But neither religion nor nationalism will unfailingly stand the test. Invented institutions often crumble and fall, particularly those not built upon solid cornerstones of noble ideals. Countrymen and parishioners may very well turn against their own – if scarce food, land or fortune are on the line.

Providence: God and/or Nature

Many people appear to demonstrate an unwavering loyalty to their particular ideology, quite sure that their way of thinking is the only true path – perhaps mistakenly confusing perspective with absolute truth. Can nearly eight billion humans each be exclusively correct in their various spiritual convictions? I may have hope in my own personal beliefs; however, it would be illogical to assume that all others are wrong in theirs.

So, I like the idea of Providence.

If you look up its meaning, you would find that Providence has been defined as:

"The protective care of God or of Nature as a spiritual power."

God or Nature. The guiding force of our universe may be called

151

God, or any of the many possible names used for God. It may also be called Nature. It serves no cosmic purpose to retreat to tribalism; quibbling over different points of view, none of which can be proven with any degree of certainty.

Maybe it is fair to consider the idea of Providence as a unifying beginning, a somewhat imprecise conception that can be interpreted in a number of different ways. The vagueness is intentional, and not meant to be an apology for individual conviction. An artist will paint an image of a meadow in her own fashion, while another may portray the same scene differently. Each demonstrates fidelity to their own vision, and one rendition is perhaps no truer than the other.

Universal and Personal

I am not sure that Providence can be perceived directly with precise clarity. It is as if each person possesses their own unique prism through which to see its light. Each glass piece unveils an exclusive rainbow of colors and patterns; each revealing an inimitable spectrum of Providence – one Source viewed from an infinite number of perspectives.

Providence may be seen as the mystery of existence that many of us call God, instilling a sense of calm and happiness. We may also see Providence in the realm of Nature, with all its splendid forces and energy. Perhaps we see God and Nature as one. Each person possesses their own individual vision.

Providence is at once universal and personal.

Providence is *universal*, as there is likely only one true explanation of the universe, and how or why we got here. Whether you want to call it Physics or Nature or the divine will of God, the force that guides the universe is the same entity for every creature on this planet. Providence is universal.

Yet Providence is also *personal*, because even though no one knows all of the answers exactly, each of us is free to develop our own ideas about God and Nature. Providence is perhaps one entity, yet each person will experience Providence in their own individual way.

Providence is personal.

A Spectrum of Color and Design

When asked what religion he believed in, philosopher Ralph Trine offered an interesting perspective, suggesting that there is only one religion – what he called the religion of the living God. He believed that there have been many inspired Scriptures from many different faiths, and that through these writings God has revealed Himself at different times and places. He did not believe that God created prophets or chosen people, rather that certain individuals merely recognized a universal oneness with a common Source, just as ocean inlets open to a much greater sea.

Trine offered this beautiful excerpt from Alfred Lord Tennyson's poem, Akbar's Dream:

"Well, I dreamed that stone by stone I reared a sacred fane, a temple, neither pagoda, mosque, nor church, but loftier, simpler, always open-doored to every breath from heaven, and Truth and Peace and Love and Justice came and dwelt therein."

Motivational writer Napoleon Hill held a somewhat different yet equally intriguing view. Hill intuited that there is an Infinite Intelligence permeating every atom of matter in the universe:

"...the stars, the planets suspended in the heavens, the elements above and around us, every blade of grass, and every form of life within our view."

Hill hinted that the "secret" of success in life is learning how to tap into the infinite energy source of creation that Nature herself advertises.

And different yet, is the idea of the Dalai Lama who has said:

"My religion is simple. My religion is kindness."

At once universal and personal, here are some of the various names for Providence:

God, Allah, Holy Spirit, Jesus, Yahweh, Nature, Infinite Intelligence, Creator, The Source, Lord, The Way, Krishna, Almighty, Teacher, Father in Heaven.

Philosophers, prophets, books, and institutions may offer relevant ideas for each man or woman to consider. But perhaps these are all only intermediaries of Providence, offering interesting and often helpful guidance and perspective, but not necessarily absolute Truth revealed.

Whether you believe in God or in Nature, or even if you are not quite sure what it is that you believe in, you may find calmness and peace in surrendering to an Agency that is greater than yourself.

You can drop to your knees in a church, if that is what you feel. You can sit beside a glistening mountain lake, watching midday sunrays shimmer across its tiny ripples. You can stand on a mountain ridge, high above a hawk gliding on currents below. Just know that there is something larger than self and humanity, even if you do not know exactly who or what that is.

Offer up your deepest sorrows, if you wish. Let a breeze dry your tears and carry your burdens far away. If you ask for anything, ask for the strength to weather the storms of a random world, where fairness was never promised. Ask for Truth revealed.

And then, perhaps most importantly, express joy and gratitude. Give thanks for your family and your friends. Give thanks for the privilege of living on such a magnificent planet.

Maybe Providence is listening.

The Best of All Possible Worlds

I have often wondered why mankind has been subjected to so much pain. We suffer losses, some minor, but some exceedingly severe. In our everyday world there are innumerable atrocities.

If Providence is indeed a Deity, why would such tragedies be allowed to happen?

It is certainly possible that the seventeenth century philosopher Gottfried Leibniz was correct – perhaps ours really is "The best of all possible worlds." Maybe our universe, with all of its apparent unfairness, is as good a universe as one can possibly be.

It is possible that Providence fashioned the universe in one Big Bang, breathing life into the formulas and equations that would govern the galaxies and their inhabitants; and then simply let go, allowing the world to unfold from relatively simple beginnings into extraordinary levels of complexity, permitting us to be human, revealing all of our strengths and frailties.

It is possible that Providence is heartened by human achievements and triumphs, as parents are by the successes of their children. Perhaps Providence enjoys observing civilization advance in medicine, the arts, civic structures and governance, computers, and rocket ships.

But with human achievement comes human failure. Jealousy, mistrust, and greed lead to wars, hunger, and other crises. Many individuals are born with mental or physical handicaps. There are frequent senseless acts of brutal violence against innocent individuals. It certainly is not fair.

I offer up no easy answers. Perhaps there are no simple explanations. However, it is possible that some dark clouds of our existence may have a faint silver lining. Human trials, although very painful, could maybe serve some purpose – as even difficult situations may sometimes present opportunity.

Perhaps we have been given the chance to reveal our strength of character in times of personal turmoil. Ennobled by our own travails, maybe we will now choose to help others who have been similarly struck by hardship or cruelty.

I am reminded of a comment Earl Woods once made regarding his son, the talented golfer Tiger Woods. He said that Tiger prefers to play difficult golf courses. Tough venues demand the ultimate in shot-making and will eventually separate out the better players. Any pro can win on an easy golf course. Our response to the plight of those less fortunate, and to our personal tribulations, gives us the opportunity to better define ourselves, strengthening our will and resolve. Perhaps we have to earn our victory, managing our game over a very difficult course.

Maybe we should not expect life to be a straight, flat line. On an EKG monitor, a flat line is seen only with death. Just as without darkness we could not comprehend light, without sorrow, joy would have no meaning. If a fisherman caught a fish on every cast, he would soon become bored, his learned skills rendered useless, and the exhilaration of the catch quickly diminished. It is the struggle and the fruitless casts that make the successful cast meaningful. Continuous divine intervention could possibly take away the very fabric of human life; blunting the laughter, fear, sadness, and joy that make us human, essentially rendering our existence a lifeless flat line.

Even if these are the rules of the game, it is still painful to think of the acute fear and suffering experienced by many. Perhaps Providence is with us at times of great fear, pain, and suffering. Perhaps Providence envelops and protects an unseen part of us, even as our bodies succumb to the pain and indignities placed upon us by others, or by the frailty of our human physical tissues.

Shoulder to Shoulder

It is all quite difficult to understand. I know that I have far more questions than answers. I think that love fits in somewhere; perhaps the one true constant of a unifying equation describing the cosmos, if there is such a thing.

As with attempting to comprehend the vastness of the infinite universe, some concepts may simply exceed human levels of understanding. Sometimes we are just left with uncertainty, and there is no real choice but to yield to a design that we ourselves did not create.

Collectively, humankind often exposes its lonely heart, looking for someone or something to make sense of its existence. One must recognize that faith or religion, or whatever you want to call it, has provided comfort to countless individuals throughout the ages. It may be reasonable to question the logic of mindlessly following ritual and seemingly senseless traditions, but it is wrong to attempt to rob the faithful of their beliefs. For the wounded soul, faith can be a much better salve than the numbing medications currently dispensed to a bewildered populace.

Some who long for a sense of meaning may look to those who possess a brilliant intellect, hoping that they can help find elusive answers to our questions. Those who are searching could consider the humble statements of Albert Einstein, one of the greatest intellectuals of all time. Although he did not believe in a personal God, nor did he necessarily believe in an afterlife, Einstein strongly rejected being labeled an atheist.

A professed agnostic, Einstein said the following:

"The problem involved is too vast for our limited minds. We are in the position of a little child entering a huge library filled with books in many languages. The child knows someone must have written these books. It does not know how. It does not understand the languages in which they are written. The child dimly suspects a mysterious order in the arrangement of the books but doesn't know what it is. That, it seems to me, is the attitude of the most intelligent human being toward God. We see the universe marvelously arranged and obeying certain laws but only dimly understand the laws."

At least in this life, humans will not find an answer to every question. It is fruitless to seek consensus conclusions, as absolute Truth may remain forever beyond our mortal reach. I think this is okay. Individually, we will each try to find our own way.

We move forward, cloaked in an innate unique desire to find Truth, a yearning perhaps bestowed by an unseen Presence awaiting us at the end of our Earthly journey. We do not have to be afraid. We can submit to something greater than ourselves, and embrace the intrigue of the unknown.

What we do know is that we are each a living part of the fantastic grandeur that is our very existence. We do not necessarily have to understand or agree upon how or why we got here. As unified beings existing on this Earth, together we can stand shoulder to shoulder, looking to the heavens in awe, thankful to be witness to such an extraordinary universe.

Social Justice and a Healthy Planet

A Prelude to Part II and Part III

THERE ARE NEARLY eight billion people living on Earth, although our planet may quite possibly have only enough resources to indefinitely sustain a few billion less than that number. Within a few decades we are on track to add a couple billion more to our population. Several species are becoming extinct each day, at rates one hundred times normal background levels.[34]   Water, the lifeblood of our planet, is becoming increasingly polluted. Ocean fishes harbor high levels of toxic chemicals in their tissues, and their numbers are severely threatened by overfishing. Essential tropical rainforests are leveled daily. Coral reefs are dying due to climate change and CO_2 emissions. Who will stand up to address these problems?

Much of our soil is poisoned by pesticides, and nutrient levels are becoming depleted.   Current agricultural yields are artificially and unsustainably propped up by synthetic fertilizers; inputs that are dependent on finite amounts of substrates that must be produced from natural gas or obtained from mining. Many agricultural areas are now reliant on irrigation, but water table levels are dropping and irrigation has increased soil salinity in many regions, rendering much land less productive than in years past. Agribusiness is developing genetically modified organisms for us to eat, possibly placing our health and future food supply at great risk; without just cause. Who will stand up to stop these actions?

Clean sustainable energy is available; however, we continue to burn coal, natural gas, and oil to supply most of our energy requirements; even though it is widely known that we will soon run out of all three – but quite possibly not before severely damaging our Earth. Soldiers have been sent overseas to fight and die, attempting to protect American interests; which in times past has sometimes simply meant securing the availability of cheap oil, or maintaining spheres of influence in faraway locales. Many of our business and government leaders plan only for the next quarter, focusing primarily on growth and profit, amassing tremendous debt, and dragging our nation perilously close to financial disaster. The gap between the wealthy and the poor of the world continues to expand. Individual nations fight over natural resources, each chasing the impossible dream of perpetual growth, in a maniacal race to the bottom labeled the "Tragedy of the Commons" by ecologist Garrett Harden. Who will stand up to address these challenges – who will be a voice of reason and hope for both the privileged and the oppressed; and a representative for the children of future generations?

We must not let the words of Yeats come to pass: That the best lack all conviction and the worst are full of passionate intensity. The world has no use for restless apathy or despair. Although our problems are very real, they are certainly not insurmountable. The world is dizzyingly complicated – and at times a little scary – but it is an exhilarating ride, and a fantastic time to be alive. Explosive growth in information, technology and connectivity are giving many concerned citizens the tools they need to help solve current problems. Sustainable Global Happiness is well within our reach.

Present challenges impact all citizens, but it is our youth who have the most to gain or lose. Architects of a new century, it will likely be young leaders who tear down dangerous paradigms and create new models for social justice and sustainability.

The first part of this book suggests ideas for strengthening body and mind to optimize personal health and happiness. This prepares fertile ground from which springs forth the transcendent idea that the health and happiness of person, people, and planet are inseparably connected.

The emphasis of the following two sections is on achieving this collective happiness, focusing on the general needs of other world citizens, and highlighting the importance of protecting our Earth so that future populations can live happily as well.

Our actions come back to us, touching our own lives, improving our own personal wellness. It takes a healthy planet – with rich soils, fresh air, clean water, and safe and happy fellow citizens – to make a fully healthy and happy human being.

If my friend and I are starving, I may get lucky and find a loaf of bread. If I wish, I can choose to keep my discovery secret and eat all of the bread myself. However, my happiness will be very short-lived and will soon be replaced by grief, as I must now watch my friend succumb to hunger. Alternatively, I can offer a part of the bread to my friend – which will increase her happiness, and subsequently my overall happiness as well.

Cognitive dissonance theory posits that an individual is not completely happy if he simultaneously entertains two conflicting beliefs or truths. To solve this conundrum, and to optimize his happiness, he has two choices. He can attempt to reach equilibrium by ignoring or refuting one belief, or he can alter one or both of the dissonant factors.

If I am full, but my friend is hungry, I feel internal conflict and I am not at equilibrium. I will experience cognitive dissonance and therefore I will not be fully happy. Because she lives near me and is my friend, I cannot simply ignore her, or refute the fact that she is hungry. To find equilibrium I must alter the opposing factors of my desire for fullness and her pain from hunger – which I can easily accomplish by sharing my bread.

Similarly, a wealthy citizen who has everything he wants may think of himself as a good person. But then he begins to notice that although he is rich, other world citizens have basic unmet needs. He may also begin to realize that his lifestyle is harming the Earth for future generations. He, too, will experience cognitive dissonance.

In years past he could reach equilibrium by claiming ignorance to the plight of others across the world, and by refuting the notion that human actions have had a detrimental effect on the environment, ultimately negatively impacting future generations. He therefore could still consider himself to be a good person. This is no longer possible in our new, connected world.

The wealthy citizen is now very acutely aware of global conditions, often only moments after they occur. He must merely turn on his television or computer, or look at his smartphone. He cannot simply turn away from the concerns and suffering of others, as they are present in every direction. He can no longer easily deny the reality of human-induced damage to the Earth. The evidence is far too great. His intellect demands that he must now acknowledge these truths. But he remains unwilling to significantly change his way of life or his personal comfort level.

Yet he still wants to consider himself to be a good person.

Much unhappiness can arise from attempting to live with these conflicting truths, this cognitive dissonance. Chasing an illusory personal happiness, he grasps for something he can never quite attain.

The following sections will discuss many important issues that impact the health and happiness of the Earth and all of its inhabitants. I challenge you to evaluate these issues from a panoramic perspective; attempting to find innovative and integrative solutions derived from your own unique vantage point.

I encourage you to think differently.

PART II: PEOPLE

Health and Happiness for All Earth Citizens

"All I am saying is simply this, that all life is interrelated, that somehow we are caught in an inescapable network of mutuality, tied in a single garment of destiny. Whatever affects one directly affects all indirectly."

-Martin Luther King

Randy A. Siltanen

FOURTEEN

Perspective

"The important thing is to not stop questioning. Curiosity has its own reason for existing."

-Albert Einstein

IMAGINE YOURSELF STANDING at one end zone of the Rose Bowl in Pasadena, California, gazing across the length of the field to the other end zone. Now consider the 100-yard length of this field to represent the approximately two or three million years that human like creatures have walked our planet; with you in present time at one end zone, and an ancient bipedal human ancestor at the other end zone.

In the time represented by the first 99 yards and two feet, our ancestors lived in small groups, hunting animals and eating whatever they could find. Only the final one foot of this playing field represents the amount of time (approximately 10,000 years) that man began to give up hunting and gathering in favor of agriculture and the domestication of animals. From the time of Christ to the present day is represented by the last two inches of this 100-yard-long field. If you are 25 years old, the length of your entire life is denoted by the last half millimeter of turf, just a fine sliver of the last blade of grass before the goal line.

Now if you wanted to go back in time, you could walk down the football field a few million years to the other end zone to meet your ancient ancestors. If you were to continue back from there, using the same timeline, you could walk out of the stadium, head north and continue for about one mile, just over 60 million years, before you would approach the time when dinosaurs last inhabited the Earth.

If you wished, you could continue further north and walk another 200 miles up to around Fresno, which would take about 4 days, if you did not stop to sleep or rest. You now stand at point alpha, witness to a grand explosion, back about 13.7 billion years ago – the beginning of time as we know it.

This chapter will provide a brief tour through history, to add perspective, as a sort of a backdrop or canvas to more modern times. It is certainly not my aim – or for that matter possible – to write a detailed account of world history in a single chapter. The intent of this chapter is to simply refresh the memories of the reader.

History tends to repeat itself; and it is therefore useful to be reminded of some of the general proclivities of humankind. We can outline a better course to lasting global happiness by first reviewing some of the pathways that brought us to the present day.

Approximately 100,000 years ago (the exact timeline is debated), some of our ancestors left the cradle of mankind, East Central Africa, and began to slowly migrate up to Asia Minor. They then continued east into what is now China, and then veered south into Southeast Asia and Indonesia. This was a population that subsisted on hunting and gathering, living in small groups in a nomadic existence.

Around 20,000 years ago, a northerly migration had reached the land bridge connecting Siberia to Alaska, at which time much of North America was covered in ice. Several millennia later this land bridge would become covered by water, essentially isolating the Americas. Many people then began a southerly trek, some reaching into South America.

Up until this time, humankind had become successfully adapted to many different lifestyles. This was an adaptation that was necessary, due to weather and terrain related considerations, and based on the diversity and populations of the flora and fauna that they depended on for their existence. Some groups relied more on wild game and fish for survival, others more on plant life. There had however been relatively few major changes in the daily life of an individual when compared to an ancient ancestor who lived hundreds of thousands of years earlier.

Although social structures may have matured, these were still people who had to live in small groups due to the nomadic lifestyle forced upon them. When one food source became temporarily depleted, such as fallen acorns gathered in the autumn, the group had to move on to the next treasure.

Small groups are not exposed to one of the greatest benefits of a larger congregation of people – which is the intermingling of new ideas, and the resultant advances achieved through collaborative efforts.

Humankind's journey evolved relatively slowly until about 10,000 BC, at which time the weather on Earth began to warm. The snow turned to rain, and the inhabitants of the world began to chart a markedly different course.

The exact reason of this period of warming is unknown, but the effect was the melting of enormous regions of ice and snow, and the following rise of the oceans. This resulted in the separation of the British Isles from Europe, Sri Lanka from India, the Philippines and Taiwan from Asia, and the formation of the Bering Strait between Russia and Alaska.

As ice melted in the mountains, silt-filled rivers and streams would deliver a mineral rich payload along overflowing banks in countless valleys throughout the world. The increasingly fertile soil and warmer weather allowed the proliferation and cultivation of many plants, especially various grains – an event which would markedly change the world.

Root crops, such as yams, potatoes, and taro became major food sources; but these could not be stored for long periods of time. Hard grains could be stored and eaten when needed, although approximately one third of the heads of grain would have to be saved for planting in the next spring. Wheat and barley were planted and harvested in the Middle East and Asia Minor, millet and sorghum in Africa, rice in Asia, and maize in the Americas. Hunting and gathering could now be augmented by farming.

Coinciding with this revolution in agriculture was the domestication of sheep, goats, cattle, and fowl. For the first time in history, humankind now had food sources that could be saved and safely stored in great quantities, as was the case with grains; or tended and utilized when needed, such as with a herd of sheep or cattle. This allowed for the growth of larger communities, and an eventual end to the nomadic ways of most populations.

The relative abundance of food decreased the amount of time and human power needed to feed the community. This extra time allowed members of the group to begin to develop specialized skills; first those basic for survival and advancement, such as carpentry, masonry, and metallurgy. Soon to follow would be individuals who became proficient in art, mathematics, architecture, and philosophy. This was due not only to the new luxury of time afforded to a privileged relative few, but also due to the collaboration of ideas made possible by the greater number of intelligent individuals now living in close proximity to one another.

In what is now present-day Iraq, the Tigris and Euphrates rivers descend from the mountains of Asia Minor to eventually join and empty into the Persian Gulf. In approximately 3500 BC, a great civilization once flourished in this region of fertile river valleys, an area referred to as Mesopotamia. A part of the Fertile Crescent that also includes the Nile river valley in Northern Africa, the productive soil and gentle climate in this region supported cities of up to 50,000 inhabitants.

After a few thousand years this civilization began to decline, in part due to weakening of the population by wars between the Assyrians of the north and the Babylonians of the south. The decline was also accelerated by agricultural land degradation issues. These same problems – nutrient depletion, soil erosion, and increased soil salinity – would be mirrored in countless times and global locations in the millennia to come. The diminished crop yields, especially those of wheat, could no longer support such a great mass of people.

Today, much of the marshlands of the Fertile Crescent region have dried and turned to salt encrusted desert, mostly due to diversion of water supplies. Its agricultural areas are currently threatened by climate change, which computer models predict will result in markedly less rainfall in this region by the end of this century. This is an ominous prediction for an area that already suffers from political instability, and currently exists only barely above the margin of economic viability.

Around 2,000 BC, the roots of many of the major religions began to take hold in the masses; many of whom, like present day citizens, longed for a sense of meaning and understanding of their existence. These early religions included Christianity, which today claims just over two billion followers; Hinduism, with about one billion believers; and Judaism, with a much smaller following of approximately 14 million.

Of note, there are now also nearly two billion followers of Islam, 400 million adherents of Folk religion, and 500 million believers of Buddhism. Over one billion people today consider themselves non-religious.[35]

Many current world borders, regional conflicts, customs, and beliefs have obviously been tremendously influenced by differences in religious views. A large part of our current societal direction has been wrought by the spiritual belief systems of our ancestors and their leaders. For thousands of years, many have unquestioningly followed the traditions of their culture – rather than assimilating their own knowledge, and shaping their own personal interpretation of spirituality. Briefly examining the various starting points of some of the major religions can help to shed light on current circumstances.

Probably the oldest major religion, Hinduism originated on the Indian subcontinent. An institution with no single founder, Hinduism is considered to represent a set of principles and traditions of morality; acknowledging that there are many different approaches to God. Hindus may worship many gods, which some consider to be various manifestations of the one true Brahman. The Rigveda, an ancient Hindu scripture, was written as early as 1,500 years B.C.

In approximately 2,000 BC, Abraham was born in the Middle East, perhaps somewhere in present day Iraq, but the exact location is unknown. In the Jewish and Christian traditions, Abraham is the father of the Israelites through his son Isaac. In Islamic tradition, Abraham is considered to be a prophet of Islam and an ancestor of Muhammad. Although they each espouse somewhat different beliefs, these three branches of religion do acknowledge Abraham as a common trunk.

Of note, the Baha'i faith also affirms Abraham as a Messenger of God; one of many messengers that include Krishna, Zoroaster, Moses, Buddha, Jesus, and Muhammad. The Baha'i faithful today number 7 million.

In approximately 550 BC, Confucius was born in Central China. He espoused no religion, but extolled the virtues of good citizenship. At nearly the same time, Taoism also emerged in China. Proponents of Taoism revered all things natural, believing that one should be humble and live passively with Nature. Today there are some Chinese faithful who proclaim their religion as strictly Confucianism or Taoism; however, many can be included under a more general umbrella of Chinese Traditional Religion, which has been considered as a blend of Confucianism, Taoism, Chinese Buddhism, and Chinese folk religion.[36]

In approximately 500 BC, Siddhartha Gautama was born in India, and became known as Buddha, "The Enlightened One." Never endorsing the notion of a Creator deity, Buddha instead promoted the interconnectedness of Nature, the importance of compassion and goodness toward others, and the development of mindfulness and meditation. Buddhism gained a major foothold in India when its leader, King Ashoka, became a convert. In approximately 250 BC the newly converted Ashoka controlled most of India, honoring Buddha by dutifully erecting many shrines across the countryside.

It is of interest to note that many of us today are of a certain faith because that is what our parents taught us; which is often what their parents taught them, going back many generations. However, if we continue back far enough, we find that our ancestors often accepted a religion that was decreed upon them by the ruler of their country. King Ashoka was but one of many rulers whose religious beliefs would influence his subjects, some of whom had no real choice but to subjugate themselves to the will of their leader.

Buddhism eventually spread outside of India; however, the numbers of faithful eventually waned within its place of birth, and presently over eighty percent of the current citizens of India are of the Hindu faith. Although it lost influence in India, by AD 900 Buddhism had spread throughout China, Korea, Japan, Cambodia, Thailand, and Burma (Myanmar).

Approximately 2000 years ago, in what is now Israel, Christ was born. Such was the influence of Jesus that, at least in the Western world, the timing of all historical events would be recorded relative to the time of his birth. A superb orator, his message was to love God, whom he proclaimed to be his Father, and to love others as we love ourselves. He was said to heal the sick with a mere command or touch of his hand. It has also been claimed that he foretold his own death to his disciples, proclaiming that his death would absolve the sins of mankind.

Christ's disciples claimed to have seen him after he died, and described his ascension into the heavens. His followers took immense personal risks, traveling widely to spread a message of peace, forgiveness, and selflessness. Most of his disciples suffered violent deaths. His life was written about in the New Testament of the Bible, some by authors who knew him, but also in large part by Paul, a convert who probably had never met Christ.

In AD 285, the Roman Empire was divided into a Western Empire ruled from Milan in present day Italy, and an Eastern Empire ruled from Nicomedia, which was located to the east of present-day Istanbul, Turkey. The western regions began a slow demise, while the eastern (Byzantine) regions continued to thrive.

Born in Nicomedia, the Roman Emperor Constantine converted to Christianity in AD 320. This conversion was an extremely important event in the history of the Christian church. Previously a persecuted minority, Christians could now worship openly, and their numbers quickly multiplied.

Similar to King Ashoka's importance in the proliferation of Buddhism in Asia, Constantine demonstrated once again how the religious views of a powerful leader can shape the beliefs of millions of citizens in the centuries to follow. Without Constantine and Ashoka, it is quite likely that neither Christianity nor Buddhism would today be practiced by such large numbers of people. Some of the faithful found true peace in a message of divine inspiration. Others were simply following the route taken by their family, as that was often the easiest way; never truly contemplating whether other paths could lead to the same destination.

Today, many people still identify with a particular religion for reasons more to do with loyalty than conviction.

Constantine developed a new city, Constantinople, within the older city of Byzantium. Strategically located along a vital trade route at the entrance to the Black Sea, Constantinople linked together the distinct cultures of East and West. Currently named Istanbul, this Turkish city has witnessed the rise and fall of four major empires within its borders. The Eastern Church grew in this region, eventually separating from the Western (Catholic) Church, to become the Orthodox Church.

The Western Roman Empire remained in power until AD 476. Besieged by many attacks at the far outposts of its borders, including incursions by an East Germanic tribe, the Vandals, and also by the warriors of Attila the Hun, centuries of Roman rule eventually came to an end.

But the fall of Rome was considered more likely due to a slow collapse from within, rather than as a result of extrinsic factors. The cause of the downfall was probably multifactorial, the summation of various possible etiologies – political instability, a government paradigm of excessive taxation of the citizenry and looting of conquered lands to support an expensive military, environmental degradation, and even possibly a lack of civic virtue among its citizens. It is of course quite common to hear echoes of similar concerns expressed in various locales throughout the world today.

The Eastern (Byzantine) Roman Empire would prove to be more resilient, outlasting the Western Empire by roughly one thousand years, surviving until the fall of Constantinople to the Ottoman Turks in 1453.

The year AD 570 marked the birth of another momentous figure, Muhammad, the founder of Islam. Born in Mecca, located in present day Saudi Arabia near the Red Sea, Muhammad was orphaned at a young age. He wed his employer, a woman 15 years his senior, who conceived four daughters. After her death, Muhammad had several more wives, and by some accounts had three sons who died in childhood. Descendants from his daughter Fatima are still today given the honorable title of sharif or sayyid.

In AD 610, Muhammad had a religious experience in which he claimed to receive a message that there is only one God. He saw himself as the last of a great line of prophets, from Adam to Jesus. His words were brought together in the Quran, the sacred text of Islam. Islam means "Peace through submission to God." As with all religious texts, the meaning of certain passages can sometimes be subject to individual interpretation, which has unfortunately engendered a small minority of vocal Islamic extremists to distort the overall message of peace.

The vast majority of the Muslim faithful continue to promote peace in the world, often demonstrating a selfless devotion to God, practiced through the Five Pillars of their faith. The Five Pillars of the Muslim faith are these: 1) adhere to the belief in one God, whose message was delivered by the prophet Muhammad; 2) pray five times daily while facing Mecca; 3) give alms, offering at least 2.5% of income to the poor; 4) fast during the lunar calendar month of Ramadan, at which time they consume no food or drink between sunrise and sunset; and 5) make at least one lifetime pilgrimage to Mecca.

The creed preached by Muhammad was not welcome in Mecca (then a tourist haven for pagan pilgrims) so he moved north to Medina, where his following grew larger. Often attacked by those unreceptive to their beliefs, his troops would in turn plunder the caravans which delivered goods to and from the merchants of the south. In AD 630, with a following of approximately 10,000 faithful, Muhammad captured the city of Mecca. Muhammad's army continued to grow in size, claiming many victories (even after his death in AD 632) including the capture of Jerusalem in AD 636.

By AD 945 Islam controlled what are now Spain, Northern Africa, the Arabian Peninsula, Iraq, and the western part of India. Islam would also eventually spread to the Malay Peninsula and Indonesia, which are now home to the greatest number of Muslims in the world (however, the island of Bali remains a small enclave of Hinduism in the Indonesian archipelago).

Half a world away, the centuries prior to AD 900 marked the time of the development of numerous successful agriculturally intensive city-states in the central portion of the Americas, on the Yucatan peninsula. Magnificent palaces and temples dotted the landscape, built by a Mayan populace that was also advanced enough to develop an elaborate writing system; utilizing a form of paper manufactured from the bark of a fig tree on which to write. Quite proficient in the crafting of copper into tools, weapons, and art forms, the Mayans also possessed superb skills in mathematics and astronomy.

Although they hunted game and grew vegetables, the main source of subsistence for the Mayans was maize. After thriving for centuries, in about AD 900 the Mayan civilization began a slow collapse from which it never fully recovered. Many of the southern communities died off, likely due to environmental problems such as deforestation – which among other problems would exacerbate periods of drought, as fewer trees were available to add water back to the atmosphere through transpiration, ultimately resulting in decreased rainfall. Northern communities survived, but the Maya never regained their previous level of glory. Their numbers were even further attenuated many centuries later by the Spanish Colonization. As a testament to their tenacity, Mayan culture persists to this day, albeit only as a faint glimmer of its former past.

Across the globe, also around AD 900, a group of intrepid explorers set sail in small outrigger canoes into a vast blue expanse, not knowing where the winds, currents, and stars would lead them. There had certainly been numerous other similar endeavors; for some a fatal misadventure, and for others the chance to be vanguards of a new Polynesian civilization. This particular party landed on Easter Island, a home that their descendants would eventually turn into a thriving community.

The early inhabitants of Easter Island are well known for the large stone statues they constructed – first employing the efforts of thousands of villagers to sculpt, transport and erect the figures, and later indirectly employing hundreds of later-day archeologists who would study these silent sentinels, and the culture of the people who created them.

The intrigue of Easter Island is accentuated by the sad tale of a people who themselves were instrumental in their own demise, mostly due to lack of proper care of their environment. The island population simply outran its available resources, and within a few centuries began a precipitous decline. The once lush island was eventually stripped of its last tree, leaving only a stark landscape; a chilling reminder to any later generation that would dare to repeat the same mistakes.

Unfortunately, the lesson has not been well heeded, as presently approximately one-half of the world's original forests have been destroyed. The last few decades have witnessed an incredible destruction of rain forests in tropical climates, with tremendous attendant losses of animal and plant species, and a marked reduction in the sequestration of atmospheric carbon dioxide.

Approximately ten to twenty percent of current deforestation is due to commercial logging or removal for firewood. Most of the remainder is to clear land for subsistence farming (sometimes necessary to support increasing population numbers) or commercial agriculture. Commercial uses include planting soy beans for consumption by livestock, creating pasture land for cattle, and planting sugar cane and palm plants for food or biofuel production. Over one-third of the palm oil exported to Europe in 2014 was used as biofuel for automobiles. On an encouraging note, members of the European parliament voted in 2017 to ban palm oil use for biofuel by 2020.[37]

Perhaps somewhat surprisingly, many tropical rain forest soils are not very fertile, and rapid nutrient depletion often soon renders the land unsuitable for continued farming. Much destruction is currently being wrought, while providing only a short term non-sustainable benefit; one that can only be measured in increased profit for relatively few numbers of people, and for just a few years.

Worldwide, rates of deforestation are decreasing; however, there are still extraordinarily large losses of forest each year. The World Wildlife Fund estimates that forest land the equivalent of about 27 soccer fields in size is lost every minute.[38]

Some countries are taking appropriate action: India and Costa Rica are replanting forests that they once cut down (this is certainly a helpful process, but near monoculture regrown forests lack the diversity of the primary forests they replaced). And, encouragingly, in 2006, Brazilian soybean traders and beef industry leaders placed moratoriums on soya bean production and cattle operations linked to deforestation in the Amazon. Unfortunately, in 2019, numerous wildfires burned vast amounts of the Amazonian rainforest. Protesters attribute these fires to pro-business policies of the current Brazilian government leadership, which have weakened environmental protection and encouraged deforestation.

Just after AD 1200, the nomadic peoples occupying the cold grassy expanses to the north of the Silk Route were united by the Mongolian leader, Genghis Khan. To the south lived the Chinese, who were more prosperous than the Mongols, and whose land supported higher populations – which spurred early technological advances. By that time, Chinese alchemists had already discovered that if they mixed charcoal, sulfur, and potassium nitrate in proper proportions, and then exposed this to an open flame, a flash and powerful explosion would occur. Gunpowder would of course later be used in various forms of weaponry throughout the world. Also, in earlier centuries, a Chinese citizen had noted that if a lodestone (a naturally magnetized iron ore) was suspended and allowed to turn freely, it would always point to the same direction. The Song Dynasty would eventually utilize this finding to build a rudimentary compass to assist in navigation.

It is interesting that, as in many western civilizations, advancement in technology was not accompanied by a similar leap in the value of the inherent dignity and equality of all peoples, as millions of the Chinese were enslaved by their own people during this time.

With an army of over 100,000 men, Genghis Kahn and his skilled horsemen attacked many Chinese villages and captured the vast lands to the south, east, and west. Noted for their savagery, his troops must have terrified the peasants working in the fields, when the quiet of the day was broken by the thundering sound of rapidly approaching mounted warriors. Eventually the Mongols would control an immense expanse of land from coastal China to the Black Sea.

To the west, in AD 1200, Christians had been fighting Muslims for about one hundred years, and the Crusades would continue for one hundred more. Sanctioned by the Pope and the Catholic Church, Christian soldiers were charged to regain the Holy Lands, and to fight the expansion of Islam into the Byzantine Empire. The reward to those who would fight was a promise, by Pope Urban II, of the remission of sins and entry into heaven upon death in battle. Approximately 3 million people perished in these wars.

In the Middle Ages, the Holy Lands were considered to be of great importance to the three major monotheistic religions; Christianity, Islam, and Judaism. In the Christian belief, these lands are today still regarded as holy as they are the birthplace of their savior, Jesus, and the land of his ministry, death, and resurrection. Islam also considers Jerusalem to be a holy place, along with Mecca and Medina, as this is where Muslims believe Muhammad ascended into heaven. Jewish people still regard Jerusalem as their ancestral homeland, and it is where the sacred Western Wall and Temple Mount are located.

By AD 1300 the weather in the Northern Hemisphere had begun cooling, and Europe was experiencing increased rains. The once dependably warm summers arrived less often, and years of famine became frequent. Greenland, its southern region inhabited by the Norse approximately 300 years earlier (an area that could only marginally sustain an agriculturally based society even in the best of weather), also became cooler. The inhabitants failed to adapt their livelihood to the constraints placed upon them by the changing climate, and food became scarce. They continued to grow hay for their sheep and cattle, spurning the ways of the Inuit people to the north, a group who had embraced a lifestyle that could weather a varied climate. Only four centuries after their ancestors first landed on southern shores, there were no Vikings left in Greenland. Those that did not move back to Iceland or Europe eventually succumbed to starvation.

In AD 1348, the Black Death descended upon Europe, leaving in its wake the corpses of approximately one in three of the population, totaling 20 million deaths. *Yersinia pestis* was the unknown culprit, a bacterium transmitted by the bite of an infected flea. The fleas were carried by rats, which were ubiquitous in the crowded unsanitary streets of medieval Europe. Victims were usually dead within a week of the arrival of symptoms.

In some places Jewish people were mistakenly thought to be responsible for the plague, and many were killed. This disease would recur throughout later centuries in many places of the world; and a relatively few cases are still diagnosed in the present day. A massive return of this scourge is unlikely due to the introduction of antibiotics. However, a resistant strain could possibly arise – a fact well known by the research scientists and care providers who today still battle against our old foes, malaria and tuberculosis.

In AD 1492, Christopher Columbus, an Italian, set sail west from Spain to find eastern lands. Thinking he had sailed to India, he instead landed on an island in the West Indies. After several millennia of what were essentially non-intersecting courses, the paths of the inhabitants of two major land masses would now cross, due to the relative taming of the seas. A tall hurdle in the seminal race to globalization had been cleared, setting the stage for a sprint to the finish.

In AD 1517, Martin Luther, a German priest, posted his protests against the Catholic leadership on the door of the church in his town of Wittenberg. His chief concern was the practice of selling indulgences by Catholic priests, which were essentially tickets to heaven exchanged for money donated to the church. The Reformation sparked by Luther was further galvanized by John Calvin, a Frenchman who preached that the fate of man was predestined.

Catholics believed salvation would be the fruit of good works, the followers of Luther believed salvation was achieved by faith in God, while the advocates of Calvin believed the decision to be saved or not had already been made by God.

Somewhat chastened by Luther, a slightly more introspective Catholic Church stopped the selling of indulgences. Heresy to the church, however, was still considered a grievous offense. Various Inquisitions had been sanctioned for centuries by the church, to keep the faithful from straying from its precepts. These would continue for centuries longer. Through the church, the inquisitors could typically sentence those convicted of heresy to a maximum punishment of life imprisonment; but through the often-intertwined secular courts the sentence could be increased to the death penalty, which could mean being burned at the stake.

Religious fervor was at a boiling point, and the spiritual convictions of the populace were often inextricably joined to the proclaimed faith of the leaders of their countries. Often under the guise of religious principle, wars against believers of a different creed were undertaken, with the spoils of battle going to the nobility of the victorious nations. Christians, once united against a common Islamic foe, now took up arms against each other. In Paris, on St. Bartholomew's day in 1572, several thousand Protestants were slaughtered by Catholics. Protestants would also be bloodthirsty. Neither side had a monopoly on misguided religious extremism, a fire often stoked by nationalism and cultural differences.

In AD 1519, the Spaniard Hernan Cortes first entered the city of Tenochtitlan, in central Mexico. The capital of the Aztec Empire, this city claimed an estimated 200,000 inhabitants. Constructed approximately two hundred years earlier, Tenochtitlan was built on an island located in a large shallow lake. Aztec citizens paddled canoes across the warm waters of the lake, and also through a series of canals that transected the city. Causeways interrupted by bridges led north, south, and west out of the city to the shores of the lake. In the center of the metropolis was a great square, which measured 300 meters along each wall, and contained many public buildings and temples. Outside of the square was the palace of the Aztec leader Montezuma. This was said to house a zoo, a botanical garden, and an aquarium. Water arrived to the city via two aqueducts, and some buildings even contained toilets.

Crops were grown on raised rectangular beds in the lake, as well as in surrounding regions. Maize, the mainstay of the Aztec diet, originated from this region and had been cultivated for over 7,000 years.

Of note, this part of Mesoamerica is considered to be one of Earth's relatively few centers of origin and diversity. These centers of diversity give rise to a tremendous number of hardy varieties of plants. Over several millennia, many of these plants have naturally mutated and evolved resistance to pathogens and climatic challenges; adding a definite measure of global food security.

This incredible biodiversity is however now being threatened by a few large international agribusinesses, who are presently attempting to introduce genetically modified monoculture corn into Mexico. It is extremely difficult to stop altered genetic material from contaminating adjacent hardy native crops. Not only would this practice be very disruptive to local markets and culture, it could also possibly result in widespread perilous consequences, as corn is one of the world's three most widely consumed crops.

In AD 1521, with the help of neighboring tribes not enamored with the Aztecs (perhaps in part due to their penchant for human sacrifice) Cortes attacked and completely dismantled Tenochtitlan. Most of the lake was drained, and present-day Mexico City was built upon the ruins of the old city. The colonization of Central America by the Spanish had begun.

In AD 1527, an expedition led by the Spaniard Francisco Pizarro sailed south of the equator in the Pacific Ocean. In their travels, the Spaniards met a group of natives who possessed beautiful textiles, and other indicators of great wealth. The natives were members of the Inca Empire, a civilization inhabiting a 2500 mile stretch of the western coast of South America along the Andes Mountains, from what is now Ecuador to central Chile.

The Inca maintained an impressively long system of roads upon which runners could deliver news and goods to and from the capital, Cuzco, located high in the Andes Mountains in present day Peru. Never discovered by the conquering Spaniards, the now frequently visited tourist attraction Machu Picchu stands as an enduring testament to the engineering and masonry skills of the Inca. Similar to the Maya and Aztecs, they too practiced human sacrifice. It is also quite interesting that, like the Europeans, they also used bronze, the combination of copper with small amounts of tin. Although bronze was first invented centuries earlier in Eurasia, it is intriguing that humans who were apparently unaware of each other's existence could each independently discover and fabricate a substance so unique and valuable.

In AD 1532, the solidarity and numbers of the Inca were attenuated by a civil war and smallpox, as well as by other diseases brought by the Europeans – maladies to which the natives had no natural immunity.

The number of those who died would reach into the millions, similar to losses suffered by the natives of the Mexico region a decade earlier. These problems left the Inca vulnerable to an attack, and Pizarro would soon capitalize on their misfortune.

With an army of less than 200 men, Pizarro captured the Inca chief, Atahualpa, and held him for ransom. To pay the ransom, the Inca army delivered tremendous amounts of gold and silver; often in the form of beautiful artifacts, which were subsequently melted down by the Spaniards. Despite the acquiescence of the Inca people, Atahualpa was killed by Pizarro. Assisted by weaponry that was novel to the indigenous people (horses, guns, and disease), a handful of men were able to annihilate a nation whose inhabitants numbered approximately ten million.

In AD 1615, the Italian Galileo Galilei, often considered to be the father of modern science, was investigated by the Roman Inquisition. A gifted physicist, mathematician, and astronomer, it was Galileo's support of the heliocentric model of the universe (first espoused by Copernicus in the previous century) that drew the ire of the Catholic Church. That the Earth and planets could revolve around the Sun was considered contradictory to biblical passages. The court found him suspect of heresy. Galileo was forced to recant his views and spent the rest of his life under house arrest.

In AD 1632, in northern India, a woman named Mumtaz Mahal died during the birth of her 14th child. Her grief-stricken husband, the emperor Shah Jahan, employed thousands of gifted artisans to construct a white marble mausoleum in her honor. The Taj Mahal, a jewel of Muslim art, still stands in Agra, located in the predominantly Hindu nation of India.

In AD 1674, utilizing a microscope with a magnification power of 270X, the Dutchman Anton van Leeuwenhoek was the first to see and describe bacteria. This would set the stage for remarkable advances in the treatment of disease. The magnification bestowed by the microscope was due to the collaborative efforts of many artisans who for centuries had exploited the refractive power of expertly milled glass. Although glass had been utilized before the time of Christ, and its magnification powers were noted, it was not until about AD 1300 that the refractive powers of lenses were utilized in glass spectacles, and later in telescopes around AD 1600. One hundred years earlier, around AD 1500, mirrors were constructed in Venice. Prior to the introduction of the mirror, most people likely had only a vague idea of the image of their own face, occasionally glimpsed as a watery reflection.

In AD 1687, the Englishman Isaac Newton published his Principia, a text that laid the foundation for most of classical mechanics; a field of study still used today to describe physical laws that govern macroscopic (visible and measurable to the naked eye) objects. These concepts are useful for understanding the workings of various types of machinery, and also the properties of astronomical bodies. Newton's work on gravity was indeed likely inspired by observing an apple as it fell from a tree, although the part about the apple landing on his head was probably an embellishment. Gifted in many subjects, Newton was a co-inventor of calculus, and was also a philosopher and theologian.

In the 1690's, poor weather and subsequent lower grain yields caused one-third of the population of Finland to die in a famine – highlighting the importance of humankind's relationship with climate, and emphasizing just how disastrous a crop failure can be to a population that exists near the edge of sustainability.

There would be many more famines throughout the world: In the late 1700's over 20 million would die of starvation in Northern India, largely due to drought; in the early to middle 1800's over 40 million would perish in China; and as recently as 1959 another 15 million more would also die in China from lack of food, brought on by poor weather and governmental mismanagement. More widely known to those in the west was the Irish potato famine, which was caused by potato blight – underscoring the danger of becoming largely dependent upon monoculture farming techniques. It is estimated that approximately 1 million people died from starvation in Ireland between 1845 and 1852.

There have been thousands of other famines of lesser magnitude throughout time, many associated with social chaos, war, and even cannibalism. Several decades removed from these tragedies, many today fail to realize that another widespread famine is still a possibility.

In 1776, rebels from the British colonies of North America created and signed a Declaration of Independence from British rule. With some help from France and Spain, the United States became free and independent. The war weary British accepted defeat in 1782.

The words of the Declaration have since been regarded as a bright beacon of human rights. The second sentence states: "We hold these truths to be self-evident, that *all men are created equal*, that they are endowed by their Creator with certain unalienable Rights; that among these are Life, Liberty and the Pursuit of Happiness."

When viewed today, these words, crafted so eloquently centuries ago by Thomas Jefferson, reveal the duality of the human spirit. Harmonious ideals of the heart are often countered by selfish motives from darker places; intentions arising from otherwise brilliant minds that refuse to examine their own conscience or question preconceived notions. Jefferson depended on hundreds of slaves to maintain his wealth. Upon his death, he had only freed seven of the six hundred slaves that he held captive (five of those freed were thought to be children he had fathered). Two hundred of his slaves were sold after his death.

To a slave, and to many abolitionists as well, Jefferson's words of equality rang hollow. Future generations will likely look back similarly upon ours, noting how we also often foolishly clung to outdated ideas, our own flames of brilliance often extinguished in part by selfish concerns.

In 1804, members of the Nez Perce tribe greatly aided the Lewis and Clark contingent during its westward expedition to the Pacific Ocean. In 1855, tribal members signed a treaty with the government of the United States which entitled them to approximately 12,000 square miles in Oregon, Washington, and Idaho. During the gold rush of 1860, thousands of settlers ignored the treaty and formed the town of Lewiston, on Nez Perce land. A group of Nez Perce, purportedly mostly Christian converts, ceded ninety percent of their land back to the United States for a price of eight cents per acre. Many of the Nez Perce, including a band led by Chief Joseph in the Wallowa Valley of Oregon, did not agree with this decision, and refused to leave their native lands.

In June of 1877, the Nez Perce began an arduous fighting retreat with U.S. cavalry forces, tracing a twelve-hundred-mile circuitous route from the Pacific Northwest through what is now Yellowstone Park and into Northern Montana. The band consisted of approximately 250 warriors, 500 women and children, their horses and a few other possessions. Greatly outnumbered, the Nez Perce engaged in several battles with cavalry troops as they attempted to retreat into Canada, hoping to find sanctuary with the Lakota group of the Sioux tribes, led by Sitting Bull. Only 40 miles from the Canadian border, in November of 1877, they were forced to surrender.

In his famous surrender speech, Chief Joseph said the following: "I am tired of fighting... It is cold and we have no blankets. The little children are freezing to death. I want to have time to look for my children, and see how many I can find. Maybe I shall find them among the dead... My heart is sick and sad. From where the sun now stands, I shall fight no more forever."

The Indian Wars, a series of battles between settlers of mostly European descent and Native Americans, lasted approximately 300 years; beginning at Jamestown in 1622, and ending in the Apache Wars with a final battle in 1924.

It is quite ironic that the citizens of the United States, a nation whose very charter declares the equality of all men, would forcibly displace Native American people from their own lands. Many U.S. citizens convinced themselves of the morality of their actions. A general notion of the time was that of American exceptionalism; i.e. that this country was somehow different and better than others. This nationalistic ideology even evoked in some people a religious proclamation that it was the manifest destiny of the United States to expand into western territories.

Some of these same characteristics still persist in many U.S. citizens. We frequently hear the words "God Bless America," particularly during election years. Perhaps it is a somewhat vainglorious assertion to suggest that a Creator would play favorites, and that any particular group of people would be elevated over others. I saw a bumper sticker the other day that said: "God Bless everyone. No exceptions!"

By 1850, steam-driven locomotives were commonplace in the United States and Europe, and they soon began to reach into more remote places of the world. The burning of carbon, found in coal, would power these locomotives and other steam engines. The energy in carbon would later be exploited in motors powered by oil. Human muscle power, so often augmented by domesticated beasts of burden, was no longer at a premium. Propelled forward by inexpensive energy, the world of commerce would never look back.

In 1853, the city of Nanking, China was captured by a rebel army led by Hung Hsui-chuan. This army destroyed the beautiful Porcelain Tower, a 260-foot-tall Buddhist pagoda that had stood for over four centuries, and was heralded as one of the architectural wonders of its time. A village teacher turned Christian nationalist reformer, Hung Hsui-chuan preached equality to a population of peasants subordinated by rich landlords. The Taiping Rebellion lasted over a decade and resulted in over 20 million deaths.

In 1859, Charles Darwin published his book On the Origin of Species. The subsequent maelstrom of controversy was likely not welcomed by Darwin, a man who was simply committed to recounting a truthful summary and interpretation of his findings; which happened to be at odds with the religious beliefs of many, including those of his wife.

1865 marked the end of the four-year-long Civil War in the United States, a war precipitated by the secession of the Confederate States from the rest of the nation. President Abraham Lincoln's objective was to keep a strong nation from splintering into two weaker fragments, and also to end the practice of slavery.

Slavery was prevalent not only in the United States, but throughout many other countries as well. Besides the more widely known practice in many European colonies, there also existed a large African slave trade to Muslim regions, as well as within the African continent itself.

The end result of the Civil War was the abolition of slavery, and a once again physically unified nation. The price of victory was paid with the spilled blood of over 600,000 slain Americans at war with each other.

In his Gettysburg address, Lincoln concludes with the sentence: "We here highly resolve that these dead shall not have died in vain – that this nation, under God, shall have a new birth of freedom – and that government of the people, by the people, for the people, shall not perish from the earth."

America was not the first country, nor the last, to abolish slavery. But now a great message, conceived by a more unified nation poised to become the most influential in the world, could be broadcast to all: An initial battle toward true democracy, where all men (although not yet women) were deemed equal, could be won.

As in all wars, many in the Civil War did indeed perish in vain, acting on motives forged by a sense of clannish duty, or vengeance, rather than by more rarified ideals. Whether any death is validated by meritorious results is highly subjective, often depending on whether or not it was one's own son or daughter who was killed in battle.

Of course, the battle for equal rights did not end with the Civil War. The end of the war was a momentous starting point, indeed; but the journey toward equality has been slow and arduous, with many setbacks. Between 1870 and 1950, in a reign of terror and intimidation, over four thousand black people were lynched in America – an indelible blood stain upon the history of humankind.

Slavery was replaced in part by convict leasing, consisting of incarcerated individuals (mostly black men) lent out by the state to work the fields of landowners, often with no government supervision. Segregation became law (it did not end in the U.S. until the Civil Rights Act of 1964 was enacted) and racial abuse was rampant.

Some southern states also erected monuments to the vanquished leaders of the Confederate troops; in an attempt to rewrite the narrative of a troubling past. Many of these statues are still allowed to stand. The journey toward racial equality continues; and there is of course much further to go.

In 1869, Leo Tolstoy published War and Peace. Born into a wealthy family, Tolstoy was later enlisted as a soldier in the Russian army, fighting in the Patriotic war against the French invasion led by Napoleon. Later in life he developed an ascetic lifestyle based upon the teachings of Christ, particularly the Sermon on the Mount. Critical of its institutions, he was excommunicated from the Russian Orthodox Church. His pacifism lead to rejection of the state, an organization that he thought owed its power to the use of physical force; and he was therefore considered an anarchist.

Tolstoy's later works promoted peaceful protest. His ideas influenced Mahatma Gandhi, a man who decades later pioneered the use of civil disobedience and non-violent resistance to fight tyranny in South Africa and India. In turn, the teachings of Gandhi would later significantly influence the views of the American civil rights leader Martin Luther King, Jr.

In 1870, the 15th Amendment granted African Americans the right to vote, preceding by fifty years the passing of the 19th Amendment granting that same right to women.

Universal suffrage was however not a true reality in the United States until 1965, with the passing of the Voting Rights Act. Prior to that time many southern states disenfranchised the poor and minorities by using poll taxes and literacy testing, in an attempt to exclude these groups from the voting process. The first large nation to practice complete universal suffrage, where a person of any sex, color, or religion could not only vote but also hold office, was the Grand Principality of Finland, in 1906.

In 1876, the telephone was invented. Although its merits are obvious, this device is however likely responsible for the demise of the love letter, whose author once possessed the requisite time to first collect his thoughts, and then elegantly construct a prose that could sway the passions of the heart.

In 1882, the American inventor Thomas Edison switched on his Pearl Street electrical generating station and delivered DC electricity to 59 customers in lower Manhattan. Edison proclaimed that "We will make electricity so cheap that only the rich will burn candles."

In 1908, Henry Ford began production of the Model T automobile, continuing until 1927, by which time 15 million had been produced. Ford intended to market his car to the middle class, stating that "….it will be so low in price that no man making a good salary will be unable to own one – and enjoy with his family the blessing of hours of pleasure in God's great open places." Around 1940, my father, along with his siblings and parents, migrated to California from West Yellowstone in a broken-down old Model T, obtained in a trade for a shotgun.

In 1914, Archduke Ferdinand, heir to the Austria-Hungary throne, and this wife Sophie, were assassinated by a Serbian nationalist. This was to be the spark that ignited World War I. Within a month Austria declared war on Serbia. Due to complicated treaty arrangements, soon Germany was also at war with France, Belgium, Russia, and the United Kingdom.

Continuing its isolationist policy, the U.S. at first declared itself neutral in this war. In 1915, a civilian British ocean liner with 156 Americans on board was sunk by a German U-boat, raising the ire of the United States. Later, in 1917, a coded message sent from Germany to Mexico was also intercepted by the British, and then shown to U.S. officials. The German message promised the delivery of some American lands if Mexico would join forces with them. Now directly threatened, the U.S. joined the fight, declaring war on Germany later in 1917.

World War I was fought mostly in muddy trenches in Europe. Soldiers attempting to overtake small bits of land would leave the relative safety of their foxhole, exposing themselves to machine gun fire. A total of 10 million died; killed in a war that had no clearly visible agenda or positive outcome for any of those involved.

The war ended with the Treaty of Versailles in 1919, an agreement containing arguably unreasonable terms that would later help to propagate World War II.

Although he is more widely known for his magnificent paintings of lily pads in his gardens at Giverny, the Impressionist artist Claude Monet would paint a series of weeping willows during the war, in honor of fallen French soldiers.

In 1928, Scottish biologist Alexander Fleming returned from holiday to his laboratory, to resume his studies of the bacteria *Staphylococcus*. In his absence, one of the petri dishes had serendipitously grown some mold, and the astute scientist noted that the mold had somehow inhibited the growth of adjacent bacterial colonies. He found that the fungus produced an antibacterial toxin, which he named Penicillin. In the early 1940's, other scientists expanded on Fleming's work, and large-scale production of Penicillin commenced; which was of course tremendously valuable to those wounded in World War II. Sulfonamides, a different drug class that was developed in Germany in the 1930's, preceded the introduction of Penicillin, but did not cover as large of a spectrum of disease.

Many of us are alive today due to these and other antibiotics. Hundreds of millions of people have been treated for infections that in years past may have proved fatal. Most of us cannot imagine the sense of helplessness and anguish many parents must have felt, able only to offer a cool cloth and comforting words, as they watched their child succumb to what is now an easily treatable infection.

It remains possible that this scenario could again be revisited. In a process hastened by their overuse in humans, and especially livestock and poultry, many antibiotics are much less effective than in years past. Bacteria, viruses, and fungi have the ability to mutate very quickly, and many pathogenic varieties have now developed resistance to the drugs intended to kill them. Much research is being done, but we have not kept pace, and humankind is steadily losing ground to many of our old foes.

In 1929, the U.S. stock market crashed, marking the beginning of the Great Depression, an era where one person in four was unemployed and the gross domestic product (GDP) dropped fifty percent. This affected nearly every country in the world, with the negative economic effects lasting until the start of World War II.

In 1939, German troops invaded Poland, marking the commencement of World War II. The war eventually escalated to involve nearly all nations of the world. The Germans would soon sign an agreement, the Tripartite Pact, with Japan and Italy. These three nations would come to be called the Axis powers.

The Soviet Union, a country who had just aggressively annexed nearby neighboring lands, initially publicly espoused a neutral position – although they had previously signed a secret agreement with Germany to share spheres of influence in the event of war. Prior to the war, during his years of Soviet leadership, Joseph Stalin was responsible for the deaths of millions of Soviets, through execution of those he considered enemies, as well as by engineered famines in populations he wished to suppress.

Germany had felt humiliated by the terms of the Treaty of Versailles, and many of its nationalistic citizens were quite eager for their nation to assume its previous glory. Convinced of the supremacy of an Aryan-Nordic race, the goal of their leaders was the annihilation of the Jews, expulsion or death of Slavic peoples, and domination of Europe and eventually the world.

Citizens of Italy, under leader Benito Mussolini, were also disgruntled by the terms of the Treaty of Versailles, which did not grant them territory that they felt they deserved. Italy had also recently signed a treaty with Germany, called the Pact of Steel. A fascist dictator, Mussolini espoused the expansion of Italian territories, an objective to be fueled by intense nationalism. His wish was to achieve his goal through violent conquests won by a warrior population.

Japan, a small island archipelago with a large population, lacked sufficient natural resources. A prelude to the war was their invasion of China in 1937, a country that itself was involved in a civil war between the Communists and Nationalists. Among the conquests of the Japanese was the city of Nanking. This was the site of widespread rape of citizens by Japanese soldiers, and the brutal massacre of 200,000 Chinese civilians including women and children.

In 1940, Germany invaded Denmark, Norway, France, Belgium and the Netherlands. In 1941, proving that there is no honor among thieves, Adolf Hitler double crossed Joseph Stalin. Ignoring the treaty of non-aggression that he had drawn up just two years prior, Hitler ordered the invasion of the Soviet Union. Coveting the rich grain producing fields and the Baku oilfield of the Ukraine, he wanted to capture these lands to ensure a self-sufficient Germany. Part of his attack was called the Hunger Plan, a plan which would cut off food supplies to the large cities of the Soviet Union, with the goal of using starvation as a weapon of war.

German troops encircled Leningrad, and succeeded in starving one million people to death. By the end of the war, four million Soviet citizens would succumb from starvation. The Russians eventually joined forces with the Allies, who were led by the United Kingdom, under the leadership of Prime Minister Winston Churchill. Taking the war to Russia turned out to be a major tactical error for the Germans.

In 1941, Vichy France, the new government formed in France after the takeover by Germany, allowed the occupation of French Indonesia by the Japanese. The United States responded with an oil embargo, at a time when the Japanese relied on the U.S. for 80 percent of its oil. The Japanese considered this tantamount to a declaration of war. On December 8, 1941, the U.S. naval forces at Pearl Harbor were attacked by the Japanese, and the U.S. officially entered the conflict.

Latecomers to the fighting, prior to 1941 the United States citizens were not interested in engaging in another overseas war. President Franklin D. Roosevelt was hoping to be re-elected, and the isolationist policies of the U.S. had also been formally outlined in the Neutrality Act penned three years prior.

During the war, German Nazis killed over 6 million Jewish people. Thousands of others, including the mentally ill, the handicapped, and those of other religions and ethnicities, were deemed "unworthy of life" and were also executed.

In August 1943, Allied troops captured the island of Sicily. The demoralized Italians soon deposed Mussolini, and the new government leaders surrendered on September 3, 1943, agreeing to cooperate with the Allied forces. Mussolini became a puppet leader for the Germans in northern Italy, but was later captured and executed.

Facing imminent defeat, on April 30, 1945 Hitler committed suicide. On May 7, 1945, Germany surrendered.

Two months later, the Allied forces called for the surrender of the Japanese or else "the alternative for Japan is prompt and utter destruction." The request was ignored, which led to the very controversial dropping of a nuclear bomb on the Japanese city of Hiroshima, and then later another on the city of Nagasaki; stunning the bewildered populace. On September 2, 1945, on the deck of the USS Missouri, surrender documents were signed by the Japanese. World War II was ended. Approximately 60 million people died as a result of this war.

After the war, in 1945, the Allies formed the United Nations; an effort designed to maintain peace. The United Nations is an international organization that now includes 195 different member states. The mission of the U.N. is to facilitate international cooperation in law, security, economic development, and human rights. There are several agencies under the umbrella of the United Nations, some of which include the World Health Organization (WHO), the World Food Programme (WFP), the United Nations Children's Fund (UNICEF), the Economic and Social Council, the International Court of Justice, and the Security Council.

The mandate of the U.N. Security Council is to maintain international peace and security through peacekeeping actions, economic sanctions, and authorization of military force. The United Nations maintains a Peacekeeping Force of approximately 100,000 police and military personnel, coming from approximately 115 of the member nations. If it is deemed necessary, the Security Council can ask for the assistance of regional organizations, as they did during the Bosnian War and the 2011 conflict in Libya, at which times they authorized North American Treaty Organization (NATO) air strikes.

The Security Council includes 5 permanent members: China, Russia, United States, France, and the United Kingdom. Each of these countries has veto power over any significant resolution; a privilege that they have not failed to utilize when faced with issues that directly impact their individual national concerns. There are also 10 non-permanent members of the Security Council, each elected for two-year terms. These countries have no veto power.

In 1947, the U.S. offered up the Marshall Plan to Europe. Lasting until 1951, this financial aid greatly helped European countries to rebuild their war-ravaged economies.

Following the war, Germany was physically divided into an eastern half under Soviet control, and a western half under Allied control. The dividing wall in Berlin did not come down until 1989. Eastern Europe would fall within the sphere of Soviet influence. The west formed the NATO alliance in 1949, whilst the Soviets formed the Warsaw Pact with eight communist nations. In 1991, the Warsaw Pact was declared disbanded. NATO members included the United States, Canada, and most of the western European countries.

Today, the NATO alliance continues to grow and now claims 29 member nations, some of which were previously affiliated with the Warsaw Pact. NATO members agree to defend any individual member nation collectively if it is attacked, i.e. an attack on one is an attack on all. Recent expansion to involve Eastern European countries has met with disapproval from Russia, who considers this to be a revival and expansion of cold war politics. Although not a member of NATO, Ukraine has today become a political football, with opposing forces from west and east each trying to gain influence and control.

Soon after World War II, tensions would escalate and result in the Cold War between the Soviet Union and the U.S. and its NATO allies. These years also spawned the massive proliferation of nuclear weapons. Although never directly at war, the two superpowers would engage in proxy wars to maintain their ideological influences.

Korea, previously occupied by Japan, was split into a northern region under Soviet influence and a southern region under western influence. This would later result in the Korean War and the formation of two distinct nations.

The Chinese would resume their civil war, and the Communist forces would emerge victorious. The Nationalist forces retained control of the island of Taiwan; however, this is not currently recognized as a separate sovereign nation by most of the international community.

In 1947, in the Middle East, Arab nations would reject the terms of the United Nations Partition Plan for Palestine. Sympathetic to the plight of Jewish people, the Allies were tolerant of Zionism – the controversial determination of Jewish people to exist in a sovereign national homeland. The partition plan called for the United Kingdom to exit Palestine (a region it had controlled since World War I) and for the division of Palestine into separate Jewish and Arab regions, each of whom had laid claim to the region. Delighted with the terms of the partition, the Jewish people declared themselves citizens of the new sovereign state of Israel. Tensions have persisted for seven decades and obviously continue today.

1955 marked the passing of Albert Einstein – one of my personal heroes – who died of complications from a ruptured aortic aneurysm at the age of 76. Well known for his numerous contributions to science, Einstein also displayed a remarkable understanding of non-scientific matters as well. My favorite photograph of him was taken near the end of his life – an iconic image depicting a kindly professor with hair unshorn and wild, and eyes that sparkle bright against an old and wrinkled face; portals to a world of wisdom and intrigue. A subtle smile completes the image, suggesting that he knew secrets that the rest of us may not.

Born in Germany in 1879, Einstein first found fame in 1905 when he proposed his special theory of relativity, at which time he introduced to the world the famous equation $e=mc^2$. His later work on the photoelectric effect was instrumental in the future development of quantum physics (quantum physics explains matter and energy at the level of atoms and subatomic particles).

Einstein became a U.S. citizen in 1940. Lending his prestige, he signed a letter written by Leo Sziland and Eugene Wigner to President Franklin D. Roosevelt, warning that the Germans were in the planning stages of the creation of atomic weapons. This led to the Manhattan Project, the massive research and development program (jointly embarked on by the United States, the United Kingdom, and Canada) that produced the first atomic bomb. Einstein apparently later expressed some regret at signing that letter, but acknowledged that it was a decision influenced by pressure to achieve nuclear capability before the Germans, whose actions indicated that they would not hesitate to use these weapons. Although he is most remembered as a theoretical physicist, Einstein arguably had an equal impact as a philosopher, socialist, and pacifist.

In 1960, Sirimavo Bandaranaike became the Prime Minister of Sri Lanka. Sirimavo possessed a characteristic that until then was only rarely seen in a head of state, although over the next 50 years there would be about 50 more leaders displaying this same distinction. As of this writing, the leaders of 15 nations, including Bangladesh, Chile, Germany, Norway, Switzerland and the United Kingdom all share this same trait, as does over half of the world population – these Presidents, Chancellors and Prime Ministers are female.

Although much progress has been made, there is still much work to be done to improve the rights of women and female children. Worldwide, female children still receive less education and health care than their male counterparts. The World Economic Forum noted that less than 20 percent of the world's land is owned by women. Women generally earn less pay than men with comparable jobs and, in many countries, they do not have equal inheritance rights.

There have been, and still currently are, countless episodes of many forms of abuse toward women. Indeed, gender discrimination occurs even in the womb, as female fetuses are selectively aborted at much higher rates than males. In many regions, particularly in China and the Caucasus, this has created large gender imbalances – a formula for social unrest. There are now millions of men in these regions that cannot find a female partner with whom to share their life and start a family.

In 1964, Martin Luther King, Jr., at the age of 35, became the youngest recipient of the Nobel Peace Prize, awarded for leading non-violent resistance to racial prejudice in the United States. A phenomenal orator, he is best known for his "I had a dream" speech.

King had his detractors; however, his message continued to ring true. In 1968, King delivered the prescient words: "Like anybody, I would like to live a long life. Longevity has its place. But I am not concerned about that now. I just want to do God's will. And He's allowed me to go up to the mountain. And I've looked over. And I've seen the Promised Land. I may not get there with you. But I want you to know tonight that we, as a people, will get to the Promised Land."

King would be killed by an assassin's bullet the following day in Memphis, Tennessee. Eventually, however, his message would begin to be realized. The mountain would be climbed by American people of all colors, and eventually some promise was found on the other side.

Over four decades after King's death, the U.S. citizenry would elect a man of color, Barack Obama, as their nation's leader and representative to the world – a tremendous step forward toward the goal of equality of all people.

In 1965, a team led by Norman Borlaug introduced hundreds of tons of seed of a new high yielding wheat variety into India and Pakistan, two countries that faced possible extreme food shortages at the time. Within 5 years, the wheat production in both countries nearly doubled, and it has been estimated that the work of Borlaug may have been responsible for saving a billion people from starvation.

The new techniques employed by Borlaug and colleagues were part of what was called the Green Revolution, which markedly changed agricultural practices. Although overall extremely beneficial at the time, the new practices encouraged the use of large amounts of pesticides and fertilizer, heavy irrigation, and mechanized farming methods. This has resulted in the present situation in which we find ourselves; which is a world whose food production is quite dependent on fossil fuels, facing water shortages and increased salinity in nutrient depleted soil, and combating new environmental damages exacerbated by the overuse of pesticides and fertilizers. The Green Revolution was certainly a necessary lifesaving bandage at the time, but is not likely a sustainable cure for the problem of feeding a continuously enlarging world population for millennia to come.

In 1975, Communist North Vietnamese forces captured Saigon, marking the end of the Vietnam War. The United States initially became involved in the war in an attempt to prevent a communist takeover of Vietnam, as part of their overall strategy of containment of communism. Bruised and defeated, a chastened U.S. government would have to re-examine and refine its strategies of warfare and interventionist policies.

News and images of the brutality of war were brought into the living rooms of America for the first time. In a massacre at My Lai, American troops slaughtered as many as 500 unarmed villagers, including women and children ranging in age from one year to eighty, bringing shame to our nation.

Many of us will never forget the iconic photograph of Phan Thi Kim Phuc, age 9, running naked with her brothers and cousins away from the burning village of Trang Bang, which was lit on fire by a napalm bomb. She had survived the firestorm by tearing off her burning clothes. The anguished expressions of terrified running children stand in stark contrast to the nonchalance of U.S. soldiers walking calmly away from the village.

It is estimated that as many as 2 million civilians and over 1 million soldiers died in the Vietnam War. This included over 58,000 Americans. Another 150,000 American soldiers were injured, many of them losing limbs. Hundreds of thousands would later suffer from posttraumatic stress disorder.

During the war, the United States military sprayed an estimated 20 million gallons of herbicide on the Vietnamese countryside, in regions considered to make up over ten percent of the land of South Vietnam. This herbicide was used as a defoliant so that the enemy would have fewer places to hide, but was also sprayed over rice paddies, which took away guerrilla rural food supplies. The Aspen Institute estimates that this spraying resulted in serious birth defects in over 150,000 Vietnamese children. The devastating health effects of this strategy are still present in veterans and Vietnamese citizens today.

In 1987, United States President Ronal Reagan stood on the Berlin Wall, and challenged Mikhail Gorbachev, the General Secretary of the Communist Party of the Soviet Union, to "Tear down this wall!" Two years later, in 1989, the iconic physical and ideological barrier did fall, leading to a reunification of Germany. Not all were in favor of this. British Prime Minister Margaret Thatcher and French President Francois Mitterrand expressed concerns about the threat posed by a more powerful unified Germany. In 1991, the Cold War officially ended with the dissolution of the Union of Soviet Socialist Republics (USSR) into fifteen separate sovereign states. Russia was recognized as the successor state of the Soviet Union.

In 2001, nineteen terrorists from the Islamist militant group al-Qaeda hijacked 4 passenger jets, crashing two of them into the twin towers of the World Trade Center in New York City. The third jet crashed into the Pentagon, and the fourth into a field in Pennsylvania, missing an intended target due to the heroic actions of passengers on the plane. 15 of the 19 terrorists were citizens of Saudi Arabia, a U.S. ally. Two were from the Union of Arab Emirates, one from Egypt, and one from Lebanon.

Interestingly, many Americans incorrectly thought that the hijackers were Iraqis, a belief that some U.S. government officials may have used as political capital to garner support for an invasion of Iraq. This invasion did lead to the demise of Saddam Hussein and his brutal regime, if not necessarily for the reasons that some U. S. citizens were led to believe. In 2011, the leader of al-Qaeda, Osama Bin Laden, was captured and killed in his compound in Pakistan, during a daring mission performed by U.S. Navy Seals.

Three of the major motives for the al-Qaeda attack on September 11 were: 1) resentment over the presence of American troops in Saudi Arabia, 2) anger regarding U.N. sanctions of Iraq (it has been estimated that these sanctions resulted in the deaths of up to half a million Iraqi children, due to malnutrition and lack of medical care), and 3) ire over U.S. support of Israel.

The slaughter of blameless American civilians led to appropriate outrage in the Western world, and to a surge of patriotism in the U.S. The attack also, however, brought under scrutiny many of the U.S. policies in the Middle East.

Control of a continuous supply of petroleum is currently crucial for the economy of America, and also for the continuation of U.S. military superiority in the world. When Iraq invaded its fellow Arab state Kuwait, to obtain its rich oil fields, the United States quickly intervened and defeated Iraq in the Persian Gulf War. Many U.S. citizens have pointed out the obvious need to wean ourselves from our dependency on oil, but few have proved willing to make the personal sacrifice of absorbing part of the initial increased cost of developing and utilizing alternative resources.

The reasons for US involvement in the Middle East are complex. The issues are contentious – not the least of which is America's ongoing relationship with Israel. It could be considered politically and geographically advantageous to have a democratic friend physically located within the Arab sphere of influence. Another reason for support of Israel is that most citizens of the United States agree with the claim of the Jewish people that they have the right to exist as a sovereign nation, in what they consider to be their native homeland. Most Arabic countries strongly oppose this claim and, astonishingly, some of their leaders would even deny Jewish people the right to exist in any place at all.

Persecuted for centuries, the Jewish people were considered by many in the West to be deserving of a land of their own. In a series of conflicts with its Arab neighbors, with disagreements as to who was the aggressor in many of these skirmishes, Israel eventually obtained more land than was initially granted to them by the United Nations in 1947. The Israeli government went on to approve the construction of Jewish neighborhoods and office buildings in regions still inhabited by Palestinians. Some of these regions are considered by the international community to be occupied, but not owned, by Israel. Israel annexed some of these lands, angering many nations, especially Muslim regions.

In 2003, the United States and the United Kingdom claimed that the country of Iraq possessed weapons of mass destruction, which posed a threat to their security and that of their allies. The United Nations appointed weapons inspector Hans Blix, a Swedish diplomat who was the Director General of the International Atomic Energy Agency, to find any evidence of nuclear, biological, or chemical weapons. Although Blix claimed to be only months away from being able to verify disarmament of Iraq, the U.S. government announced that diplomacy had failed, and immediately ordered an invasion of Iraq, which was the beginning of the Iraq war. Other motives for the attack were to stop documented horrific human rights abuses perpetrated by the regime of Saddam Hussein, truly noble intentions to spread democracy, and to fight a global war on terrorism.

The Iraq war officially ended in 2011. The United States did accomplish one of the stated goals, which was to remove Saddam Hussein from power. Although Hussein is dead, Iraq of course remains a very unstable country with a tenuous government. As far as locating weapons of mass destruction, none were ever found.

Regarding U.S. intentions to spread democracy and fight the global war on terror, the actual results were also quite poor. The attempt to forcefully introduce an ideology that many of the Iraqi people were not interested in, particularly without the support of the world community, did little but tarnish the reputation of democracy. No substantial ties to Al Qaeda or other terrorist networks were ever discovered in Iraq.

Rather than decrease the threat of terrorism, the war likely had the effect of cultivating greater support for the global jihadist movement, galvanizing the resolve of extremist groups such as ISIS, and placing America at an arguably greater risk than before the invasion. Many considered it a grievous mistake to attempt to link the situation in Iraq with the fight against global terrorism, two distinctly separate issues.

The Iraq War led to the loss of over 190,000 lives. The monetary cost of the wars in Iraq, Pakistan, and Afghanistan has been estimated to be nearly 5 trillion dollars.[39]   As a comparison, the 2019 U.S. GDP – essentially our country's yearly income – was approximately 21 trillion dollars, and the U.S. National debt is about 23 trillion dollars.

Of note, in fiscal year 2016, the Department of Defense budget accounted for approximately 15 percent of U.S. Federal government spending.[40]   However, this does not include costs for the Veterans Administration, the Department of Homeland Security, interest paid on prior debts from numerous previous military conflicts, and the cost of projects performed by the Department of Energy and NASA that are considered useful to the military.

From 2008 to 2016, Barack Obama served as the 44th President of the United States, the first African American to hold that office. President Obama inherited an economy on the brink of collapse, and ended his tenure with it running on all cylinders. His time in office was of course not mistake-free – no presidency can be.

Governing with a dignity and grace befitting the most powerful office of the planet, President Obama elevated the stature of the U.S. in the world. Other countries recognized that we would honor our commitment to treaties, to peace and social justice, and a to a sustainable environment for global citizens today and tomorrow.

Presently, in 2020, global health and happiness are threatened by many of the same troubles of previous times: political divisiveness, xenophobia, overpopulation, a worrisome pandemic (coronavirus) environmental degradation, food security issues, a fragile economy, dangerous world leaders, numerous armed conflicts, wealth disparity, religious extremism, and many more.

These recurrent issues are much the same as in years past, but humanity now has more tools with which to challenge them. Brandishing weapons of capital, awareness, tolerance, increased knowledge and imagination, new generations of global citizens are willing to fight for sustainable global happiness.

It will likely be mostly younger people who will unite together to confront the challenges of this century. It is typically much easier for young global citizens to unchain themselves from tired dogma, examine and correct many of the preconceived notions and habits taught to them by previous generations, and embrace a new way of viewing the world.

Leo Tolstoy once wrote: "The most difficult subjects can be explained to the most slow-witted man if he has not formed any idea of them already; but the simplest thing cannot be made clear to the most intelligent man if he is firmly persuaded that he knows already, without a shadow of a doubt, what is laid before him."

Many people in older generations – and some in younger ones, too – are often too enmeshed in outdated ideas. It is they who currently wield much of the power through their positions as corporate executives, lobbyists, and politicians. Many of these people fear that they have too much to lose, and they are therefore often reluctant to allow any meaningful change; unwilling to reconsider their point of view.

They are becoming outnumbered.

There are increasing legions of forward-thinking citizens joining the ranks of power and influence today. Unlike many of their predecessors, these visionary leaders in industry, politics, health care, social sciences, and technology are willing to challenge previous ways of thinking, unafraid to embrace change.

By organizing and voting, younger generations can elect people with fresh ideas, leaders whose minds are not cluttered with notions of war, greed, and intolerance. Young people in great numbers can also influence large corporations, which are often inseparably entwined with our government leaders. Corporations follow money, and they are therefore ultimately controlled by the consumers of their products. Young people can refuse to spend their money on items that degrade the Earth. They can unite against policies that threaten peace in their world.

It will likely be the younger generations who will realize the great strength of their numbers – the power of the collective – and flex their combined muscles to create positive change.

Despite the many challenges that exist today, there are many reasons for optimism. Literally thousands of non-government organizations (NGO's) are working throughout the world. These groups help those in need by providing clean water, food, medicines, and vaccines; and by assisting in education and developing infrastructure. Many billionaires are also sharing much of their wealth and intellect to help solve current problems; helping to create lasting happiness for countless future generations.

Although there are still tremendous needs to be met, the last several decades have witnessed noteworthy improvement in the health and welfare of disadvantaged citizens of numerous developing nations. There have been many missteps along the way, but these programs are definitely working, and they are helping to create a stable base upon which citizens can build paradigms of self-sufficient prosperity.

Technology is greatly improving numerous lives throughout the world, despite a few drawbacks. The introduction of cell phones and personal laptop computers in developing nations has been unimaginably useful for improving education, communication, and economic efficiencies – while also improving government transparency and assisting necessary regime change.

Many advances in medicine continue to be made at an incredible pace. A few decades ago, smallpox was completely eradicated; a remarkable event that foreshadowed what is possible when the fruits of scientific research are applied in a globally concerted effort.

Medications to treat patients with HIV/AIDS have become markedly more affordable and effective. New point-of-care diagnostic tools are on the horizon; designed to offer inexpensive and accurate diagnoses of multiple medical conditions – obtained by simply evaluating a few drops of blood or urine, or even a single breath. First envisioned to help rural patients in developing countries, these will eventually decrease costs and improve patient health in our own country as well.

Over two decades ago, environmental activists successfully collaborated with big business, instituting a cap-and-trade plan that markedly reduced sulfur dioxide emissions and resultant acid rain.

Today, several companies are forming bonds with environmental groups such as the Nature Conservancy and the Rainforest Alliance, realizing that is good business to adopt sustainable practices. Even latte drinkers are joining the charge for environmental and social responsibility, demanding that their coffee be shade grown and fair trade.

I think we can be cautiously optimistic for the future. We cannot ignore the many problems that we presently face, but we can be confident that there are many world citizens who are up to the challenge of achieving lasting global happiness. I am impressed and encouraged by the intelligence, tolerance, and selflessness displayed by many members of the younger generations.

A very insightful young man told me the other day, "We will figure something out." I believe he is right.

FIFTEEN

One Tribe

"We must learn to see the world anew."

-Albert Einstein

A SUNFLOWER FOLLOWS a design of simple elegance. Obtaining sustenance from sun and soil, it creates seeds to propagate its genes, and then eventually decomposes back into the Earth. Humans follow this same general pattern – just over a longer time frame and with a few more added details.

Our bodies are of this Earth; indeed, they are living extensions of it. Every speck of matter on our planet is constructed from the same pool of elementary particles, each forged in the heat of an exploding star.

The air in our lungs, the calcium in our bones, and the water in our tissues are not ours alone. We borrow from a giant repository of reusable eternal building blocks – such as oxygen, carbon, hydrogen, and nitrogen. We share these atoms with the atmosphere and the oceans, with rocky cliffs and valley floors, and with all other creatures, great and small.

A lotus flower graces a quiet garden pond. As Autumn nears, a petal falls into the water, creating tiny concentric ripples that vanish into the surface. Sinking to the bottom, the petal soon relinquishes its component parts back to the biosphere.

A decade later, one of the hydrogen atoms of the petal has moved on. Now residing in a myocardial cell of a young elk, it helps pump blood to muscles coiled and ready for combat with an older bull.

Over millennia, this same atom will bounce through time and space, briefly incorporated into the bodies of great leaders, and humble peasants, too. It will ascend high into fluffy clouds, and tumble-down pristine mountain streams. In a never-ending random regenerative cycle, it may once again help bring color to an exquisite lotus flower, floating on the still waters of yet another garden pond.

Using a relatively limited number of different elements as building blocks, arranged in myriad combinations, the creative cosmos moves unceasingly towards increasing complexity and diversity. Sharing a common genesis, all entities of the universe remain connected.

Our bodies and subconscious minds, and those of all creatures, remain at least loosely tethered to this common starting point – and change comes slowly. Evolutionary processes meander at a leisurely pace; at least on a human time scale. Following Darwinian rules, random mutations that produce profitable change are rewarded, helping each species to secure their niche in highly competitive ecosystems.

Somewhat different than our bodies and subconscious minds, our conscious minds do not appear to be as temporally constrained by the typical processes of evolution. The rate of development of human consciousness seemingly outpaces that of evolving human physical structures. Consciousness is also an evolutionary process, but it does not wait patiently for random mutations that rely on chance alone to offer profitable change. Possessing the ability to shape itself, consciousness can determine the course of its own evolution.

Human beings have been endowed with the ability to think, to reason, and to ponder. We can even think about our thoughts. We can, therefore, direct our future. This has afforded humanity the luxury – and attendant possible peril – of charting the destiny of all present and future life on our planet.

Hunter-Gatherer DNA

As with many other species, early hunter-gatherer humans fared better when they organized into small groups. Being a member of a tribe meant that an individual could benefit from the ideas and works of others. This also provided a measure of protection against dangerous animals and competing clans. Learning to cooperate with other tribal members increased the odds that an individual would survive to mate and pass on his or her genes.

Genetic predilections of cooperation and collaboration were thus selected for; and these traits persist in our human bodies today. It is indeed hard-wired into our neural connections to find joy in helping and interacting with others. When we lend a hand to a fellow member of our tribe, neurotransmitters are released across synapses, landing in receptors located in pleasure and reward centers of our brain. This reward-based system appears to be a primitive mechanism of the evolutionary process of survival – as the act of helping others benefits both the individual and the group.

It is perhaps likely that early human tribal members may not have been as inclined to perform actions intended to help others, if there was not a subconscious knowledge of a tasty neurotransmitter morsel to follow. Our DNA directs those actions which are most likely to perpetuate itself and the species in which it resides; creating frameworks of neural connections that incentivize behaviors to improve the well-being of the individual and the tribe.

But is that all there is to *being*? Are we human beings simply under the control of a subconscious brain, one that follows a script handed to it by its DNA; mere automatons responding to treats tossed across neural connections? This is certainly not a very romantic version of life. If this is indeed the case, then love itself is just a mechanistic extension of this same subconscious evolutionary process; wherein I love someone only if I expect to get something in return.

I believe that there is more to life than that.

There truly are some elements of human behavior that function on autopilot, at a subconscious level. However, the evolving tapestry of humanity's existence is becoming increasingly interwoven with threads of consciousness. We continue to develop ever-greater levels of awareness, self-actualization, and transcendence; and not simply because these conditions are scripted determinants of species perpetuity.

It seems that we have learned to live, and laugh, and love – just for the pure joy of it.

The Genesis of Consciousness

Does a self-organizing universe have the intrinsic potential to create consciousness out of novel configurations of elementary and atomic particles? At the time of this writing, no one knows how consciousness (or life for that matter) began on this planet. Perhaps consciousness arises inherently from the potentiality of atomic and subatomic particles; a chance accident of the cosmos. Or perhaps Providence created the blueprint for a self-organizing universe, one that was designed to develop creatures who possess consciousness. No one knows for sure.

The very idea of consciousness evokes the possibility of an ethereal living process, one that is difficult to quantify. Many questions arise. Is consciousness immortal? Could consciousness even perhaps be equivalent to (or a constituent of) a human soul? And then what of an immortal human soul? There are many intellectuals, often writing popular books, who are quite certain that an immortal human soul does not exist. For the most part, I will leave that discussion to others. However, I will note that absence of evidence is not evidence of absence. Many of history's greatest and most creative thinkers have tended to expand their notion of the possible.

Elementary particles are immortal, or at the very least they are 14 billion years old. It is not beyond the realm of reason to suggest that a part of consciousness, perhaps apportioned in some way amongst all who possess it – you can call it a soul if you wish – might possibly in some way be immortal as well.

Consider relativity, non-locality, entropy, or even gravity. We have experiments that prove their existence; but it took humankind about two million years to explain what they are (we still do not know *why* they are). These phenomena were always present, but only relatively recently did they become measurable by humans. Possibilities should not be discarded merely because they cannot be proven. Perhaps some things – infinity, beauty, love, wonder and awe come to mind – can never be fully explained or measured. It is not bad science to consider many perspectives, particularly when so many truths have yet to be discovered.

Evolving Consciousness

Learning to interact well with others may have been an introductory step into consciousness; one that allowed humans to cross a threshold to a more intricate and purposeful network of existence.

As consciousness took its first tentative steps, our ancestors developed a greater awareness of their surroundings. They observed a magenta sky over a setting Sun, chased down by a rising Moon and Stars. They stood silent, watching meteors trace patterns of light across the developing darkness of the evening.

It was not likely fear that they felt, nor any emotion that could be construed as helpful to the survival of the species. It was wonder. It was awe. It was a recognition of beauty – to be appreciated simply for beauty's sake, and nothing else. It was as if the universe had offered humanity a gift; for no apparent reason but to imbue happiness.

The evolution of consciousness has perhaps paralleled the evolution of happiness. And there is more to the story. Consciousness has given humans the ability to not only feel happiness, but also to create happiness – for ourselves and for others, too.

To Henry, With Love

Consciousness allows humanity to give love and to deeply feel love. Perhaps Homo sapiens are not alone in this regard. It is possible that early humans were merely the first users of consciousness, and therefore we are further immersed into its complexities than are other species.

Our beloved dog, Henry, succumbed to an apparent heart attack, at only four years of age. We have experienced the death of other pets, but it was remarkably more painful this time; as Henry was so very bonded to our family.

It may sound silly, but Henry appeared to truly manifest the human emotion of love, or at least something that closely resembled love. I am not certain that this was simply a learned behavior, one developed only to increase the likelihood that we might add a little gravy to his food bowl.

It is true that some of us may tend to overly anthropomorphize our pets; but perhaps some creatures are more similar to humans than is commonly realized. Maybe Henry and others animals like him are vanguards of their species, just beginning to dip their paws and wings into the global pool of consciousness.

Expanding the Notion of Tribe

We are born alone, hungry and naked; but we are immediately fed and clothed by a loving mother and father. In the beginning, this is our tribe.

Soon we are also cared for by an extended family or clan. As time progresses, we interact with other members of our larger community. We learn local customs. We exchange food, ideas, and love with those whom we interact with each day.

As we continue to grow, we develop increasing levels of consciousness. We begin to further expand our idea of tribe; to now include our town, our state, and our nation. We learn from the works of others in this larger circle; listening to gifted orators and reading books written by wise women and men.

We learn of great blue whales and trumpeter swans, who migrate fantastic distances from north to south and back again, through oceans and atmospheres unencumbered by boundaries or jurisdictions. We then may begin to think differently about nation-states and invented land borders. We consider the idea that *all* humans are in our tribe;

even those living in far-away places and speaking unfamiliar languages. We may notice that some of these people suffer greatly.

The evolution of consciousness may then carry us to yet another vantage point; to a place of wide perspective, where a living panorama of all Earth's creatures is displayed. It is from here that we see that our group, *Homo sapiens*, is but one of millions of species on this planet – perhaps each with a purpose. We realize that it is not just humans who are important and special.

Humankind seemingly trudges slowly onward, head down, mindlessly following the ruts of the wagons of yesterday. Shackled by customs and traditions, we remain prisoners of social conditioning and the madness of crowd opinion. We march ahead, often unquestioningly, never far deviating from the path laid before us.

...Until someone dares to think differently.

Perhaps we can thoughtfully turn our pencils around. Perhaps we can begin to erase restrictive boundaries of long-held ideas; expanding our circumscribed perceptions of things such as time and distance.

Albert Einstein said, "We must learn to see the world anew."

The Relative Nature of Time and Distance

The evolution of consciousness is not complete. As humanity further immerses into consciousness, we become aware that our planet is just one of many formed from the accreted dust of an exploding star, one of billions of such stars in an impossibly vast universe. Our tribe is even more expansive than imagined; expanding into all spatial directions and all dimensions of time.

In 1989, the spacecraft Voyager I turned its cameras around and took one last image of Earth, just as it was leaving our solar system. The Earth appeared as a tiny pale blue dot, illuminated by a sunray against the darkness of space.

Here is as excerpt of what the famed scientist and astronomer Carl Sagan said about this pale blue dot:

"From this distant vantage point, the Earth might not seem of any particular interest. But for us, it's different. Consider again that dot. That's here. That's home. That's us.

On it everyone you love, everyone you know, everyone you ever heard of, every human being who ever was, lived out their lives.

The aggregate of our joy and suffering, thousands of confident religions, ideologies, and economic doctrines, every hunter and forager, every hero and coward, every creator and destroyer of civilization, every king and peasant, every young couple in love, every mother and father, hopeful child, inventor and explorer, every teacher of morals, every corrupt politician, every 'superstar,' every 'supreme leader,' every saint and sinner in the history of our species lived there – on a mote of dust suspended in a sunbeam.

The Earth is a very small stage in a vast cosmic arena. Think of the rivers of blood spilled by all those generals and emperors so that in glory and triumph they could become the momentary masters of a fraction of a dot. Think of the endless cruelties visited by the inhabitants of one corner of this pixel on the scarcely distinguishable inhabitants of some other corner."

Voyager was launched over 40 years ago and is now in interstellar space over 12 billion miles away from Earth. Traveling at over 35,000 mph, it will take 40,000 years before it approaches the nearest star. It is barely out of our solar system. And ours is but one of billions of solar systems in our Milky Way galaxy, itself one of over 100 billion galaxies in the known universe.

Other continents on Earth, once considered so very far away, now seem to be quite close. And it requires only a small cognitive shift to consider the idea that a young girl dying across the globe – from violence, hunger, or treatable disease – is really no different than if she perishes on my own doorstep. Distance is relative.

As we enter even more deeply into consciousness, we may begin to see that time, like distance, is simply another variable that is poorly conceptualized by humans. And this variable does not far separate us from entities that exist in moments other than the present.

My present actions have tremendous influence on the safety, health, and happiness of future generations. If I fail today to support an agenda of peace and environmental sustainability, I may in part be responsible for a child succumbing to the ravages of warfare or hunger one hundred years from now. And this is no less a tragedy than if he dies in my arms today. Time is relative.

Perhaps this idea about time is not so far-fetched. For millennia, many cultures have acknowledged the spirits of ancestors, listening hopefully for voices from a prior age; immortal echoes reverberating across the universe.

Evolving perceptions about time may allow us to sharply envision the lives of all generations to follow. We may imagine future Earth inhabitants going about their lives; working and playing, sharing the same joys and sorrows that we do today. We may see children walking safely home from school, past verdant fields and clear waters.

The idea of intergenerational equity is now unveiled. We see that all of these future citizens are also our brothers and sisters, and that their concerns are equally as important as our own.

Our eyes are fully open, and our view is unobstructed. We see quite clearly now.

We see beyond self and family; beyond gender and sexual orientation; beyond age, color and creed; beyond political affiliations, nation-states, and borders; beyond time and distance. Before us is the whole of our universe and all of creation – past, present and future.

It is from here that we can now comprehend our station in this fantastic existence. It is from this place that we understand the importance of treating all of Earth's inhabitants with dignity and respect. It is from this vantage point that we can see the fragility of our planet, and realize just how carefully we must preserve its beauty and bounty.

This impossible immensity, this limitless universe, is us. This is what and who we are. This is our tribe. It is to the totality of the cosmos that we belong. It is within this expanded notion of tribe and community that we can create lasting global happiness.

Randy A. Siltanen

SIXTEEN

Pacifism

"The unleashed power of the atom has changed everything save our modes of thinking, and thus we drift toward unparalleled catastrophe."

-Albert Einstein

"The young recruits, moving about in lines yonder, are destined to death like the flocks of sheep driven by the butcher along the road. They will fall in some plain with a saber cut in the head, or a bullet through the breast. And these are young men who might work, be productive and useful. Their mothers, who have loved them for twenty years, worshiped them as none but mothers can, will learn in six months' time, or a year perhaps, that their son, their boy, the big boy reared with so much labor, so much expense, so much love, has been thrown, in a hole like some dead dog, after being disemboweled by a bullet, and trampled, crushed, to a mass of pulp by the charges of cavalry. Why have they killed her boy, her handsome boy, her one hope, her pride, her life? She does not know. Ah, why?"

THESE WORDS WERE written by the 19th century French writer Henri Guy de Maupassant, as he observed the military drills of French soldiers.[42] Similar sentiments could have been penned at nearly any time over the past ten thousand years.

211

In November of 1519, Ferdinand Magellan crossed around the tip of South America, emerging into a beautiful and peaceful ocean. Thus, it was named the Pacific Ocean; pacific meaning peaceful.

The word pacifism is defined in the Merriam-Webster dictionary as "Opposition to war or violence as a means of settling disputes." Pacifism covers a wide spectrum of views; however, some may consider it to be an unconditional rejection of all forms of warfare; a much narrower definition that suggests something absolute.

There is danger in absolutism, and the broader Merriam-Webster definition suggesting a principle of non-aggression is therefore probably preferable.

Although the word pacifism shares an unfortunate similarity to our ears as the word passivity, the two should not be confused. The pacifist is not a languid, spiritless soul. It is a mistake to correlate an outwardly calm demeanor with a lack of inner passion. Beneath the calm surface of the serene Pacific Ocean lay tremendous depth and power.

Conceptually, a condition of absolute rejection of all violence could be considered ideal; a world where there is no need for the use of force in any circumstance. Unfortunately, it is difficult to envision a world where all citizens are willing to submit to an innate peacefulness of the spirit; therefore, the reed of moral absolutism must yield somewhat, and bend to the winds of practicality and reason.

There may be situations where small focused actions of force may be needed, such as defense against immediate bodily harm or death. This does not however include the use of preemptive actions to diminish the possibility of harm. The preemptive action may be of greater evil than the true or perceived intentions of the enemy. The principle of non-aggression rejects initiation of violence, and posits that force may be used only in immediate self-defense or in the delegated defense of others.

World War II has been called by many a "just" war. Although there were many unjust atrocities that were committed by each of the belligerents, including the United States, a reasonable argument can be made that, overall, the war effort was validated by a just cause. This argument is fair enough.

Many of our previous and subsequent wars have however often been fought for reasons of vengeance, ideology, hegemony, or protection of resources that were not our own. We have sometimes strayed from the precept of defending ourselves and others from immediate bodily harm or death. We have included ourselves in conflicts that involve our "national interests" – which has sometimes appeared to mean anything that threatens to raise the monetary cost of the lifestyle to which we have become accustomed. Although it was an unwritten strategy, the United States policy has sometimes been one of engaging in war and violence as a means of settling disputes. This is the policy of a non-pacifist. At times, we have not demonstrated a peace policy, rather a policy of war.

The policy of war will be attacked, and the proponents thereof, using three spearheads to engage and encircle them. The argument against a war policy will utilize the following three precepts: spiritual principles, morality, and wisdom.

Spiritual Principles

Interestingly, many professed religious individuals are fiercely and uncompromisingly nationalistic; holding the seemingly incongruous values of virtue in one hand, and violence – as a legitimate means of maintaining wealth and sovereign power – in the other.

However, the spiritual principles and scriptures of all of the major faiths espouse a life of peacefulness:

Psalms 34:15 from the Jewish Hebrew Bible states, "Turn away from evil and do good, seek peace and pursue it."

Verse 25:63 of the Quran says "The servants of the Most Merciful are those who walk upon the earth easily, and when the ignorant address them harshly, they say words of peace."

In the Hindu sacred text Yajurveda, verse 36:17, one finds the following message: "May there be peace in everything, everything be full of peace, and peace pervade everywhere."

Buddhist writings in Dhammapada 129, teach: "All tremble at force. Dear is life to all. Likening others to oneself, kill not nor cause to kill."

A few of Christ's words from the Christian Bible can also be examined – as many U.S. politicians, military leaders, and citizens identify their religious affiliation as Christian. Being a Christian certainly means different things to different people. As Leo Tolstoy once stated, many have invented a Christianity and Christ of their own. Some choose to affiliate themselves with a particular denomination, and then let their leaders or congregation do their thinking for them. Others choose to pass over certain religious scriptures that contradict their personal actions or desires.

It is a valid suggestion to ask those who proclaim a Christian faith to consider verses that directly quote the spoken words of Christ. One can read the historical recollections of the biblical authors Mathew and Luke, as each separately referred to the words Christ spoke at the Sermon on the Mount. The following is a passage from Luke 6:29:

"To him who strikes you on the cheek, offer the other also, and from him who takes away your cloak do not withhold your coat as well. Give to everyone who begs from you; and of he who takes away your goods, do not ask them again. And as you wish that men would do to you, do so to him."

This is followed a few verses later by the passage from Luke 6:46: "Why do you call me 'Lord, Lord,' and not do what I tell you?"

The instructions seem clear: Live in peace and give to others. So how does a predominantly Christian nation reconcile the words of Christ with a contradicting national policy of war? One way is to invent a new version of Christianity, picking and choosing the parts that fit with preconceived notions and desires.

It is interesting to note that there is one commandment of the Christian faith that many religious leaders instruct us to not take too literally: Thou shall not kill. Perhaps this commandment should be taken literally; but most would admit that they, too, would resort to killing, if an assailant was ruthlessly attacking a loved one in their presence, and they had no other means with which to stop them. The conscience of most people would allow that as keeping within the spirit of the law.

It is, however, quite a herculean leap to take one step further and now find no crisis in conscience when killing for vengeance, ideology, resources, or hegemony; all disguised as acts of patriotism. It is yet quite another enormous bound to condone preemptive killing in the hopes of possibly preventing further killing. This is all the worse knowing that there will definitely be "collateral damage," which is the death of civilians and their children whose fate it is to live in the crossfire.

What does it mean to be peaceable and turn the other cheek? It may mean that I should first examine my own actions, to see if I may have in some way incited an incident. If I have been attacked, either figuratively or physically, it may have not been without provocation. Although my assailant may have responded in a manner that is quite disproportionate to the severity of my offensive actions, he or she may indeed have some valid grievances against me.

If our assailants continue to harm us, we can raise an arm to stop them. We can protect ourselves. If pierced in the back with a knife, we need not turn and offer our belly as well. Instructions should be taken in the spirit that they are given. Children are instructed to not talk with strangers, but if lost in the forest it would be foolish for a little one to not respond to the calls of her rescuers. Christ did not forbid his followers to defend themselves from death. Perhaps the message is simply to not fight evil with evil.

Many people wonder why some Middle Eastern citizens appear to despise Westerners. Some reasons are perhaps valid, and many are of course not. We support Israel, a country whose citizens still occupy Arab land not granted to them by the United Nations. We supported sanctions that reportedly indirectly resulted in the tragic deaths of thousands of Muslim children, due to inadequate nutrition and lack of health care. We have lived luxuriously while many of their people have lived with hardship, and we have had a large military presence in what they consider to be their holy land.

Our actions certainly do not justify any vengeful terrorist acts of violence leveled against us – but we are not entirely blameless regarding many of our troubles in faraway locales. It may at times be prudent to turn the other cheek, and cautiously seek peaceful compromise with our adversaries. We have many times in previous years negotiated with unsavory leaders and governments.

What about Christ's other instruction, the one that says to give to everyone who begs from you? We do that don't we? Doesn't the United States give more foreign aid than any other country? In the private sector, there are many U.S. citizens and institutions that provide generous gifts of time and money to disadvantaged populations throughout the world. And, in absolute terms, our government does give more foreign aid than any other nation, due to the massive size of our economy.

But in relative terms, as reported by the Organization for Economic Development and Assistance (OECD), we currently rank in 20th place out of the 28 wealthiest nations of the world, when calculating the amount of aid given to foreign countries as a percentage of our Gross Domestic Income (GDI); giving a total of 0.17% of GDI to disadvantaged countries.[43]

This means that out of every $1,000 that our country earns, our government contributes about $1.70 to foreign aid. Sweden greatly outshines us by comparison, giving a greater that eight times higher percentage (1.40%) of GDI in foreign humanitarian aid than does the U.S. Of note, the figure of 0.17% of GDI for the U.S. aid delivered falls far short of a goal of 0.70% recommended by the United Nations.

It could be argued that giving away less than two bucks out of every thousand may not be entirely consistent with following the spirit of Christ's words, "Give to everyone that begs from you."

Delivering foreign aid is not merely an act of charity; it is also an essential complement to U.S. military power. More money given in aid means less money needed for ammunition. By combating food insecurity, poverty, and lack of education, we also attack the hopelessness, despair, and anger from which foreign extremist groups arise.

Suggesting that government and military leaders maintain fidelity to their stated spiritual principles, a war policy has been attacked from the right. By engaging moral principles, an attack will now come from the left flank as well.

Moral Actions?

It is at a young age that American school children begin lessons in patriotism. When displayed in a friendly and cooperative spirit, patriotism can stir the heart; inspiring fidelity to rarified principles, pushing individuals to reach beyond previous levels of excellence. A true patriot is a jewel of the nation.

But cautious awareness is in order. Like a slow virus, nationalism can insidiously infect patriotism. What begins as a comradery with fellow countrymen and a respect for local traditions, may slowly transform into an idea that one's country is better and more important than all others.

A patriot loves the citizens, culture, and noble ideals of their country. A nationalist loves their country – no matter what. There is great danger in the that way of thinking.

We teach our children to pledge allegiance to flag and country, but we do not always teach them that our nation must also fulfill its end of the bargain – earning our allegiance, by drafting laws and engaging in activities that are kind, just and noble. We also teach our children that our country is one indivisible nation under God; although most of us know that it is quite difficult to serve two masters, each with their own sets of laws or commandments.

We allow our children to play war video games on our televisions. Some in our military have encouraged these games, knowing that this young demographic will be more likely to join their forces, even though these games do not depict the true horrors of war. Bullets hurt, and when you are severely injured you cannot simply push the reset button. Is this a moral action?

We awe young soldiers with displays of military power and discipline, and tell them that their commanding officer alone is responsible for the ethical consequences of his command. The conflicted conscience of the soldier knows that this is not always true, as he surely would not kill his own brother if so commanded. But the young soldier may be placed against his will in a situation that similarly opposes his conscience. He may be intimidated by threats of court martial, imprisonment, and bodily harm or death; and he may therefore be coerced into making decisions that contradict his personal beliefs. Are these moral actions?

From an early age we teach our children to become soldiers; because it is a truly noble action to protect the lives of our countrymen. But then when they do become soldiers, we sometimes engage them in aggressive actions in distant lands, far from family and home, attempting to convince them that any military action of their country is honorable and noble – whether it is to save a citizen from bodily harm, or simply to secure the supply of cheap resources or spheres of influence in faraway places. Are these moral actions?

We take honorable and noble young men and women, valorous people who make great personal sacrifice and take great risk for all of us, and we place them in dangerous situations – at times for questionable motives. We have in past wars asked them to risk their lives not just for people, but for resources; reminiscent of what empire-building leaders once asked of their soldiers in colonial wars. Are these moral actions?

Early in my career I had the opportunity to work as a civilian general practice physician at Beale Air Force Base. It was a privilege to work with such an outstanding group of individuals. These soldiers – for all military personnel consider themselves as such – knew how to get things done efficiently and effectively, dedicating their lives to the service of others. It is not moral to take advantage of their inherent noble characteristics of duty, honor, and service, and unnecessarily place them in places of great danger.

It is also not moral to commit violence in the anticipation of preventing greater violence. It cannot be known if my preemptive action will be of greater evil than the action I wish to prevent. As noted in the writings of Leo Tolstoy, evil cannot be vanquished by evil. Although Tolstoy may have perhaps displayed an overzealous passion for anarchy and a tendency toward absolutism, there are many intriguing insights promulgated in his book, *The Kingdom of God is Within You.*

Tolstoy asked: Who is to define what is evil? He stated that those in power often declare as evil any action that they do not like. There is no unbiased party who has the power to define evil in such a way as is recognized by all. We grant our assemblies the right to define what is evil, but we know that men are not rendered infallible simply by assembling together in a Congress or any other organization. We often attempt to redefine morality in ways that further our own purposes.

Is it moral to state that all men are created equal, yet knowingly allow the widening of the chasm between the rich and poor, aware that this will foment feelings of anger and despair that lead to violence?

Is it moral to advocate justice to others, when our own lives are based on advantages that are often gained by the exhausting labors of the poor, and many of our possessions are merely a result of, as Bono calls it, an accident of latitude; born lucky citizens into affluent nations, whose lands were often obtained by the use of violence and killing?

And finally, is it truly an accident when civilians are killed again and again, day after day? If civilian casualties are a certainty, is it moral to knowingly advance our agenda, accepting the disinfected term of "collateral damage" to describe the killing of innocent children, to protect us from the mere possibility of ourselves being killed? Is it moral to allow the death of even one child in order to exact justice and revenge on an enemy?

There is no moral justification for a policy of war.

Using the two precepts of morality and spiritual principles, the war policy has been attacked from both flanks. Next, the precept of wisdom will be used as the third of three spearheads against a policy of war. It will attack directly from the front, while the two flanks link up at the rear and begin to encircle our opponent.

Gathering Pearls of Wisdom

E.M. De Vogue said the following: "War cannot be altogether suppressed so long as two men are left on earth, with bread, money, and a woman between them."

It is difficult to disagree with him. And, due to jealousy or misguided religious extremism, there may always be individuals who hate our country regardless of any benevolent actions that we direct toward them. Scattered pockets of conflict on this Earth are inevitable and, regrettably, there will likely always be a need for a military presence in the world.

It is not the concept of a military that should be argued against, which can be viewed as an unfortunate necessity. Rather the argument is against the idea of supporting an exorbitantly large military, one that oversteps its mission of defense and becomes an aggressive enforcer of a policy of hegemony. The individuals who make up our military, by and large, are a force for good in the world. It is a general strategy of maintaining a policy of war, rather than a policy of peace, that is ill-conceived.

A couple of expert characters will be introduced, to help argue the case against a strategy of maintaining a war policy.

Howard Zinn was an American historian, social activist, and political science professor at Boston University. As a young man, he joined the United States Air Force and was a bombardier for the 490th Bombardment Group in World War II. A prolific writer, Zinn would also author the widely read text, *A People's History of the United States*.

After the war, Zinn would return to the seaside French town of Royan, a village that he had dropped napalm bombs upon in 1945. During that visit he learned that the bombs he had released resulted in the deaths of over 1,000 French civilians and a few German enemy soldiers. This and other experiences made Zinn acutely aware of the ethical dilemmas faced by soldiers at war, and Zinn would become an ardent anti-war activist throughout his life.[44] I encourage you to read his essay, "*A Just Cause, Not a Just War.*" Howard Zinn died at the age of 87, at which time he was still speaking out against war.

Leo Tolstoy once wrote: "The seductions of power, and all the wealth, honor, and luxury it gives, seems a sufficient aim for men's efforts only so long as they are unattained. Directly a man reaches them he sees all their vanity, and they gradually lose all their power of attraction. They are like clouds which have form and beauty only from a distance; directly one ascends into them, all that splendor vanishes."

Late in his life, Zinn made the statement that he wanted to be known as someone who gave people a feeling of hope and power.

Howard Zinn was an active participant in war, experiencing firsthand the anguish that bombing brings. He was also a very bright historian, keenly aware of the results of war throughout history. At an old age he had nothing left to prove, no professorship to keep, no more books to sell. He had already attained the splendor of power, wealth, and luxury and he had long since reached the age where they lose their attraction; yet he still spoke out against war.

It is an enlightening exercise to compare Zinn's motives with those of individuals who favor a war policy: political leaders who wield power from the strength of our military; corporate leaders who travel through the revolving door from private sector employment to government work and then back again, profiting greatly from our nation's military commitments; and finally, the outraged citizen, bubbling over with vitriol, hell-bent on vengeance.

As Albert Einstein said, "Anger dwells only in the bosom of fools." After the terrorist attack on September 11, many of us got up like intoxicated patrons off of a tavern floor, swinging wildly at whoever was in reach – who in this case was often any person with dark-colored skin and of the Muslim faith.

Trust in the opinion of the composed and intelligent individual, who can expect no personal gain from giving his or her advice. This person does not deny that there is an enemy. They simply realize that the most sensible course of action is to accurately define their foe, calmly educate themselves in the culture of their adversary, and attempt to achieve the ultimate objective – peace.

Zinn argued that there is a difference between a "just cause" and a "just war." The cause may be just, but it does not necessarily follow that going to war for that cause is just. The argument that the end justifies the means is not always valid. Encouraging democracy is a just cause; however, obtaining democracy with bombs, while knowing with certainty there will be many children who are maimed or killed while doing so, is not a just war. Not only immoral, it plainly does not work – one has to look no further than the Vietnam War.

It is an error of strategy to employ military tactics that are known to cause civilian casualties. In an attempt to kill one terrorist, we may kill several children from a previously peaceable community. It is from these communities that the seeds of mistrust and hatred are thus sown, and for each terrorist that we kill, two or more may spring forth.

It is also incorrect to assume that destroying al-Qaeda or ISIS will end the threat of terrorism. In my garden, if I am not careful, when I remove a weed it sometimes sends out a shower of new seeds. Rather than curse and cut down every new weed, it is more logical to prevent new growth.

Nature does not like bare ground. If I amend my garden and provide water as needed, my vegetable plants will grow strong; covering the soil and outcompeting most weeds. If I do not meet the needs of the soil, nature will cover the bare ground for me – often with a plant that I do not find desirable.

One of the prime causes of terrorism is poverty, which often leads to jealousy and hatred. Many of us inadvertently help to propagate disharmony; as we may be complicit in allowing an unequal distribution of global resources. Living in relative luxury, we are often not meeting the needs of our international neighbors who struggle at the edge of survival. Terrorists, like weeds, arise from the barren soil of impoverished nations.

For every one dollar that the United States spends on humanitarian aid to other countries, at least twenty-five dollars (some estimates are higher) are spent on our military. Instead of one dollar, it may perhaps be more logical to spend five dollars on aid. If we did this, we would likely spend significantly less on the war on terror, as there would be much less need for it. Our overall expenditures could be significantly decreased. The crushing debt that we are currently incurring to financially support our military is simply not sustainable, and could ultimately make our country weaker and more vulnerable.

It is crucial to understand the supreme importance of public opinion. Like momentum in a football game, you cannot see it, but everyone can sense it. It has the power to allow an outmatched team to come together and defeat its opponent. It can move quickly to ignite passion in the hearts of humankind, coalescing into a great force of nature.

A bright older gentleman once told me that the best way to get rid of an enemy is to make him my friend. If your first inclination is to consider this statement to be sentimental babble, perhaps you should reconsider; as there is definitely truth to this idea. Acts of giving turn enemies into friends, even on a global scale.

The next expert to be introduced is Sun Tzu, a Chinese military general who lived in the 6th century B.C. Sun Tzu is considered to be the author of *The Art of War*, an ancient treatise on military strategy. This book is still widely read today, including by military officers throughout the world. Sun Tzu realized that it is wisest to avoid war, and that fighting should be used only as a last resort.

Here are some of his quotes about achieving victory by peaceful means:

"A brilliant general is one that can win without fighting."

"Supreme excellence consists in breaking the enemy's resistance without fighting."

"The supreme art of war is to subdue the enemy without fighting."

Sun Tzu also wrote that attacking the strategy of his opponent is a crucial component of victory:

"Thus, what is of supreme importance is to attack the enemy's strategy."

"Thus, it is that in war the victorious strategist only seeks battle after the victory, whereas he who is destined to defeat first fights and afterwards looks for victory."

Is it not the strategy of the terrorist, or any military leader, to encourage a hatred for the enemy? This tactic can be countered with one of our own – a campaign of goodwill, born of generous acts of giving. We can wisely attack their strategy of hate. The battle is nearly won before the fight, because public opinion is on our side.

Sun Tzu also said:

"Invincibility lies in the defense; the possibility of victory in the attack."

"The general who advances without coveting fame and retreats without fearing disgrace, whose only thought is to protect his country and do good service for his sovereign, is the jewel of the kingdom."

Experience taught Sun Tzu that one will fight more fiercely in defense, while the aggressor rests his hope on the mere possibility of victory. Fear of disgrace is a ruinous force against good; pride comes before the fall.

Here is one final quote of Sun Tzu:

"Regard your soldiers as your children, and they will follow you into the deepest valleys; look onto them as your own beloved sons, and they will stand by you even unto death."

Is it wise to send our children to unsafe lands, risking loss of life and limb, without asking ourselves for what just cause? Is the cause equal in worth to the life of my own son or daughter? Our leaders have many times made unwise decisions, placing our soldiers – our beloved children – in peril.

Live each day in gratitude for our soldiers and their families, who have sacrificed so much. Be deeply thankful for these young men and women who willingly place themselves in great danger, often surrendering their own liberty and lives to protect the lives of you and me, their neighbors. Look unto them as your own beloved children.

This essay argues for a policy of peace, attempting to defeat a policy of war from three positions – attacking from the flanks with the precepts of morality and spiritual principles, and advancing from the front with the precept of wisdom. Our opponents, those who argue for a policy of war, are now nearly surrounded.

You may have noticed that our opponents are not *completely* surrounded.

The clever general Sun Tzu would often offer an escape route for his enemy, noting that sometimes soldiers who have no hope of escape will fight the most ferociously. Although this essay is an argument for a general policy of peace, and against a general policy of war, one must be cautious of absolutes. It must be acknowledged that life is messy; that unfortunately there are times when the gate of a small escape route must be left open, recognizing that even with a policy of peace there will likely be times when force must be used.

It is incumbent upon the citizenry and leaders of any nation to monitor this gate quite closely, allowing the use of military action typically only in cases of self-defense, or in defense of the life of a disadvantaged neighbor.

Any mission should also ideally be part of a worldwide contingent assembled by the United Nations, under the command of leadership appointed by the Security Council. Unfortunately, this is not always possible, as the five permanent members – particularly Russia and China as of late – make frequent use of their veto power over war resolutions.

At times the United States has invoked Article 51 of the UN Charter, which begins with: "Nothing in the present charter should impair the inherent right of individual or collective self-defense if an armed attack occurs against a member of the United Nations."

This argument can be used as justification to engage in war, for any nation that feels that its safety is threatened. However, Article 51 can also be used to circumvent the authority of the Security Council.

Amid numerous global pockets of chaos, many world leaders are currently working tirelessly to establish the coalitions that they can, attempting to empower all parties in regional conflicts to seek compromise and peace.

All nations have much work to do to maintain peace. For some, this may mean swallowing a bit of nationalist pride, and scaling back spheres of influence gained by force or intimidation.

Every nation should consider relinquishing vanquished territories that they consider holy. Every cubic meter of our evolving universe is of equal sanctity. Temples and sacred monuments will fall and one day be covered by dust. Every mountaintop will crumble onto a valley floor, only to rise again at a later time and place. There is impermanence in the creative destruction of Nature, and no exception is made for that deemed holy by humankind.

Pride and humility can coexist. We can certainly be proud of the many valorous accomplishments of our soldiers and our great country, but we must also humbly admit and apologize for our missteps. To not do so would be an immoral act – and also a grave tactical error. Garnering favorable global opinion is of critical importance.

Wealthy countries must give substantially more assistance to poorer regions. All citizens must forgive prior injustices inflicted upon them or their ancestors. Policies of generosity and reconciliation harness the tremendous momentum of favorable public opinion. Peace is attainable.

The combined regenerative forces of goodwill, diplomacy, and optimism are the key determinants of a safe and nonviolent Earth. Do not underestimate their power. Together, these coalesced energies can outmatch the destructive forces of bombs, nationalism, and fear.

Randy A. Siltanen

SEVENTEEN

Precepts for Prosperity

"Imagination is more important than knowledge."

-Albert Einstein

MOST PEOPLE WOULD agree that our prosperity, our happiness, and our very existence are ultimately dependent upon the health of our planet and its abundant resources. The Earth is our principal source of wealth; the very wellspring of all health and happiness. We know this is an immutable truth – yet there is a wide chasm between what we know and what we do.

We know what to do. We are just not doing it.

Viewed in total, it would be difficult to choose a better time for humanity than today. Although pockets of tremendous global suffering persist, collectively we are considerably less ravaged by war, hunger and disease than in times past. Indeed, with a few notable exceptions, most decades have proven to be more prosperous than the one preceding. With a few fits and starts, and an occasional slide backwards, humankind continues to head up the mountainside.

However, this ascension of the human condition stands in stark contrast to the attendant free-fall of the Earth itself. Bruised and bloodied by relentless assaults on imperiled ecosystems, a falling Earth cannot forever sustain a rising populace. Tethered firmly together, person, people and planet ultimately trace the same curve, destined to experience a similar fate.

Our planet has many times witnessed the rise and fall of numerous human civilizations, as well as the appearance and disappearance of entire species. We are presently at another crucial inflection point – what some have called the sixth extinction – and, from here, the trajectory of life on Earth can rapidly change in either direction.

It is quite possible that we will choose to steepen and extend the ascending curve, nudging the arc of human existence to even greater heights of health and happiness. However, it is also quite possible that we will not.

Without adaptive behavior and visionary leadership, a planetary free-for-all could commence; one in which all parties desperately claw for their share of the prize, eventually leading to an exhausted and polluted Earth – each corner covered by a mass of humanity at war with itself. If appropriate changes are not made, future historians may wistfully look back on the present decades as the halcyon days of old; the zenith of the human experience on Earth.

A world of enmity and resource scarcity are certainly not foregone conclusions. Humankind is the author of its own story. Collectively, we write our destiny; acting out our script through our combined personal efforts and actions. We assign the most vital roles of the story to the elected leaders for whom we cast our vote. The actions of everyday people are of great significance; however, they can be exponentially magnified by one visionary leader who creates beneficial laws for hundreds of millions of citizens to follow. Likewise, one great country can provide guidance and inspiration to billions of global inhabitants of other nations.

Present government administration missteps notwithstanding, in the last several decades America has arguably performed the role of Earth's guardian and leader as well or better than any other nation would have. Although not perfect, we may still be the best that the world has to offer. If we lose our position of influence and authority, a less benevolent and broad-thinking regime could easily take our place, and the wellness of our planet and its inhabitants could suffer.

Due to integrated world markets, global health and happiness are greatly influenced by the health and happiness of the United States. This means that we must remain strong in all respects – and this includes remaining financially solvent.

It may seem out of place to discuss the idea of money, even at a national level, in a book that attempts to illuminate many other (perhaps nobler) pathways to happiness. But a robust American economy is indeed critical to the health and happiness of the U.S. population; and the global citizenry as well.

Money actually can buy happiness – if it is shared with others. Food, shelter, and medical care are fundamental to a healthy and happy life. It takes capital and commerce to provide basic life necessities to a global populace.

It is imperative that the U.S. expertly leads a network of many global economies. Our current policies of debt-driven fiscal growth are not sustainable. We are jeopardizing our position of leadership and thus the goal of lasting global happiness.

As with all world economies, the U.S. economy is reliant on energy. This is a necessary and inescapable relationship. However, our economies have become reliant on *fossil fuel-based* energy – which is an unnecessary and dangerous association. Our current choices of energy sources are not sustainable.

From a financial outlook, it does not make sense to promote fossil fuels; products that will soon become depleted. And from an environmental viewpoint, it is illogical to utilize a product whose continued use will damage our Earth; perhaps irreparably, at least in a human time frame.

In an association expertly elucidated by economic researcher and author Chris Martenson, the environment, the economy, and energy are all very interrelated.[45] How we choose to manage this complex relationship will greatly affect our personal health and happiness, as well as that of our international neighbors and all generations to follow.

The effects of the economy, energy, and the environment on personal and global health and happiness may at first appear to be merely tangential influences; but they are not. If one wishes to make impactful changes – bringing together person, people and planet for the benefit of all – it is necessary to gain an understanding of these and many other diverse and interrelated issues.

Knowledge is power. It is the creative synthesis of the efforts and achievements of those who have come before us; the sum of the successes and failures of our ancestors. Integrated and applied knowledge creates a foundation for *imagination*, which is even more powerful than knowledge itself.

Imagination may sometimes be thought of as flashes of inspiration and brilliance, often seemingly created out of thin air – but it is more than that.

A master chef imagines and creates a culinary delight not merely by chance alone, rather by drawing upon her vast knowledge of cooking and baking; perusing through her mental catalog of food ingredients, proportions, aesthetics, and timing; all coming together to create an original masterpiece. The process is the same with any great endeavor.

Imagination arises from a base layer of accrued knowledge. And it does this most spectacularly so when emanating from the mind of the transcendent individual – one who wishes to become a meaningful part of something greater than oneself.

There are many leaders in government and business who may know a great deal about energy, the economy, or the environment. They often have much expertise in a particular area; but many lack the broad and integrated knowledge necessary for a panoramic understanding of events. More importantly, many lack a transcendent nature – and therefore they have little imagination or vision for a path to sustainable global happiness.

Many of these leaders are focused inward; motivated predominantly by personal concerns, often money related. They are not nearly as interested in the health and happiness of the planet and all of its inhabitants. If they are not challenged, the world could easily descend into one of conflict and environmental destruction.

To be uninformed and silent means to acquiesce to the apathy and indifference of the masses, surrendering to the oft-present madness and selfishness of many of our leaders.

It is imperative to gain a level of integrated knowledge that exceeds that of individuals who are concerned chiefly about person, and who show little concern for people or planet. Armed with this knowledge, we are then ready to imagine a path to lasting global health and happiness; well-equipped to run into the fray and to fight our best fight.

We can then create a better future not only for ourselves, but for our Earth and all of its inhabitants as well.

Here are three precepts for world prosperity:

First Precept: The Earth is our primary source of wealth. Without it, we have nothing.

Second Precept: A noble and strong nation is necessary to protect the Earth and its inhabitants.

Third Precept: Human existence is dependent upon inexhaustible sources of clean energy.

The **First Precept** must be emphasized, the idea that the Earth itself is our key source of wealth. First and foremost, it is in every citizen's best interest to protect our planet. Without clean air, fresh water and rich soils, our civilization will cease to exist.

The **Second Precept**, the need for strong and noble leadership, is also essential: World prosperity – as measured by health, happiness, freedom, clean sustainable ecosystems, and GDP – is dependent on a great nation to act as leader.

To remain effective, it is imperative that our country remains financially strong – we cannot give from emptiness. We must maintain a robust economy. We must abandon the current shortsighted paradigm of excessive debt-driven continuous growth, which is doomed to failure.

The United States must also maintain its role as an environmental world leader; an ardent protector of our Earth, our primary source of wealth. We have recently encountered a few obstacles that have slowed our progress forward in this regard – as many of our present government leaders show little interest in advancing responsible interrelated fiscal and environmental policies.

Some U.S. government officials rebuff overwhelming scientific evidence of climate change and environmental destruction. Denying the truth is a calculated political strategy; one that many politicians find preferable to admitting that they value wealth and power over lasting global happiness.

Our nation's guiding principle must not be "America First" or "Make America Great Again" – at least not in the economic and military sense that these slogans presently imply. We are already tremendously strong and wealthy. The pursuit of even more power and money at the expense of other nations is misdirected at best, and dangerous at its worst. It is far nobler, and easier, to lead a contingent of friends than to crush a rebellion of enemies. A true leader offers a hand up, not a boot on the throat.

The reputation of America was recently jolted off stride by our federal government's declaration to break promises made at the 2015 Paris Climate Agreement. However, there are many forward-thinking private sector and state government leaders who wish to set straight our course; unwilling to abdicate our role of responsible leadership.

The citizens of the state of California, home of the world's sixth largest economy, are steadfastly adhering to policies that ensure a safe and sustainable future for its citizens. Championing planet-friendly policies at local and national levels, there are many other visionary political and business leaders throughout the world who are also choosing a sustainable course. These leaders have discovered that environmental responsibility comes with another very desirable added perk: It will save their economies and businesses an extraordinarily large amount of money in the long run.

Led by Paul Hawkins, *Project Drawdown* was created by a consortium of world environmental experts, comprising seventy individuals from twenty-two countries. The objective of the project: To identify, measure and model one hundred substantive solutions to achieve a decline in yearly greenhouse gas emissions over a three-decade period. One of the pertinent findings of the project was that by implementing appropriate climate change solutions, there will be an estimated global net operation *savings* of $74 trillion over the next thirty-year period.[46]

The U.S. must lead by principled example. Some members of government suggest otherwise, even stating that our efforts at environmental protection are relatively meaningless, as other nations will continue to pollute. This is, however, an indefensible and narrowly focused argument.

It is true that the United States cannot alone avert climate change, keep the environment clean, or steady the world economy. It was also true that the United States could not alone win World War II – yet it was our assistance and leadership that were crucial components in winning that war. Noble and intelligent actions will encourage others to follow.

The guiding goal, Sustainable Global Happiness, is unassailable; a promontory holding firm against the elements. Truth, honor, and intellect will prevail. New leadership will be elected, and America will find its stride again.

Also essential for global prosperity is the **Third Precept**, which is the need for *inexhaustible* sources of *clean* energy.

Just like us, our ancient ancestors were dependent on energy; reliant on the Sun to provide fuel for plant photosynthesis. Humanity obviously remains connected to this process, but our present society is also extremely dependent on the conversion of raw energy to power.

Assisted by photovoltaic panels and solar concentrating arrays, we can now harness the energy of the Sun to create electricity. The Sun also indirectly gives us another form of energy – Wind. Created by the uneven heating of the Earth by sunrays and resultant differences in air pressure, wind can be used to turn turbines to generate even more electricity.

Presently, the most commonly used sources of energy – fossil fuels – are not inexhaustible or clean. Soon they will all be depleted; but perhaps not soon enough, as the utilization of these fuels continues to damage the Earth – which violates the First Precept (the Earth is our primary source of wealth).

World happiness and prosperity is threatened by three problems, each related to the others: 1) a fragile world economy, 2) a global marketplace that must compete over a dwindling and increasingly expensive supply of energy and mineral resources, and 3) an environment that is rapidly becoming damaged by the utilization of fossil fuels.

There is one solution that can solve all three of these problems and it is this: **We can embark upon a rapid and complete transition to clean, renewable energies – utilizing wind, water, and solar energy technologies.**

This course of action will help mitigate the environmental damages caused by fossil fuels, while also providing sustainable clean energy for millennia to come. This will also become an engine for economic prosperity – providing jobs for those who will design, construct, and maintain the wind turbines, solar panels, grid infrastructure, and electric transportation vehicles that the world will need. This surge to our economy will help free us from the current unsustainable model of using exorbitant debt to fuel perpetual growth.

Building infrastructure for renewable energy solutions, such as wind and solar, is presently dependent on natural resources that are available in only limited amounts. The Chinese government has come to this realization long before we have, and they are rapidly acquiring the resources necessary to make the momentous change to renewable energy. The longer we wait, the more expensive and increasingly scarce resources will become – and the planet may also be irreparably damaged in the meantime.

We find ourselves pushed to the edge of a sea cliff. There is no real choice but to jump. The longer we wait, the more the tide recedes and the rougher will be the landing. If we jump now, we may sprain an ankle or break a leg. If we wait, we will likely break our neck......or worse. Either way, eventually we will have no choice but to leap off of the edge. Complacency provides merely an illusion of safety.

We have ways to soften the landing. We have the technology and intellect, but we are only just beginning to develop the vision and political will to utilize it. The choices we make will each act as determinants of present and future global happiness.

We must quickly shift to an economy powered by clean renewable energy, and free of deficit spending and reliance on growth. The tide is quickly receding and it will not come back in.

Our forefathers wrote the U.S. Constitution nearly 250 years ago, and we continue to benefit from their actions to this day. Demonstrating a commitment to intergenerational equity, it is now our turn to advance policies that will benefit all future populations.

When our nation makes plans for the future, it is important to consider the effects of our actions over a long time-frame; perhaps at least one thousand years – merely a blink of the eye in geologic time.

Indeed, if one postulates that we are but halfway along the arc of human existence, it may be a valid suggestion to consider the needs of our descendants two million years hence.

Let's take a look at some economic concepts as they pertain to sustainable global health and happiness.

Wealth

All real wealth originates from the Earth and Sun. Money is just a claim on wealth, not actual wealth itself. Our paper currency is a promise that we will get something valuable in exchange; however, it is merely a promise.......and promises are often broken.

All wealth originates from the Earth and Sun. This is an extremely simple yet very profound truth that has been largely overlooked by recent generations.

The discovery of oil as a remarkably inexpensive form of energy has allowed most of us to live a life completely removed from the soil and water that our lives depend upon for sustenance, as most of us now toil in office buildings rather than in fields or oceans. It is easy to forget the source of our true wealth.

Fossil fuels will certainly not last forever. It may be three years, or it may be thirty, but we may soon be much more acutely aware of the real economic value of oil. Just as the proliferation of agriculture 10,000 years ago resulted in a tremendous leap forward for humanity, the discovery of oil has allowed gains of a similar degree.

The advent of agriculture provided food in a way that was much less energy intensive for humans than hunting and gathering, allowing more time for humanity to branch out into new endeavors. There was also more time available to collaborate with increased numbers of people, whose larger populations could be supported by fields of grain, and the milk and meat of domesticated animals.

The availability of inexpensive oil and natural gas brought about a similar tremendous leap in population; by revolutionizing agriculture via mechanized planting and harvesting, providing energy to pump water for irrigation, and providing inputs for the production of fertilizers. Fewer people were required to work the fields, and society became much more specialized and service oriented; and subsequently more disconnected from the Earth – our primary source of wealth.

There are many forms of wealth; some more real than others. Real wealth consists of rich soils, mineral deposits, clean water with abundant fisheries, forest land, and even two other resources to which every global citizen lay claim – sunlight and wind.

These tangible forms of wealth also include the materials and structures derived from the above resources; such as steel from mined ore, food grown from rich soil, lumber milled from forest trees, and wind turbines, dams, and solar panels that create electricity from wind, water, and sunlight.

Paper wealth is a more intangible form of wealth; comprised of human inventions that serve as proxies for resource-based wealth. This includes currency, stocks, bonds, derivatives and other forms of paper that are a claim on wealth – but not actually wealth itself.

One should remember that a claim on wealth rests merely upon a promise of repayment. Paper wealth seems very real, but new money can be, and recently was (by quantitative easing), literally created out of thin air by our government.

The Earth itself is our prime source of wealth. This point should be emphasized: Without a clean, verdant, and sustainable planet, there will be no wealth at all. We must protect our soils, air, water, and forests as if our children's lives depend on it......because they do.

Economic Growth

If we turn on the news, or read the financial pages, we will undoubtedly hear or see something about growth in our economy. An increasing size of our economy is reflexively lauded as a measure of success and prosperity, while a steady-state economy or slow growth is disparagingly referred to as a recession. But why do we love growth so much?

In past years, economic growth was heralded as the savior of humanity, bringing increased affluence to all citizens throughout the world. Growth has certainly brought more wealth and improved health care to impoverished nations; there is no denying that. However, increased growth has also widened the gap between the rich and the poor. Increased growth has not brought a *commensurate* increase in prosperity to all; a fact that has not gone unnoticed by those who are the least prosperous – a potent recipe for fomenting global discord.

Continuous growth in most systems is impossible, particularly in those with finite boundaries. A swarm of locusts will keep feeding until a field is laid bare, and then may soon collapse from lack of food. Such is likely the case in a world limited by finite resources – the substrates typically needed to fuel continued growth.

Proponents of a continuous growth model argue that economic growth can be decoupled from its association with an increased use of resources; and that advances in technology will solve many of the current problems related to increased growth. It is certainly true that many knowledge-based and service-oriented industries are not particularly resource intensive, and they may therefore continue to grow. However, this may likely eventually occur within a backdrop of a near steady-state economy.

It is also true that technology will likely find recyclable, cheaper, lighter, and more ubiquitous materials – and develop ways to utilize them in a more efficient fashion. But some material will still be needed, no matter how cheap or light, and there are inherent limits to efficiency improvements. At some point, a steady-state economy may likely be our most desirable course of action.

Of note, there is an economic phenomenon known as Jevons Paradox, which proposes that the rate of resource consumption *increases* as technology progresses. Increased energy efficiency can actually cause a rebound effect of increased consumption, by lowering costs and accelerating economic growth, further increasing the demand for even more resources.

This phenomenon is currently playing out in many present-day scenarios. Although resources continue to be utilized more efficiently, world economies continue to use greater amounts of them. Unless the boundaries of space travel can suddenly increase by several orders of magnitude, limitless resource-dependent economic growth is simply not possible in the long run. Even if it was, business as usual would result in the environmental destruction of the planet.

Many notable economists, including Adam Smith and John Maynard Keynes, recognized limits to economic growth. And 19th century economist, philosopher and scholar John Stuart Mill once stated: "...a stationary condition of capital and population implies no stationary state of human improvement. There would be as much scope as ever for all kinds of mental culture, and moral and social progress; as much room for improving the art of living, and much more likelihood of it being improved, when minds ceased to be engrossed by the art of getting on."

Most economists today adhere to an economic model of perpetual growth, using complicated mathematical equations to bolster their arguments. They believe that economic growth can be decoupled from its dependence on natural resources – hitching its wagon instead to technological advances. They may possibly be correct, but this opinion is not unanimous among all economists, especially those who understand the existential threat of environmental destruction.

Presently, most economists are chasing the wrong dream – that of perpetual growth in GDP (Gross Domestic Product). They would do better to aim for Sustainable Global Happiness (SGH), which is a much better indicator of prosperity. If humanity does indeed have a cosmic purpose, it is not to merely increase the bank accounts of a select few, rather it is to create health and happiness for all Earth inhabitants, present and future.

Certainly, humankind will continue to leverage technology, and we will of course continue to look for new economic opportunities. But we must do so while ensuring that all present and future citizens have the opportunity to live healthy and happy lives on a safe and beautiful planet.

Presently, this is not happening. The current U.S. government administration appears to value GDP over SGH – i.e. they value money and power over social justice, intergenerational equity, and the health of the planet.

Inflation adjusted GDP could possibly perpetually go up – although that is unlikely – or it may settle into a steady-state. It may even go down. No one knows for sure – and it really does not matter as much as people think. Gross Domestic Product is a primary *economic* indicator, but it is only a secondary indicator of *prosperity*. To focus exclusively on GDP is to lack panoramic vision.

It is not perpetual growth of an economy that is the point of life; rather it is happiness. Economic well-being is a component of happiness, to be sure, but it is only one of many. The wealthiest family on Easter Island was not happy when overfished waters no longer yielded a catch, or when the land was stripped of its last tree.

The Earth is our primary source of wealth and happiness. The worthy dream of a transcendent economist is to attain growth in SGH – Sustainable Global Happiness. This will only be possible on a clean, safe, and sustainable Earth. The GDP will be whatever it will be.

If growth does not necessarily bring commensurate levels of prosperity, and we know that growth cannot continue forever, why do our economists and governments continue to push for continuous growth? Probably the most important reason is that governments have long planned expenditures based on a paradigm of a continuously growing economy, and therefore a continuously growing tax base. If a government is to keep its monetary commitments, it must rely on ever-growing tax revenues from an ever-enlarging economy – a plan eventually doomed to failure due to resource constraints and environmental damage that will likely limit growth.

It is also not just governments that desire growth, but private business and individuals as well. Businesses sell stocks to investors who demand high returns on their investments, achieved mostly through growth of the company. Money is lent into existence with interest rates attached, and repayment of this debt is reliant on growth. Easy credit has fueled growth to artificially and unsustainably high levels, as we are now experiencing.

There is great power in exponential growth. A properly invested financial portfolio can grow very quickly due to the effects of compound interest. Danger, however, lurks in the shadows, as the curve not only applies to systems that benefit from growth, it also applies to those that we do not necessarily want to grow, such as with our human population.

Exponential growth also works in reverse with respect to utilizing a finite pool of resources. Resources can become depleted in an exponential rather than linear fashion.

Gross Domestic Product

The Gross Domestic Product (GDP) is the market value of all final goods and services produced in a country for a given year. The U.S. GDP was approximately $21.4 trillion in 2019, about a quarter of global GDP. This is a good ballpark number to remember; as it places other numbers – such as our national debt, money spent on wars, stimulus packages, and future necessary allocations needed for infrastructure – into a more understandable context.

Growth in our GDP! That is what our government, economists, stockholders, and businesses are so interested in achieving each year. As discussed, whether or not GDP is a good yardstick with which to measure prosperity is definitely a point of contention (the New Economics Foundation introduced the Happy Planet Index in 2006, and the country of Bhutan utilizes a Gross National Happiness index). For now, understanding what is included in the calculation of GDP gives insight as to why governments use somewhat predictable methods to increase it.

Here is the basic equation[47]:

GDP = Consumption + Investment + Government Spending + Net Exports (Exports minus Imports)

To raise GDP, at least one of the four elements on the right side of the equation must be increased.

In a troubled economy, citizens are not likely to increase their **consumption** of goods and services, because they simply do not have enough money to buy them. If one can barely pay his rent, he is not likely to go out and buy a new car. The government sometimes tries to encourage increased consumption by lowering taxes, so the consumer has more money to spend.

The next option for a government that wants to increase GDP is to attempt to increase business **investment** in capital expenditures. However, business people are usually pretty smart, and they do not want to increase the size of their factory if there is not a growing customer base to buy their product. By lowering interest rates, governments can try to increase the funds that businesses have available to add or upgrade equipment, as credit is much more affordable. Lowered interest rates also make investors more likely to buy stocks in these companies, as they search for higher returns on their personal investments.

The third option that is utilized to attempt to increase GDP is to increase **government spending**. That can help, if it is properly applied. But a citizenry soon grows weary of paying increased taxes to support government spending, particularly when no noticeable benefit is achieved.

This often leaves an economically troubled country with only one good option to increase its GDP, and that is to increase its **net exports**. To increase its GDP, a country wants to have a positive trade balance, i.e. export more goods to other countries than they import in. There are both good ways and bad ways to increase net exports. One good way for a country to increase its exports is to efficiently produce a quality product that a foreign customer wants or, more preferably, needs. One bad way for a country to increase its exports is to devalue its currency; which is what the U.S. recently did through its actions of "quantitative easing" (essentially money printing). A devalued currency makes a country's exports cheaper for customers in other countries.

Easy credit and debt have fueled growth to artificially high and unsustainable levels. To repay this debt, without significant sacrifice, requires continued growth – a course of action that may very likely be impossible. Sacrifices will therefore have to be made. The next few decades may be significantly more challenging than the last.

Debt

In years past, ours was mostly a society that would first save money, and then subsequently spend a portion of it on a desired item; typically, a product that was necessary for survival. This mentality has changed dramatically. We are now a society that saves very little money; instead going into debt to purchase items that are often luxuries rather than necessities. We have been living beyond our means, and the painful readjustment to equilibrium may soon occur. The bills are due, we have no money, and our creditors may soon be coming to break our kneecaps if we do not start paying off our obligations.

Some debt is justifiable, such as buying a reasonably sized home, at a price commensurate with the buyer's income. Incurring debt for education purposes, or to start or grow a business venture, is often necessary (a farmer is usually far more prosperous financing a tractor than continuing to use a shovel). Much other indebtedness, however, is quite imprudent. Borrowing money for wants rather than needs is at least somewhat understandable at an individual level, as human beings often make irrational decisions. The desire to get something for nothing but a promise is simply too irresistible for many people. Fueled by easy credit, our level of consumer debt has now reached astronomical levels.

What is more surprising than individual consumer debt is when debt is taken on by an entire country, an entity made up of millions of people, typically governed by intelligent leaders who collectively should definitely know better. This is particularly troubling when funds are borrowed to pay for unnecessary and unsustainable practices, as is currently the case in the United States. Even more disturbing is that the citizenry that benefits from the easy money is not usually the same generation that will have to pay it back.

Present generations often pay for the imprudent decisions of their predecessors. Our current actions are like those of elderly parents who borrow money and spend it all on a lavish Mediterranean cruise, knowing that they will soon pass away, leaving a debt burden squarely on the shoulders of their children.

Deficit spending confiscates wealth from future generations. It is a stealthy – and legal – way to rob the future bank accounts of our children.

At the beginning of 2020, the U.S. national debt was approximately $23 trillion – greater than our GDP of $21 trillion. Of the 195 countries in the world, only 16 have a debt that is greater than their GDP. Of the $23 trillion in debt, roughly one-fourth is owed to other U.S. government agencies, and the rest is public debt. About 30% of the national debt is owed to foreign entities (the largest are China and Japan, which are each owed over $1.1 trillion).

To get an idea of just how large a number a trillion is, consider that it would take over 30,000 years to count to that number (if you counted one number per second and did not stop to sleep or rest).

Our national debt continues to increase by over $10,000 per second, and the interest we pay on our debt is over $1 billion per day. About 15 cents of every tax dollar paid is lost in interest payments. The amount now owed by each individual U.S. citizen is over $70,000. Each taxpayer owes over $188,000. (www.usdebtclock.org).

It gets worse. Total credit market debt, which includes debt held by households, businesses, and government exceeds $50 trillion. There are also unfunded liabilities of the U.S. government that are not included in the national debt. These include future payments for Social Security, Medicare, and Medicaid. Although these are not legal debts, they are ethical liabilities, and the total is estimated anywhere between $50 trillion and $200 trillion (representing an individual liability of somewhere around $1 million for each U.S. taxpayer).[48] This does not even include the many unfunded liabilities of states and municipalities. Remember that the U.S. GDP, essentially equivalent to our yearly paycheck, is about $21 trillion per year. Where will the money come from to honor all of the promises that have been made?

For an individual there are two ways to get rid of a debt:

1. Default (break your promise).
2. Pay it off.

Governments typically do not like these two options.

Defaulting will render a nation an international pariah, and other countries will no longer be very willing to trade with them, at least not with their devalued currency. Defaulting on our national debt would also not likely be tolerated by the U.S. citizenry that holds about one-third of all Treasury bonds.

Paying off a debt is also a politically unsavory choice, as it involves decreasing government spending and raising the taxes of one's constituents. No one likes paying for a dead horse. And few politicians are elected on a platform that promises higher taxes and decreased benefits.

Governments have, however, found a third option to pay off debts; one that is not available to the rest of us. They can print money. This passes the problem on to future generations. This also weakens the currency, which often leads to inflation. A country can essentially inflate much of its debt away, as they are now paying off a debt with dollars that are worth much less than they were when they were borrowed. Engineered inflation may help reduce the debt owed to other countries, but it harms citizens who hold Treasury bonds, and does not decrease future unfunded liabilities, because future Social Security and Medicare/Medicaid payments will also have to rise to levels commensurate with rising prices.

The best and most honorable way to pay our debt is to reduce government spending and increase taxes. This action is simple, honest.......and often painful. We have paid our debt down before; after WWII our national debt also exceeded our GDP. This action was easier back then, as we had a growing economy unlimited by resource constraints. It will be more difficult this time. This makes it crucially important that our government drastically tightens its belt.

Our government must also encourage the correct sectors to flourish and add income to our economy. This will increase tax revenues and help to decrease our national debt. The chief industry that our government must champion is that of clean and renewable energy technologies. This is by far our best bet to create a thriving US and global economy – while also ensuring an inexhaustible energy supply and a sustainable planet.

The most appropriate future mix of clean and renewable global energy options will be determined by many factors such as environmental impacts, cost, efficiency, siting issues, and resource scarcity.

Limited Resources

Oil has had a remarkable impact on the ease with which we live our lives. But when plotting its use against a timeline of human existence, the age of oil is merely a blip on the screen; a barely noticeable aberration impacting but a relatively few generations. It will soon be gone, nearly as quickly as it appeared. And it is currently worth far more than you may think.

It is quite interesting that many people do not think twice about paying $6 for a glass of wine or a pint of beer. Keep this number in mind when considering the time and cost involved in sending very bright individuals to engineering school for advanced degrees; teaching some of them how to find deep pockets of oil sequestered often far beneath the land or ocean floor, and instructing others how to drill down into the depths to retrieve it. Business people must spend billions of dollars to finance the equipment needed for these ventures. The oil must then be shipped across the world to a refinery for processing, and then shipped once again after that to a gasoline filling station.

Note that a single gallon of gasoline can propel a nearly 3,000-pound vehicle, and its 4 passengers, about 50 miles down a highway. Consider again that $6 *pint* of beer. Maybe $3 or $4 for a *gallon* of gas isn't so bad after all.

The amazing economic value of oil should soon be clear to all. Some may think of this oil age as an incredible one-time gift, a bonanza that has allowed the proliferation of great numbers of people to live in relative ease. It may however eventually turn out to be a curse, a Faustian bargain that has artificially inflated world population to numbers that are not sustainable, and whose use continues to foul our air and warm our oceans to levels that may soon not be compatible with life as we know it.

No one knows exactly when we will reach Peak Oil, the time at which more than half of all obtainable oil has already been extracted. We may have already reached that point, or it may be a few decades away. In any event, each remaining barrel of oil remaining in the world will become more difficult and expensive to retrieve than the one before it. The low hanging fruit has already been picked.

Perhaps equally relevant to the timing of Peak Oil is the time at which the demand for oil exceeds the supply. That time may be quickly approaching. It may be one year or it may be twenty, but if it comes, the price of gasoline will likely rapidly rise – unless there are viable alternative energy sources.

It is of utmost importance that our government not only immediately embarks on a path of renewable energies, but also intelligently chooses the best renewable energy technologies in which to delegate resources. The renewable energy sectors that deserve the majority of our attention are currently wind and solar; but there are smaller niche energy technologies that will need encouragement as well.

We are currently dependent upon diminishing supplies of fossil fuels to develop alternative energy. At this time, fossil fuels are often needed to power the machines needed to mine and refine the metals needed to build wind turbines and solar panels.

Possible shortages and rapidly rising costs of materials (such as copper, platinum, lithium, cobalt and rare earth elements) could severely limit the transition to a renewable energy economy for countries who wait too long to embark down this path.

Copper is presently essential for the transmission of electricity. Platinum is needed for the production of hydrogen fuel cells; which will likely be needed as a necessary adjunct to a clean energy system powered by electricity. Lithium and cobalt are currently necessary elements utilized in the production of batteries needed to run electric cars and provide energy storage. The majority of lithium supplies are located in politically and geologically challenging areas such as Bolivia and Chile.

Estimates of extractable world supplies of these minerals differ greatly and are dependent on many variables, including possible future mining efficiency improvements and population growth. Any estimates based on current usage could be wildly optimistic; as the use of copper and other minerals may possibly grow exponentially.

Rare earth elements such as neodymium, dysprosium, and terbium are essential for the production of magnets used in electric cars and wind turbines. Many rare minerals are also currently needed to produce photovoltaic panels. Presently, China controls over 95 percent of world production of rare earth elements.[49]

If we wait too long, important minerals could become prohibitively expensive to obtain, and then perhaps unavailable due to resource nationalism or exhausted supplies.

Interestingly – and striking an optimistic note for the future – human creativity has thus far ameliorated resource scarcity to a remarkable degree. New technologies continue to replace one resource with a more abundant or less expensive resource. Energy efficiency continues to improve, and energy use per dollar of increased GDP has been decreasing. Products have also been redesigned to utilize fewer raw materials.

There are even ambitious projects currently underway that hope to one day mine asteroids for minerals (this may indeed be quite possible; however, there are many dangers involved, and the cost may prove to be prohibitively high). It is imperative that funding for continued research and innovation continues, which will undoubtedly lead to many new and exciting breakthroughs.

But despite heartening historical patterns of technological advancement, there are no guarantees that continued adaptation to scarcity can keep pace with resource demand. Population growth and the desire for a higher standard of living in developing countries will continue to put even greater demands on technology to prevent worsening resource scarcity. And even if fueled by an inexhaustible and clean energy source such as the Sun, mineral recycling is never perfectly efficient.

It is difficult to imagine a scenario of unending resource-dependent economic growth, particularly with increasing population numbers. At some point, the supply of natural resources is ultimately limited by immutable physical laws of nature.

Although technology has successfully delayed the effects of resource scarcity, the world has not been similarly adept at preserving the natural ecosystems that yield these resources. Continued economic and population growth will increase ecological pressures on our environment. Transitioning rapidly to renewable energies is necessary due to eventual resource constraints, but it is also an essential action if humankind is to prevent further environmental degradation and climate change.

The current economic paradigm depends on growth, and our Earth's population continues to grow exponentially. This is problematic, as growth in GDP, population, and energy demand are also associated with increasing CO_2 emissions and environmental degradation. Due to swelling population numbers and increasing energy usage in many nations (led by China and India), there is an expected increase in energy demand of 30% by 2035.[50]

The point is that any decrease in CO_2 emissions achieved by adopting alternative energies, efficiency gains, and conservation may be offset by increased demand from global growth. This is a crucial point.

Continuous growth in GDP or world population is therefore not an option. The Earth, our primary source of wealth, can simply not withstand the punishment that additional growth would deliver. First and foremost, our Earth must be protected. Other issues are by definition secondary concerns.

New Directions

We must stop trying to manipulate the system to create illusory wealth. Reliable wealth comes from innovation, calculated risk taking, and producing a dependable product that people need and want – at a fair price. This involves capital investment from everyday citizens who believe in the product that a company sells.

It is imperative that we wisely choose the correct sectors to flourish, as there may be no second chance. We must avoid the temptation of narrowly focusing on solutions that offer only immediate national financial reward. We must instead broaden our field of view to consider long term and global considerations.

What the world does not need is to limit ourselves to making more trinkets, toys, or electronic gadgets – purchases that are dependent on disposable income. We cannot afford to think small. What is needed is a new and courageous sweeping vision, a colossal venture that can propel us successfully through this century and far beyond.

The industry that would most likely deliver the jobs and financial prosperity we need today is that of clean and renewable energy technology. It is imperative that we make this transformation in rapid fashion. This will be a massive undertaking. Due to resource constraints, this may not necessarily engender continuous long-term growth into the second half of this century and beyond, but rather reach a steady-state; indefinitely supporting a wide cadre of engineers, scientists, retailers, and maintenance/repair workers.

America can produce and sell clean energy products and technology to a world populace that is starved for energy – and who live on a planet that is currently threatened by the burning of fossil fuels. Embarking on this endeavor is the best bet to improve our economy and our environment.

Not everyone realizes it yet, but the world *needs* alternative energy – we will soon have no other reasonable viable option. We now have the perfect opportunity to be a vanguard of this industry; developing technologies in wind, solar, hydroelectric, wave, and geothermal energy.

We can build wind turbines, solar panels, electric cars, electric trains and infrastructure, smart grids, charging stations, energy efficiency improving devices, batteries, and hydrogen fuel cells – which will provide millions of jobs. Although still in its infancy, there are already nearly 300,000 people employed in the solar industry.

This energy transformation will require an educated populace, tremendous political will, and numerous government mandates. It will be much more difficult to develop scalable clean energy technologies without government assistance and the support of the American citizenry.

As we make this transition, it will be imperative to not sell our natural gas, coal, or oil to other countries; except in case of an international emergency. Continuing to export fossil fuels does not decrease pollution – someone else will be burning these fuels with less restrictions, and the global end result is usually worse.

Selling our carbon-based fuels would also undermine our efforts to export clean energy technologies, as countries would not need them as dearly if cheap fossil fuels were also offered to them. Providing clean energy products and technology will be a much more productive and sustainable venture than simply selling off our natural resources.

Clean burning technologies may also eventually be available, and our fossil fuels may one day be much needed. Saving these fuels would provide an additional measure of energy security; and national security as well.

Although continuous growth of a population or resource-based economy is impossible, the growth of knowledge is limitless. Accrued knowledge is something other nations will want and need. We can profit from an expertise based on the collaborative efforts of American citizens, nurtured by a government that is fiercely dedicated to advancing scientific understanding. Knowledge derived from our human capital is a valuable commodity that can essentially be selectively exported for time eternal.

Our government must heavily fund the disciplines of science, technology, engineering, and mathematics (STEM). The amazing advances realized today are the fruits of basic research performed by scientists of years past. These scientists had no idea that their contributions would someday be used to build MRI scanners or cell phones. New opportunities are born of accrued knowledge in the basic sciences. The economic and subsequent military power of our nation was built upon basic research; and the fact that *we got there first* has been the principle reason that our country has flourished.

If the consequences were not so serious, it would be laughable how the present US government leadership is wasting time and resources on dying and polluting fossil fuel industries, while also thwarting opportunities for research, development and implementation of alternative energies.

By embracing and funding research and technology, other nations are now steadily chipping away at our position of dominance. It is imperative that we continue to prioritize funding for basic and advanced sciences. This is very important today in regard to sustainable energy production, and will be equally important tomorrow for other unknown challenges that humankind is certain to encounter.

The transition away from fossil fuels will be a massive undertaking, initially requiring government involvement and subsidies. Our international competitors will not necessarily be constrained by capitalist models that often necessitate making immediate profits. The Chinese government essentially subsidized their solar industry, eventually forcing some American solar energy companies into bankruptcy. American companies may also need government subsidies until economies of scale are realized. Eventually, tremendous profits will be made.

Our Energy Options

King Coal

You may have heard that the US has an abundance of coal. This may be true. However, the best grades of coal have already been mined, and the remaining reserves are of much lower quality and are more difficult to obtain. Burning coal is of course also very polluting and a major player in our climate change problem.

Coal-derived energy also uses vast amounts of water; shortages of which may be inevitable. Also, the economic cost related to adverse health effects of mining and burning coal is greater than the retail cost of electricity derived from it; more than doubling its true cost, and making it uncompetitive with renewables from a price perspective alone.[51] These adverse health effects include respiratory, cardiovascular, and neurologic disease related to breathing toxic chemicals and particulate matter in polluted air, and exposure to methylmercury in the environment.

There is the possibility that coal may someday be able to be used with minimal environmental impact. However, despite what you may have heard, the possibility of "clean" coal is at least several decades away from large scale implementation. This may also never be truly feasible, as carbon sequestration methods are extremely expensive and fraught with danger.

Coal has been an extremely valuable workhorse in providing the world's energy needs; and it has served a vital purpose. And due to the expertise of engineers in the industry, current coal burning methods are definitely far superior to those in years past. However, better energy options have now become available, and it is time to move on.

Today, approximately one-fourth of our nation's energy needs are still met by burning coal; even though this is no longer necessary. It is time to advance forward, to widely available cleaner and renewable energy sources that are eager to replace coal – and at a lower cost.

The US should hold on to our coal resources. Instead, we currently ship much of our coal to China and other countries, exporting a possible future measure of energy security, utilizing additional liquid fuels in transport. This exported coal is often burned in countries with minimal environmental regulation; fouling the air of the planet, adding mercury to the fish in our oceans, and increasing global warming through CO_2 emissions.

Coal is not a good long-term option to address world energy needs. It is imperative that we expand our horizon to much beyond the next few decades.

Is Natural Gas a Good Option?

In the U.S., coal has recently been overtaken by natural gas, the new leader in the energy mix – but not because environmentalists have convinced everyone about coal's ecologic problems. Why then? Money. Producing electricity by burning natural gas is now cheaper than producing it by burning coal.

The advent of hydraulic fracturing ("fracking") proved to be the tipping point. The fracking process involves the high-pressure injection of a chemical-laden fracking fluid into a well. This creates fissures in deep rock formations, providing access to larger collections of natural gas and petroleum, and allowing them to flow more freely.

This new means of extraction has resulted in greater supplies of cheap natural gas, which now provides about 37% of US energy needs (vs 24% for coal). But there are worrisome trade-offs. Fracking methods are dangerous to the environment, causing contamination of adjacent water supplies. You may have seen YouTube videos of people in natural gas fracking regions of Pennsylvania, who can now entertain dinner guests by lighting their kitchen tap water on fire.

Also, as reported by the Union of Concerned Scientists (UCS), the production and distribution of natural gas results in the leakage of methane, which is 34 times stronger than CO_2 at trapping heat over a 100-year period.[52] This significantly reduces, or possibly negates, the potential climate advantage that natural gas has over coal. UCS analysis also showed that a natural gas-dominated electricity system would generate CO_2 emissions up to three times higher than the level below which we may limit some of the worst consequences of climate change.

Another issue is that natural gas supplies are limited. If we constructed or expanded infrastructure to support a natural gas energy model, as some propose, we would then have to subsequently soon construct a second infrastructure to support an economy powered by electricity from renewable resources.

Natural gas is no new bonanza, just another distraction that keeps us from focusing on long-term sustainable solutions. We cannot entrust our future to a resource that is polluting and finite in supply. We need solutions that will last many centuries and far beyond. Narrowing our scope to the next few decades does not make sense.

Nor does it make any sense to ship this natural gas in liquefied form to other countries. This uses even more energy, and causes even more pollution. As mentioned, readily available fossil fuels also act as a financial disincentive for developing countries to pursue clean and renewable options.

U.S. government leaders often complain that other countries are not doing their part in fighting climate change, yet they see no irony in selling them our fossil fuels – as long as the money keeps rolling in.

Natural gas is not the best fuel to meet world energy needs.

What About Nuclear Energy?

In 1951 a group of scientists at the Arco Reactor in Idaho first created electricity from a nuclear reactor. Three years later, a nuclear power plant in Obninsk, Russia was the first to crank up its generators and deliver electricity to the power grid. Hailed as a miracle of technology, power generated from nuclear fission did indeed offer many advantages over other forms of energy production. A single uranium pellet could deliver nearly as much energy as 150 gallons of oil or a ton of coal. Nuclear reactors utilized relatively little land mass, produced less greenhouse gas emissions than carbon sources, and offered continuous flow of electricity that was not dependent on weather conditions.

However, similar to coal generated electricity, nuclear power generation involves the use of tremendous amounts of water. Nuclear power also results in 25 times more carbon emissions than wind energy, when reactor construction and uranium refining and transport are considered. There also remains the possibility of more disasters like those that have occurred in Chernobyl, Three Mile Island and, more recently, Fukushima. There is also the potential for terrorist or state sponsored abuse or theft of nuclear material for weaponry, or a direct attack on nuclear power plants.

And lastly, there is no place in the universe to safely store nuclear waste. You cannot throw it away, as there is no "away." The cosmos is one vast interconnected system. The nuclear energy community therefore just sweeps the dirt under the carpet, looking for remote locations to bury the spent uranium fuel rods underground. No matter how efficient the process becomes, there will always be some dangerous nuclear waste created, and there will never be any place to put it. This fact alone makes nuclear energy a very poor option for generating electricity.

Until an international ban in 1993, many countries dumped their nuclear waste into the oceans, and there have been reports since then of illegal dumping off of the coast of Somalia. There are no good solutions for the problem of dealing with nuclear waste; however, scientists have determined that the safest option is to bury it underground.

Located approximately 100 miles north of Las Vegas, Yucca Mountain was chosen by Congress as the permanent geological repository for U.S. generated nuclear waste. However due to various concerns, including the possible effects of earthquakes and contamination of water sources, the project has been abandoned.

Even if it were to reopen, it has been estimated that Yucca Mountain would reach its full storage capacity in a relatively few years, and the 98 nuclear reactors operating in the U.S. would still continue to produce nuclear waste, with no permanent place to store it. Other countries also face the same problem, and some are planning to build extremely expensive geologic repositories within the Earth over the next few decades.

For lack of another option, nuclear waste is now temporarily stored on site at the nuclear reactor facilities that produce it; either in storage pools or in dry cask cylindrical storage containers made of steel and concrete. Problems arise, as storage pools are vulnerable to terrorist attacks. And dry cask storage cylinders are designed to last only up to 100 years. However, due to extremely long decay half-lives, their radioactive contents remain lethal for over 200,000 years, and sometimes for much longer. Due to the above concerns, many European countries have made plans to phase out nuclear energy.

Nuclear power plants currently deliver much needed electricity to many communities (meeting 19% of U.S. electricity needs), but there are currently far safer, and cheaper, alternatives.

The use of nuclear energy is a dangerous and expensive exercise that is best considered only as an option of last resort.

Are Biofuels the Answer?

Probably the most well-known and ubiquitous biofuel is corn. Roughly 40% of the over 90 million acres of corn grown in the U.S.

are used to produce ethanol.[53]

Corn ethanol is predominantly utilized to add to gasoline, to fuel motor vehicles, as part of a controversial mandate initially designed to help America become more energy independent. However, producing ethanol from corn is an absurd exercise – as ethanol use is polluting and is also an inefficient fuel source (ethanol takes a little over 2 BTU's to produce for every 3 BTU's that it provides).

We are currently utilizing about 35 million acres of prime American farmland to grow corn for ethanol, even though it is less efficient than gasoline (and far less efficient than electric batteries). This means that, in a hungry world with a growing population, 35 million acres of valuable soil are having nutrients unnecessarily extracted each year. This vast land expanse is also typically sprayed with biome-altering pesticides, and treated with synthetic fertilizers – much of which leaches into the Mississippi River and Gulf of Mexico, contributing greatly to the formation of an enormous nitrogen-induced dead zone.

All of this, to feed cars instead of people; the only real benefit of which is to keep a small sub-segment of farmers and their communities happy.

Biofuel produced from sugarcane is more efficiently produced than is fuel from corn; but it is likewise quite polluting, and it also utilizes land that could be better used for food production. Presently, to grow sugarcane biofuel, vast amounts of Amazonian rainforests are being cleared away – removing a natural carbon sink, hastening climate change, and resulting in the loss of many animal species.

Cellulosic biofuels (obtained from switchgrass, woodchips, yard debris, and municipal waste) can be utilized to create electricity. These fuels may hold some promise, but likely in small niche markets only. Cellulosic biofuels offer advantages over current biofuels, as food-producing farmland is not used, and they are much less polluting than fossil fuels. There are still significant potential concerns; however, as growing cellulosic crops utilizes land that could perhaps be better used for grazing. Also, scalability issues loom large.

Today, biofuels are being used to provide a large proportion of Europe's renewable energy. Much of this fuel comes from wood pellets manufactured from American trees grown specifically for this purpose. This process may indeed result in some improvement in total greenhouse gas emissions when compared to burning coal or natural gas. However, the bottom line is this: Utilizing biofuels means burning carbon – plain and simple.

There is also some fuzzy accounting about achieving net carbon neutrality with biofuels. And even if the math were solid, the positive effects on climate are calculated to occur only several decades from now – time that we do not have. Warming temperatures today will have lasting impacts tomorrow.

We need rapid, sweeping changes now. Biofuels may play a role, but they are not a major solution to the energy problem.

Clean, Safe and Renewable Energy

So, how should we meet global energy needs? The title above provides the answer. To be most accurate, it should really say "Clean, Safe, Renewable, and *Inexpensive* Energy," because renewables have reached grid parity (and better) in most locales, and prices continue to decrease.

Any method used to provide electricity must use some sort of "fuel" input to do so. Most of the electricity used in the U.S. comes from large utility plants that burn coal or natural gas. These natural resources must first be extracted from the Earth, and then burned to provide the energy needed to boil water into steam, which is then used to turn electricity-producing turbines – causing pollution and global warming as unwanted byproducts. As noted, the amount of carbon-based fuel remaining in the ground is a finite supply. And these fuels are certainly not free of charge.

This is not the case with renewables. Not only are they clean, **wind** and **solar** energy technologies use "fuel" inputs that are *inexhaustible* and *free*. Free sunlight shines upon solar panels every day; and the breezes that turn wind turbines will never cost a dime. Clean energy sources are already cost competitive with carbon-based energy sources, and in many regions are now the least expensive form of energy.

Currently, only 8% of US electricity generation comes from wind, and 2% from solar, but they are each gaining market share. In 2018, wind and solar respectively made up 13% and 29% of all new electric capacity.

In a clean energy future, it will likely be necessary to continue the production of hydroelectric energy, at least for the next few decades. Hydropower presently accounts for about 7% of US electricity production. Technological advances can increase efficiency in existing hydroelectric facilities; however, the potential for major growth in hydropower is limited, as most of the suitable waterways have already been utilized.

Hydroelectric dams have certainly imperiled many fish populations. At some time in the future, it may be best for the environment if dams were no longer necessary. That time will likely come. But, presently, hydroelectric generated energy is a better option than using carbon burning sources to generate power.

Hydropower is likely needed as an adjunct to wind and solar; at least for the short term. Dams also of course serve purposes other than energy production – such as flood control, recreational opportunities, and creating repositories of water for irrigation. Hydropower may not be a perfect energy option; but it is a good option for the next decade, and maybe even a couple more.

Geothermal and wave energy may play a role in niche markets, hopefully someday expanding greatly as new innovations develop. These clean energy technologies also utilize free fuel. Geothermal and wave-produced energy are promising energy-producing adjuncts to solar and wind, but presently operate at a much smaller scale.

When utilizing clean energy technologies, one must of course still pay for the hardware – wind turbines and solar panels – just like the coal and natural gas industries must pay for their turbines and factories. But, again, a very enormous difference remains: with wind and solar energy technologies the fuel is free – forever. This fact alone has the fossil fuel and nuclear energy industry very concerned, and they are thus ready to use propaganda, lobbying, and any other weapon they can find to delay the inevitable change to clean, safe, and renewable energy sources.

A rapid and complete transition to clean energy sources is an absolute necessity if we are to avoid many of the catastrophic effects of climate change. For this reason alone, there is no real choice but to commit to rapidly eliminating the use of fossil fuels. The fact that clean energy sources are also the most economical in the long term is just an added benefit.

Clean energy sources are not perfect. Any time you use any power source there will always be some price to pay. Some forms of geothermal energy development can increase the risk of earthquakes; and hydroelectric dams still endanger anadromous fish populations.

Wind turbines have indeed caused migratory and raptor bird deaths; however, the industry is well aware of this issue and is making appropriate considerations when siting new towers. Also, the number of wind turbine-related bird deaths is far less than from other causes (collisions with automobiles and home windows; transmission line electrocutions, capture by house cats, etc.).

Solar energy production has been associated with land use issues; however, panels can be placed in unobtrusive areas such as the current use of rooftops. Photovoltaic panels can also be installed on land that is otherwise unusable, such as retired landfills or abandoned mining areas. They can also be placed along existing transmission and transportation corridors.

Both wind and solar technologies face intermittency issues, during nighttime, or when the wind is not blowing. This problem is presently being mitigated by using interconnected networks and energy storage devices, which are becoming much more ubiquitous and much less expensive.

Not to trivialize the above important obstacles, but the problems related to clean and renewable energy technologies have been greatly exaggerated – mostly by desperate and dying fossil fuel and nuclear energy industries, whose own ecological downsides are far worse.

The concerns associated with the use of wind and solar technologies are minimal when compared to the problems associated with the use of nuclear or fossil fuel-based power production. It is really no contest; when evaluated against these other energy sources, clean and sustainable energy technologies are by far the better choice.

Here are some additional advantages of wind and solar power:

1.   Clean air. Obtaining electricity from wind turbines and solar panels instead of carbon-based sources markedly reduces pollution.

2.   Energy security. The U.S. will no longer be dependent upon imports from other nations for fuel.

3.   Beneficiaries of technology. Wind and solar energy efficiencies will continue to advance in step with technology. Solar panels and wind turbines continue to become more efficient – while also decreasing in price. Wind and solar will soon be the least expensive power source in almost all locales worldwide (in many places they already are).

4.   Employment opportunities. The solar and wind industries have created an enormous number of new jobs. The Department of Energy reports far more new jobs in the solar industry compared to the coal industry, and solar power is still in its infancy. Although its use is growing extremely rapidly, solar generated power currently provides only 2 percent of the electricity that the U.S. consumes each year. This represents a tremendous opportunity to create an incredible number of new jobs in this industry. Compared to fossil fuels, clean energy technologies provide cleaner power at a lower cost – while also providing jobs and a paycheck to far more citizens. It is a win-win-win situation.

5.   Decentralization. Solar panels, and to some extent wind turbines, offer the opportunity to obtain energy off of the grid. Rooftop or community owned solar panels do not need to tie into massive electricity transmission networks. This can result in efficiency gains, because when electricity travels along transmission lines power is lost as a function of distance traveled. The average loss of electricity from the power plant to the consumer is around 10%.

6.   National security. Large scale utility energy production and transmission is vulnerable to the actions of terrorist groups, who could possibly use cyber malware or an electromagnetic pulse to knock out large power stations. Decentralization strategies can help mitigate risk. There will indeed need to be interconnected networks of various energy sources, however many clean energy sources (like community solar) could also function in stand-alone fashion in emergencies.

A village began to flood during a heavy rainstorm. The rain continued to fall and many of the townsfolk fled to higher ground. As the water level continued to rise, one man climbed onto his roof.

When the water was to the level of the rain gutters of his home, a fellow rowed buy in a boat, beckoning the man on the roof to join him. He was answered with the reply, "Thanks for the offer, but God will save me!" Soon the man was standing on the top of his chimney, with water up to his ankles. A helicopter showed up, hovered overhead and dropped down a rope. The man shook his head, and again yelled out "Thanks for the offer, but God will save me!" Ten minutes later the water kept rising and the man drowned.

At the pearly gates to heaven the man complained to St. Pete, "I trusted in God that He would save me, yet I still drowned!" Peter replied, "For heaven's sake, He sent you a helicopter and a boat!"

Some people say that future technology will provide humankind with answers, and that we just need to wait patiently until nuclear fusion or some other form of energy becomes available. That is wishful thinking. Nuclear fusion, or a different yet to be discovered process, could one day become a major energy source. However, at least presently, that option appears to be decades away.

We already have everything we need right now, and we need to stop waiting for something better. We have wind and solar energy – our helicopter and boat have already arrived. We just need to climb aboard.

Transitioning quickly to a renewable energy economy will be a catalyst for a new economic prosperity. This will also mitigate the environmental effects of burning fossil fuels, while providing a clean and sustainable energy source. Making this transition will improve our economy, our environment, and our energy security. We can make this *one* move and help solve *three* problems.

Mark Jacobson, Stanford professor of civil and environmental engineering, and Mark Delucchi, research scientist at the University of California, Davis, have expertly outlined an ambitious but economically feasible roadmap to achieving a clean and renewable energy economy utilizing wind, water, and solar technologies within by 2030.[54] We have the technical capability to reach this goal, but it will take tremendous political will as well.

It will be necessary to improve upon our electrical grid, building one that can handle the massive amounts of electricity that will be needed to power our nation. It must also be capable of avoiding intermittency problems; by balancing and redirecting different sources of energy generated by wind turbines, hydroelectric dams, solar panels and concentrated solar power systems.

Eventually, much of our domestic travel and transportation of goods will be by electrified high speed railway and autonomous battery-powered trucks; with local travel via small electric cars or cycles.

There will be a place in the future for hydrogen fuel cells, to be used to smooth the bumps of an electric energy economy. Hydrogen could be used as a fuel for trucks designed for long-distance hauling, as presently the weight and charging times required to power these vehicles by battery power is excessive (that may change). Hydrogen fuel cells may also be used in future air travel, in conjunction with batteries. Fuel cells can also act as an emergency backup source of electricity production in hospitals and industrial settings. In addition, hydrogen can also be used to replace coal in the iron and steel making industry, which is a major contributor to total global greenhouse gas (GHG) emissions.

The key to using hydrogen in the energy mix is to make sure it is obtained from the proper source. Historically, hydrogen has been derived from fossil fuels; which defeats the purpose in regards to using it as part of a clean and renewable energy plan. But there is an alternative process that can be used to produce hydrogen – and it is both clean and renewable.

By running an electric current through water, it can be separated into its component parts (hydrogen and oxygen) by a process called electrolysis. The hydrogen produced by electrolysis can then be stored and later used in a fuel cell, where it is recombined with oxygen to create electricity and water (a much more desirable byproduct than the CO_2 and other pollutants produced by the burning of fossil fuels). If the electricity used for the electrolysis process is produced by wind or solar sources, a carbon-free power production and storage system is created.

One of the concerns with wind and solar energy is that at times there can be excessive energy production, more than the grid can handle. At times, large systems have to be shut down, a process that the industry refers to as curtailment. But the renewable energy industry is beginning to turn this challenge into an opportunity – as they are now creating systems that can use excess electricity production to electrolyze water, producing hydrogen as a stored form of energy.

One of the major obstacles limiting solar and wind generated electricity is that sunshine and wind can be variable or absent, resulting in power intermittency issues. Many innovative ideas are currently in the works to solve this problem (some are already scalable and currently utilized). All of these solutions attempt to store excess energy when demand is low, and release it when demand is high. Hydrolyzing water to create hydrogen is a great solution, but there are many other options as well. These include pumping water to higher elevation reservoirs and releasing it through turbines when necessary, filling subterranean caverns with compressed air, storing heat in molten salts, and utilizing giant flywheels.

Large battery systems are also presently used to store excess energy, and there are many companies attempting to develop cheaper and more efficient batteries – the holy grail of a clean energy network. It has also been proposed that electric cars (envisioned to one day be located in most garages across America) could serve as a giant storage network, utilizing some of the energy stored in their batteries in times of high demand.

Many companies currently offer home battery system wall units, like the Tesla Powerwall, to store energy obtained from photovoltaic solar panels. Large utility scale batteries are also being produced, and a Tesla product is already being utilized in Australia.

Transitioning to a renewable energy economy will necessitate government oversight and significant financial resources, but there will be long term monetary and environmental benefits that dwarf initial expenditures.

In the transition period it will be essential to conserve fuel resources. The government should immediately impose a 55-mph speed limit, which would result in an approximately 20% improvement in fuel efficiency for long distance travel (there is a 7% increase in fuel use for every 5 mph increase in speed over 55-mph.).[55] Unfortunately, this is not currently happening, and many states are instead raising speed limits. Many states have increased their speed limits to 80 mph in some areas.

Perceptions need to change regarding the time it takes to travel. Traveling fifty-five miles in one hour is still an incredible luxury. Driving at this lower speed is a very minor sacrifice; however, without a government mandate most people will refuse to drive more slowly.

A large tax could be added on to the price of any new vehicle that does not achieve 50 mpg on the highway, and also on any vehicle that exceeds specified weight limitations. Some may balk at government interference, stating that we should let the market figure this out on its own, and when people really want change, big business will respond. However, history has shown that most American citizens are not willing to significantly change their individual driving habits. The automobile industry is quite willing to provide the public with the product it desires (larger vehicles), especially as this is what is most profitable. Our government must therefore step in.

Lower speed limits would also help obviate the need for heavy vehicles, often built with hefty safety features designed to withstand high speed crashes. Smaller cars require less steel and less resources. The ultimate goal is a rapid and complete transition to an electric vehicle society.

American journalist Thomas Freidman once suggested a floor price for gasoline, a price below which gasoline could not fall.[56] In essence, the difference between the market price and the floor price would be a tax. This could be earmarked for clean energy production. This would level the playing field, giving alternative energy technologies a fair chance. Investors could make prudent financial decisions as they would know the worst-case financial scenario, and plan accordingly.

As it is, when oil prices drop, they drag down the short-term economic viability of clean energy products with them; discouraging entrepreneurs and investors, and keeping citizens from get started down a sustainable path. Government intervention is needed to keep short term market phenomena from negatively influencing the long term economic and environmental viability of our country, and the rest of the world.

It is important that our government becomes more forward thinking, attempting to predict not just what people in our country and others will want, but what they will need. Humanity will need clean and renewable energy.

Helpful Individual Actions

Revolutionary social changes require action at an individual level. This often involves reevaluating perceptions of what defines a happy and successful life, and a willingness to forgo a few luxuries that our grandparents lived quite happily without.

Personal finances should be managed conservatively; by avoiding unnecessary debt, purchasing homes and cars at prices commensurate with income, and diversifying investment portfolios. All individuals should save a little money each month, and also avoid taking large financial risks. Taking great chances with a large percentage of an investment portfolio is like going to the casino…. eventually the house usually wins.

Americans should think not only of our own personal financial situations, or just that of our country, but also of the financial needs of impoverished populations throughout the world. As noted earlier, helping others in need is not just a worthy moral endeavor; it also promotes world peace and a diminished need for military expenditures. Pockets of extreme poverty, misery, and hopelessness easily turn disenchanted youths into soldiers or terrorists. When we assist our international neighbors, our actions come back to us; eventually benefiting our own nation.

Consider sponsoring a child in another country, through World Vision or one of the many other great non-governmental organizations (NGO's). This is a great segue into a more global outlook, one that acknowledges the tremendous hardships faced by many young people in developing countries.

Philosopher and Princeton University professor Peter Singer has proposed ethical arguments encouraging people to evaluate their current lifestyles in a more appropriate perspective; challenging most people to donate approximately 1% to 5% of their personal income to the extreme poor, using an income-based sliding scale. For very high-income individuals, the recommendations are to pledge a higher giving percentage; e.g. about 5% for yearly incomes of $200,000 progressing to 10% for those with an income of $500,000.[57]

Singer suggests that even if we significantly downsize our current way of life, we will still be fabulously wealthy when measured against developing world standards. GiveWell and Charity Navigator are excellent resources to help individuals better evaluate the myriad organizations dedicated to helping others throughout the world.

Personal energy use can be decreased by making a few minor changes: fly less, drive less, choose a smaller car, buy a smaller home, turn down home air conditioners in the summer, and roll car windows down when driving in warm weather (automobile air conditioning uses additional amounts of fuel). Consider turning the heater down and wearing a sweater or long underwear in the winter. Remember that changing the way you eat can also use less energy. Consider eating fewer animal products, buying local produce, and planting a garden and fruit trees in your yard.

Larger sacrifices will also have to be made. By necessity, world citizens will be asked to choose to have smaller families. Sadly, there are simply too many people dependent upon too few resources.

It is really somewhat irrelevant whether it is only one year or a hundred before our resource supplies peak and then decline, or when our Earth surface temperatures increase to dangerous levels. Relative to a time frame of total human existence, these events could each occur in a very short time from now. If we continue our present actions, these events will almost certainly come to pass, markedly constraining levels of personal and global human health and happiness.

We can change our course to mitigate the damages. Or we can collectively choose to continue our current lifestyles, continuing to pollute, fighting over the last drops of oil, possibly sacrificing the lives of our children and those of future generations as payment for our actions. These lives may be lost quickly in wars over resources, or more slowly due to starvation and disease associated with an overpopulated and overheated planet, stressed beyond its capabilities of self-repair.

A new course must be charted. We can become a fiscally responsible nation, engaging in policies that utilize a global perspective, allowing us to maintain our position of leadership. We can take the bold steps toward a world economy that eliminates the use of fossil fuels. We can transition to wind, water, and solar energy technologies by 2030. We can continue to search for efficiency gains and reduce the amount of energy that we use each day. We can realize that infinite growth in our economy is improbable, and that further population growth will also act as a very destructive force.

We will be challenged by strong headwinds.

The individuals who have the most to lose (financially) from a shift to renewable energies are also the people who are least likely to personally feel the pain of possible future catastrophic events. These individuals often live in a cocoon of wealth, sheltered from the winds of hunger and despair. Most of these individuals are also at least middle-aged, and many are chiefly concerned about their own personal comfort in the next twenty or thirty years, after which time they will be long gone. They have very deep pockets, and they will fight ferociously to protect their personal interests – often employing lobbyists to distort the truth with false propaganda. That is why our government must seek counsel predominantly from an independent scientific community rather than from entrenched industries.

Many in the oil, coal and nuclear energy community have complained vehemently about subsidies available to solar and wind energy industries. However, in today's dollars, the oil and gas industry has received an average of nearly $5 billion in subsidies every year for over 90 years, the nuclear industry received an average of $3.5 billion yearly for over 50 years, and biofuels received $1 billion yearly for over 30 years – massively exceeding subsidies to renewables.[58] The U.S. government has underwritten these mature, extremely profitable, and highly polluting industries for decades. But leaders of these industries now cry foul when clean, efficient and sustainable energy industries are finally given the initial assistance needed to become widely implemented.

Members of Congress often succumb to the will of powerful constituents, whose narrow concerns are often detrimental to our country and the world at large. Many of those in states with a large agricultural industry argue for the use of corn biofuel; those who are heavily involved in the automobile industry fight higher gas mileage requirements; and those in coal-producing states elevate the importance of maintaining a relatively few regional jobs over global environmental concerns. Everyone desperately grabs for what they consider to be their share of the bounty, even when it is obvious that this will eventually be to the detriment of all.

It is not just wealthy oil barons who will need to be convinced of the necessity of converting to renewable energy technologies. The middle-class worker may open his utility bill and possibly notice a transient small increase in his rates. This may be unavoidable, at least initially. He may forget that there are many ways to pay for energy. He can pay for fossil fuel derived energy with an initially relatively small cost to his pocketbook. But with each bill he pays for fossil fuel, a much more insidious second fee is subtracted from his primary wealth, which is the Earth itself; a small portion of which each world citizen lays claim, the intrinsic worth of which becomes less when it is altered by pollution and climate change resulting from the burning of these fuels.

Alternatively, the consumer can pay simply with money alone, if he is willing to pay a possibly slightly higher rate today for clean and renewable energies. As an added benefit, his monetary cost will soon be less than he would pay for energy derived from fossil fuels, due to eventual economies of scale and imminent scarcity of currently utilized energy resources. In many places, clean and renewable energy modalities are already the least expensive options.

Some citizens may complain of wind turbines ruining their view, even though they have already learned to mentally subtract telephone poles and power lines when looking out of their windows. They forget that just because they cannot see greenhouse gases in the air, they are in truth much less attractive than a wind turbine or solar panel, if they would evaluate with more than just their eyes.

Some conservative citizens may also lump all conversations resembling a "green" agenda together into a bundle of what they consider to be leftist hippie talk, and summarily dismiss many good ideas without due consideration. Many of these people fear change, particularly in their later years. Our youth are not as fearful. We must count on them to realize the strength in their numbers, and demand the change that is so necessary.

We are a populace that is unaccustomed to even small amounts of self-sacrifice. We live in a society where luxury and excess are revered rather than reviled. That could change, and the tipping point may be drawing near.

Many persist on viewing the world within a very short time frame, refusing to be long term thinkers if that entails any immediate loss of convenience or comfort, however small. Instead, they choose to postpone responsible actions to some later time in the future, even though each extra moment they wait will cause even greater pain when further delay becomes impossible.

There is a deep connection between energy, the economy and the environment. Energy is needed to sustain our economy, as well as to keep us warm and free from hunger. Wind and solar renewable energy technologies can provide this energy with minimal environmental impact. These technologies offer a long-term and sustainable solution to our energy needs.

Building a clean energy infrastructure will also create new jobs, lifting our economy. In turn, a healthy U.S. economy will help to protect the Earth, providing the monetary resources needed to secure our nation's leadership role in displaying environmental responsibility. The Earth is the primary source of our true wealth. The basis of all future policies must be built upon this First Precept. We must protect our true wealth.

Our government must abandon current paradigms of limitless growth, deficit spending, money printing, waste, and an economy dependent on energy derived from fossil fuels.

One hundred years from now, and a million years after that, the fossil fuels will all be gone. But the wind will still be blowing, water will still be flowing, and the Sun will continue to warm the Earth. This must be remembered when planning our energy future.

It is imperative that we are each willing to change our perceptions, and that we find new definitions for happiness. We already have what we need. There are innumerable books, museums, works of art, and sporting events to entertain me. I turn on the tap and I have clean flowing water. I have never known true hunger. I have clothes to cover and warm my body. In the morning I walk into my backyard and, depending on the season, I can harvest fresh raspberries, apricots, peaches, plums, pears, grapes, and many types of vegetables. At night I lay in bed, under a roof protecting me from rain and snow. I gaze at the exquisite beauty of a flower in a vase on our nightstand. I listen to the laughter of our adult children downstairs, who have come home for a visit. I embrace my wife, and drift off to sleep. This is true happiness. This is paradise. Everything else is just fluff and window dressing.

But the siren song beckons. Many of us have everything we need, yet we are often not satisfied. We may not recognize that a life of increasing ease and luxury often merely leaves us wanting for more; all the while increasing our levels of expectation, frustration, and worry.

Soon we may crash against a rocky shore.

We fail to realize that, like an asymptotic curve, we can approach but never quite reach a line that we ourselves have created; continuing to hopelessly pursue a prize that can never quite be grasped. We must learn that searching for complete gratification is not only an unworthy and illusory goal, it is also impossible. We must realize that we already exist in a world of lean abundance. Looking for more can actually make us less happy.

We will likely see many positive changes in the world. With less reliance on automobiles for transportation, we may improve our health by walking and bicycling more. We may choose to live closer to family and friends to avoid the high costs of transportation. Neighbors may no longer drive past, click the garage door opener and quickly isolate themselves away from others. Perhaps more people will start sitting on their front porches again, exchanging friendly conversation with passerby neighbors as they walk to work, the library, or the market. Ironically, living with less may make us happier, if we only let it do so.

The world faces daunting challenges, but these problems are not insurmountable if we act quickly and decisively. A world of strife and chaos is certainly not a foregone conclusion. Tough challenges offer the possibility of tremendous victories and exciting new discoveries. Sustainable Global Happiness is well within our reach.

Now is not the time for complacency. We must immediately make necessary changes to protect our economy, ensure a supply of clean and renewable energy, and safeguard our environment.

It is time to leap off of the cliff, accepting our fate – a fate that will be influenced by our own actions. Where we land is up to us.

Part III: PLANET

Sustaining a Healthy and Happy Earth

"And I think to myself, what a wonderful world."

-Louis Armstrong

Randy A. Siltanen

EIGHTEEN

Drowning in a Sea of Humanity

"Intellectuals solve problems, geniuses prevent them."

-Albert Einstein

EVERY TWO SECONDS there is a net increase of five people in the world population. This means one new classroom full of children every ten seconds, and enough people to fill each of the seats of a large college football stadium every eight hours. Every three weeks there are approximately four million more people on Earth, which is about equal to the population of the city of Los Angeles.

There are now over 7.7 billion inhabitants on our planet. Although the rate of increase in human population growth has diminished recently, we are still on track to have an estimated global population of approximately 9 to 10 billion by the year 2050. To stabilize our population at the current level we need a global birth rate of approximately two children per couple.

Many scientists suggest that our Earth is already on a non-sustainable course with our current numbers. Stanford University population studies professor Paul Ehrlich has suggested that an optimal and sustainable number would be about 1.5 to 2 billion people (roughly one-fourth the size of the current population).[59]

Several major countries do not have enough arable land to feed their own citizens. This is of even greater concern as current crop yields have become reliant on heavy doses of synthetic fertilizers – which cause soil acidification, worsen climate change due to nitrous oxide release, and result in oceanic dead zones. Also needed are vast amounts of water for irrigation, which requires energy to pump and distribute. There is also increasing salinity in the soils due to irrigation, rendering some farmland unproductive. Water tables are dropping at rates that are orders of magnitude higher than they can be replaced, putting future food security at risk.

There is also worldwide competition for many other natural resources – oil, metals, timber, minerals, and clean drinking water – which has the potential to greatly exacerbate geopolitical instabilities. The Global Footprint Network states that we are currently using up more resources than the Earth can continue to provide; estimating that it takes our planet one and a half years to regenerate the resources we consume in a single year.[60]

Any improvements in climate change, by conservation or the use of clean energy, could easily be erased by an increase in global population. This is especially troublesome now, as many citizens in developing nations are eager to adopt many of the luxuries currently enjoyed by their developed world counterparts. The result is greater numbers of individuals, each using increased levels of energy consumption – a recipe for disaster. The Earth simply cannot tolerate more population growth.

Unfortunately for our younger citizens, they will be the ones who must change their perceptions and actions regarding family size. It is regrettable that the model of a large family size is not sustainable for future generations, who must be encouraged to have smaller families. We ask a lot of our young people.

There are three major ways to solve the world population problem:

1) Adjust cultural perceptions regarding optimal family size.

2) Use effective birth control measures.

3) Decrease childhood mortality rates.

Adjust Cultural Perceptions

There are some religious beliefs that exacerbate the population problem, either directly or indirectly. Catholic Church doctrine discourages the use of all types of birth control other than abstinence or natural family planning – although this directive is certainly not followed by all Catholics. There are also other religions, too, that actively encourage large family sizes. Leaders of these churches should consider revisiting their stance on this issue, particularly in light of current overpopulation concerns.

In many less affluent countries, it is culturally encouraged for couples to have large families. This is often due to various forms of gender discrimination, and a lack of education. In some locales, women are often coerced by their husbands and extended family to have more children. And in many societies male offspring are favored; therefore, the birth of a female child is often followed by another pregnancy in an attempt to produce a male heir.

Empowering young couples with the idea that a woman is an equal partner in her relationship – and that a smaller family size can actually be quite beneficial for everyone in her family – is an effective way to lower population levels. This is a perception that it is successfully changing in many places throughout the world, including Iran, Mexico, India, and Indonesia.

Effective Birth Control

There are various effective forms of birth control to help control the population problem. Other than abstinence, none of these are perfect methods; therefore, there is always some risk of pregnancy with sex. Even if precautionary measures are taken, it is always possible that one could end up with a larger family size than initially planned.

As a world average, a worthy goal to aim toward would probably be just under two children per couple. However, averages are made up of many different and acceptable numbers on each side of the line so, at least at this point in time, it is probably most appropriate to simply develop a general mindset of encouraging smaller family sizes –

without picking a specific optimal number for each and every family.

Abstinence is of course a perfectly effective form of birth control. It is also free, and there is no concern of hormonal side effects. Abstinence allows potential mates to develop friendships and determine compatibility on emotional, philosophical, and intellectual issues; without the responsibility associated with a sexual relationship. However, abstinence is obviously not a realistic long-term strategy for limiting population numbers.

Barrier devices include diaphragms and condoms for females, and also condoms for males. Male condoms are quite effective at preventing pregnancy. They are also relatively inexpensive, have no hormonal side effects, and markedly decrease the risk of contracting sexually transmitted diseases – although a small risk of infection or pregnancy definitely remains.

Using a diaphragm is less effective than using a condom for preventing pregnancy, and is ineffective at preventing sexually transmitted diseases. Female condoms are not quite as reliable as male condoms; however, they are effective, and they reduce the risk of acquiring a sexually transmitted disease.

Male condoms are about 98% effective at preventing pregnancy if used consistently and correctly. If a condom is also used in addition to natural family planning methods (temperature measurements, checking cervical mucus, and using a calendar method) the chance of pregnancy becomes even less.

Sterilization is also a quite efficacious method of birth control. Vasectomy in males is a less invasive procedure than a tubal ligation is for females, although both work well. Implanted occlusive metal devices placed in the female fallopian tubes as an outpatient procedure is also a relatively new option.

Implanted intrauterine devices, IUD's, are placed in the uterus by a trained clinician. This foreign body disrupts the endometrial lining of the uterus, making it an unsuitable home for the fertilized egg. There are some possible concerns with this type of birth control, as foreign objects in this location can have rare side effects of infection or uterine perforation.

Another very effective method of birth control is that of hormonal manipulation. The methods of hormone dissemination include orally ingested pills, implanted hormone devices, injected hormones, and vaginal rings which release hormones. However, the use of these methods can occasionally be associated with unwanted side effects.

As noted in other sections, it is not always the optimal course of action to intervene in normal physiologic pathways – unless there are no other good options.

Contraceptive hormones have effects throughout the body, not just on ovarian function. Serious side effects with hormone contraceptive agents are rare; however, their use has been associated with an increased incidence of blood clots, strokes, heart attacks, benign liver tumors, and depression. There is also no protection against sexually transmitted diseases.

"Morning after" pills contain hormones that prevent an egg from being released by the ovary. These pills can also often prevent an already fertilized egg from attaching to the uterine wall.

Hormonal alteration is certainly an effective method of contraception; however, other available alternatives may be more appropriate for some people, as the risk/benefit ratio of each option can vary by individual.

The most appropriate contraceptive method for each individual depends on several factors. All options should be discussed with one's personal professional healthcare provider.

Decrease Childhood Mortality

The third major way to limit population growth involves decreasing childhood mortality, particularly by preventing common developing-nation illnesses such as malaria and diarrhea.

At first glance this statement may seem somewhat counterintuitive, but as the populace of a country becomes healthier, birth rates plummet. There are likely many reasons for this phenomenon and, tragically, one of the most prevalent is this: In many countries with poor childhood survival rates, parents realize the high likelihood that one or more of their children may die, and they therefore plan large families as a sort of insurance policy to help mitigate the personal, cultural, and economic effects of losing a child.

It is imperative that all countries make a commitment to help decrease the world population; or at the very least attempt to keep the total number at its current level of 7.7 billion inhabitants. To accomplish this objective, appropriate birth control measures must be widely accepted, inexpensive, and available.

Via educational outreach, cultural perceptions regarding optimal family size must also continue to change.

It is also important that donors and government agencies continue to focus on eradicating deadly maladies such as malaria, diarrhea, malnutrition, and vaccine-preventable diseases.

Unfortunately, the leaders of many countries are still presently trying to increase their population base; as they want to ensure that there are enough young workers to financially support an aging populace, fuel the engine of perpetual economic growth, and provide military might. But, as stated previously, chasing after continuous growth – in a population or an economy – is a fool's errand.

The paradigm these leaders suggest would necessitate even greater numbers of people to support our youth as they themselves age, adding to a mass of humanity whose numbers would continue to spiral out of control. This would of course be associated with an increase in environmental degradation and a decrease in the amount of natural resources, each occurring in exponential fashion. At some point, humanity must jump off of this dangerous ride. A system with finite resources simply cannot support continuous growth.

Austrian demographic experts Erich Striessnig and Wolfgang Lutz evaluated worldwide economic considerations as well as environmental impacts as they relate to ideal fertility rates.[61] Noting that better educated people are more productive and retire later, these demographers suggested that lowered fertility rates are indeed economically feasible, particularly if there is a concurrent increased investment in education. Overall, they concluded that optimal fertility rates are 1.5-1.8 per woman of childbearing age; a number significantly lower than the replacement level fertility rate of 2.1 (this is greater than 2.0 because some children do not live to adulthood).

Advances in technology will certainly attenuate some of the pain of continuous growth. There will be efficiency gains in energy and possibly food production, and there will certainly be improvements in water filtration systems and pollution controls. But technological advances could also serve as distractions that take our eye of the ball, giving us a false sense of security, simply delaying for a few generations the inevitable ills associated with overpopulation.

Technology is not a panacea, and it is quite likely that new advances could soon be overwhelmed by the inexorable tide of problems wrought by continued population growth. Perhaps the goal of technology should be to make lives even better for 7.7 billion (or less) people; not just tolerable for a population of 10 billion or more.

Several thousand years from now, future Earth inhabitants will still wish to enjoy bountiful food, fresh water, open spaces, and clean air. Their wellness and happiness depend on our actions.

Sustainable Global Happiness will only be possible if we limit the growth of our population. Eventually – through warfare, starvation, and disease – populations tend to limit themselves. But these scenarios are of course associated with much suffering; at which time the damage to the Earth would continue to mount. It is much wiser to avoid these problems now, rather than to look for solutions later.

As Albert Einstein said, "Intellectuals solve problems, geniuses prevent them."

Randy A. Siltanen

NINETEEN

Wild Ocean

"Our task must be to free ourselves by widening our circle of compassion to embrace all living creatures and the whole of nature and its beauty."

-Albert Einstein

MOST OF US have seen pictures of Earth from satellite cameras. Covered predominantly by water, our magnificent planet shines a brilliant blue against the darkness of space. To our ancestors, the seas were a vast expanse, too large to consider as anything but a source of endless bounty. But from a new vantage point, out in space, our oceans do not appear quite so limitless.

The ocean is the seven seas; an exquisite wilderness, rough and wild. So, too, are clouds the ocean; evaporated particles soaring up to the heavens, coalescing into beauty, and then racing to the shore. Upon mountaintops these ocean clouds will vanish, dispersed as ocean mist upon a forested ridge. Quenching the thirst of all on Earth, ocean water droplets come together to form tiny ocean water rivulets, then small ocean water streams, and then finally winding ocean water rivers, that once again reunite with their source, meeting at our ocean bays and estuaries. It is an awe-inspiring design of grandeur.

We are each an intimate part of this elegant system. So dependent are we on this water, that without it we cannot survive more than a few days. Indeed, as approximately sixty percent of our human bodies are made up of ever-changing molecules of water, in a sense, we *are* the ocean.

Our ocean waters are home to an enormously diverse population of magnificent creatures, each with its own reason for existing, and each interacting in concert with many others. Whether we believe it is the work of a Creator or merely a happenstance of Physics, we are all guardians of this splendid artistic display – a fantastic ecosystem that, on our watch, is currently under assault by overfishing, pollution, and global warming.

Au Revoir, Wild Fish

In his excellent book *Four Fish*, author Paul Greenberg uses an analogy of a bank account when describing how to best maintain sustainable fisheries. Insisting that it is crucial that we only harvest the interest off of the ocean, Greenberg suggested that we must leave the principal intact – i.e. we should not remove more fish from a population than can be replenished naturally by that species.

In prior centuries, the numbers of people in most regions were small in comparison to the vastness of the seas, and there was no real danger of overfishing an entire ocean. Unfortunately, this is no longer true. Not content to simply collect interest, we are rapidly diminishing our principal as well.

Centuries ago, groups of South Pacific islanders overfished the sea life in their lagoons; exhausting their food supply and eventually causing a collapse of their society. The current path of exploitation, played out on a much grander scale, could portend a similar misfortune.

There are simply not enough wild fish in the ocean to feed the world population – at least not at current rates of consumption. Globally, about 20 kg (44 pounds) of fish are eaten per person per year; a rate that has nearly doubled in the last fifty years, in part due to the promotion of the health benefits of eating seafood.[62] This increased rate of consumption has coincided with a population increase of about two billion people.

As greater numbers of people are each eating greater numbers of fish, the supply of the wild ocean can no longer keep up with the demand of the consumer. To make up the difference, approximately one-half of all seafood consumed is now farm-raised.

In the past, predominantly using hook and line, it was often difficult to catch great numbers of fish. Today, with trawlers, purse seine nets, fish finders, aerial surveillance and predictable fish migration patterns, it is quite easy to decimate a fish population. Also, there are far more fishing fleets than are necessary to harvest a sustainable number of fishes. Furthermore, the fishing industry has been artificially supported by various government subsidies, a practice which has worsened the pressure on fish populations.

The UN agency's State of World Fisheries and Aquaculture (SOFIA) says that almost a third of commercial fish stocks are now fished at biologically unsustainable levels.[63] Due to low numbers, in 1994 the greatest New England fishing grounds, Georges Bank, was closed to commercial cod fishing. It is expected to take more than another decade for this stock to recover. There are also many other populations that have been overfished. Currently there are concerns over the declining numbers of Pollock, a very frequently consumed whitefish that is native to the North Pacific Ocean. And except in Northern Alaska, Pacific coast salmon runs are now nearly all made up of hatchery fish.

As predatory type fisheries are collapsing, the industry has moved to pursuing a different marine population called forage fish; the small filter feeding fish that larger fish prey upon. Similar to algae and plankton, forage fish also make up the underpinnings of an ecosystem – critical elements located at the base of a very intricate production.

Forage fish now account for over one-third of all the catch taken from the ocean.[64] If this persists, it will lead to an even greater collapse of many predator species located higher up the chain.

Most of the forage fish catch is used in aquaculture and agriculture – used to feed farmed fish, pigs and poultry. Feed conversion ratios are approximately 3:1, meaning it takes three pounds of wild forage fish to make one pound of farmed fish or animal. Also, over two million metric tons of raw fishery products are used each year to produce cat food.[65]

Bycatch is the word used to describe the portion of the fisherman's catch that is inadvertently caught when fishing for a desired species. It may be that the creature is out of season or too small to be legally harvested, or it may simply not be profitable to keep; therefore, it is discarded, often injured or dead, back into the sea.

In the Gulf of Mexico there are approximately 2.5 pounds of bycatch for each pound of shrimp caught.[66] Wild shrimp are usually obtained by dragging nets across the ocean bottom, often disrupting the microenvironment of the sea floor, and inadvertently catching and harming several other species. Almost one-half of all worldwide bycatch is caught by shrimp trawlers.

In 1996, the United States passed the Sustainable Fisheries Act, which made it illegal to overfish any American fish or shellfish. This has been a successful venture; however, most other countries have not established similar laws. As over 80% of the seafood that Americans eat is imported, we are frequently eating fish or shellfish from overseas locales that often poorly manage their fishing stocks.

Unfortunately, there is no single governing body that effectively controls international waters. In the United States, most coastal waters are governed by state agencies out to a distance of 3 nautical miles (Florida and Texas govern 9 miles out from the shore). Our federal government claims as sovereign (and therefore regulates) the seas out to a distance of 200 miles or the end of the continental shelf, whichever is greater, up to a maximum distance of 350 miles. Most other countries claim sovereignty of waters in a roughly similar fashion. This leaves an immense amount of water that is governed only via a patchwork of often unenforced treaties, commonly resulting in unlicensed poaching as well as overfishing from licensed boats.

Poor global regulation is one of the major reasons that the Bluefin Tuna is now severely threatened. A magnificent apex predator, the warm-blooded Bluefin can weigh in at a thousand pounds or more. Historically, the red flesh of this creature was not considered that desirable; however, in the last few decades this fish has become a luxury food, prized for its unique flavor and texture in sushi markets throughout the world, especially in Asia. A single fish can be worth millions of dollars. No longer just simple nutritious food, the flesh of this fish is now enjoyed predominantly by the wealthy; who will briefly indulge their palates, claiming their piece of a very rare prize.

Reminiscent of the slaughter of the rhinoceros for his horn, or the elephant for her tusks, the assault continues. But unlike the case of the rhino or elephant, there has been relatively little world uproar, and it is therefore quite possible that the Bluefin could one day all be gone.

Poison in the Well

It is imperative to understand that the world water design is essentially a closed loop system. The Earth holds a finite amount of water; similar to a bathtub in which the water can never be replaced.

Marked changes have occurred in our oceans over the last several decades – a period that represents an extremely small fraction of the time that human beings have existed on our Earth. Over millions of years, the oceans remained essentially untouched and pristine; but in a very few years enormous changes have come about.

The Pacific Ocean is now home to the largest garbage dump in the world – the Great Pacific Garbage Patch. Made up of plastic and various types of debris, this collection is located in the North Pacific gyre. A gyre is a large system of rotating ocean currents, forming a vortex with calm water at the center. The environmental organization Greenpeace has estimated that this assemblage of plastic covers an area roughly the size of Texas; however, the exact borders are difficult to measure as there is no definition as to what concentration of debris should be included in the area. Most of this debris is in the form of very small plastic particles, submerged slightly below the surface.

Due to the currents of the North Pacific gyre, debris from the coastlines of North America and Asia eventually make it to its center, concentrating the debris in this area. Although they are not as large, there are similar garbage patches in the other four major gyres in the world, which include the South Pacific gyre, North and South Atlantic gyres, and the Indian Ocean gyre. Anything that goes down a storm drain can eventually make it to coastal waters, and eventually be taken by the current to the middle of an ocean gyre.

Greenpeace estimates that about ten percent of all plastic produced eventually ends up in the ocean. Much of this plastic has been broken down mechanically or by the sun into minute particles, forming a watery soup. In some places the pieces of small plastic far outnumber plankton. Small plastic pieces can absorb hazardous pollutants, and many are ingested by marine organisms, thus entering the food chain. Bigger plastic pieces are very frequently ingested by large marine animals, and are also the source of entanglement and death of whales, dolphins, turtles and seabirds.

Approximately seventy percent of the plastic debris eventually settles to the ocean bottom, altering the ecosystem and covering marine life of the sea floor. As plastic breaks down extremely slowly, the total effect on the environment, and ultimately on humans, may not be manifest until years from now.

Briefly discussed earlier, another major pollutant in our waterways and oceans is nitrogen and phosphorous from agricultural fertilization runoff. Excessive nitrogen levels in coastal regions cause the proliferation of algae, which leads to the depletion of oxygen in the water, and ultimately to the death of fish in dead zones.

It is estimated that the use of nitrogen fertilizer has increased 8-fold in the last fifty years, due to the high input/high output model of the Green Revolution.[67] The agricultural industry can help to address this problem by choosing to employ precision fertilizing techniques. These techniques include limiting total fertilizer use to only the exact needs of the crop, timing the application of fertilizer to low run-off seasons, and creating buffers between cropland and streams.

Individuals can help lower ocean nitrogen levels by buying organic foods (not grown with synthetic fertilizers), making sure that the beef they eat is grass-fed/grass- finished, and voting against the use of corn-based biofuel (Midwest corn crops use enormous amounts of fertilizer that leaches into the Mississippi river and ends up in the Gulf of Mexico).

There is some good news regarding oceanic dead zones: They can be reversible. A huge dead zone in the Black Sea has nearly completely recovered; the fortuitous unintended result of a decrease in the use of fertilizers that farmers could no longer afford after the collapse of the Soviet Union.

In 2012, testing by the US Geological Survey (USGS) of treated wastewater bound for the Columbia River in Oregon found over 100 different toxic materials.[68] The list of dangerous chemical agents discovered included flame retardants, pharmaceuticals, pesticides, and household cleaning products. Many of our oceans and waterways also contain several other nasty substances, including persistent organic pollutants and mercury.

Persistent organic pollutants include many types of chemicals, the most familiar of which are DDT, PCB's, and dioxin. These chemicals tend to demonstrate low water solubility, high fat solubility, and extremely low rates of breakdown in nature. They are also characterized by their ability to bio-magnify up the food chain; and bio-accumulate in the fatty tissues of higher-level organisms. Persistent organic pollutants are capable of traveling great distances, via ocean currents, and often by means of a process called global distillation.

Similar to the use of a still to make moonshine, global distillation works by the evaporation of chemicals in a warm location (such as from a factory in a low latitude nation like the United States) and condensation in a cooler location (such as a higher latitude Arctic region). Air currents transport these gases from south to north. This process explains why polar bears and minimally polluting native Inuit people have very high levels of persistent organic pollutants in their tissues.

Due to atmospheric and marine pathways, and extremely slow breakdown times, many contaminants are often far removed in time and space from their original source of production. Polychlorinated biphenyls (PCB's) were once used in electric transformers, lubricants, and hydraulic fluids. The production of these chemicals was banned in the United States in 1979, however in previous years large amounts of PCB's entered the atmosphere and watersheds of the United States as industrial waste.

Between 1947 and 1977, The General Electric Company (GE) discharged an estimated 1.3 million pounds of PCB's into the Hudson River. There were also other regions where these substances entered watersheds. Eventually making their way up to the Arctic, these chemicals are still present today. PCB's continue to be ingested by lower forms of marine life, their levels biomagnified as they work up the food chain, ultimately reaching greatest amounts in the tissues of the apex predators.

In humans, persistent organic pollutants can reach our fatty tissues when we eat fish and shellfish. These chemicals increase the risk of some cancers, and also demonstrate neurotoxic effects that impair learning and memory. These chemicals can also disrupt endocrine, reproductive, and immunologic function. The developing fetus is at the greatest risk, although persistent organic pollutants are dangerous to people of all age groups. In some regions, wild seafood and marine animals can no longer be consumed without concern of toxicity. Due to emissions from coal burning plants, smelting operations, and waste incineration, much marine life now also contains dangerous levels of mercury, another substance that is very toxic to humans. This problem has been recognized for decades; however, due to the actions of powerful lobbyists and industry, this pollution is still occurring in the United States, and to an even greater degree in Asia.

Our children will have to carefully choose and limit the amount of seafood that they can eat, or else risk poisoning their tissues.

It is not uncommon for a native Inuit person in the Arctic to have high levels of a toxic substance in his/her bloodstream, a chemical that was produced over 50 years ago in a factory in New York. Present and local problems expand to have future and distant effects.

Is it Hot in Here or is it Just Me?

Because of their tremendous biological diversity, coral reefs have been called the "the rainforests of the ocean." Coral are extremely ancient animals that evolved into reef-building forms over the last 25 million years. They live in a symbiotic relationship with algae, which grow within the coral and give them their bright color.

Algae supply energy to the coral via photosynthesis. In turn, coral provide food and shelter for algae, which feed off of coral waste products. Although coral reefs cover only about 0.1 percent of the ocean floor, they provide habitat to over twenty-five percent of marine species.[69] There are approximately 30 million people worldwide who are totally dependent on the coral reefs for their livelihood, and 500 million people who have some level of dependence upon coral reefs.[70]

Astonishingly, this magnificent ancient ecosystem is in danger of collapsing over the next few decades. Predominantly due to the burning of fossil fuels, tremendous amounts of CO_2 are released each day into the atmosphere. Approximately one-third of this CO_2 eventually dissolves in the sea, raising the acidity of the ocean water. At these higher acid levels coral is no longer able to build its skeletal-like structure, and can begin to dissolve.

Rising CO_2 levels also result in global warming, hitting coral reefs with a double whammy, as rising water temperatures kill the algae that they depend on. This results in the bleached look of dead or dying coral. In 2005, 80% of coral regions surveyed in the Caribbean were bleached, and half of those had died due to heat stress. At current trends, coral reefs may stop growing and disintegrate before the end of this century.

The majority consensus opinion of the scientific community is that the Earth is definitely warming, and there is an extremely high likelihood that humans are causing this through activities that increase the concentrations of CO_2 and other greenhouse gases in the atmosphere. No major scientific body of national or international standing has maintained a dissenting opinion.

Some citizens (and some leaders of government and industry) fail to understand that it is not unexpected to experience individual years of cooling of the planet, existing within an overall trend of increasing temperatures – just like the Dow Jones stock price may go down in any given year, even though the overall movement is decidedly upward for the decade.

Not all areas of the planet will be equally affected by climate change. With mild increases in temperature and increased rainfall, some regions may experience a few decades of increased agricultural production, due to longer growing seasons and more irrigation water available. Other areas will experience droughts and crop failures (the predicted net global effect of climate change is a decrease in yields).

As temperatures increase, problems will become much more severe. In our extremely interconnected world, events in seemingly remote places will have painful global consequences. Eventually, everyone will feel the effects of climate change – and humankind's thin cloak of civility may be doffed when temperatures start to rise.

Because of previous release of greenhouse gases, we will continue to experience some degree of climate change even if CO_2 emissions immediately ceased today. The key is to figure out what level of climate change could be possibly tolerated without grave consequences. That number is a point of debate, but the current consensus scientific opinion is that it is most likely less than 1.5 degrees Celsius (equal to approximately 2.7 degrees Fahrenheit).

Here is what many scientists postulate will happen with increasing levels of planetary surface temperatures:

1-2 degrees Celsius increase: Small glaciers will disappear, threatening water supplies and damaging ecosystems. There will be a substantial increase in extreme weather events, including droughts, heat waves, flooding, and cyclones. Coral reef ecosystems will be extensively and likely irreversibly damaged, devastating a tremendously large population of sea life. Not only do millions of people depend on these sea creatures for their existence, these creatures do not live sequestered away from the rest of the ocean, but instead play a vital role in the balance of the entire ocean. Even seemingly small half-degree temperature increases can result in marked non-linear worsening of climate related problems.

2-3 degrees Celsius increase: 1 billion people will likely suffer water shortages. Many small island states will disappear under water. The Amazon rainforest will begin to collapse. Up to 20-50% of Earth's species could become extinct.

3-4 degrees Celsius increase: Extensive regions will develop major declines in crop yields, leading to widespread famine. Sea level rise will threaten major cities like Miami, New York, London, Hong Kong, Shanghai, and Tokyo – and many more.

Of course, one could certainly quibble about the accuracy of these numbers, and perhaps suggest that the threat of potential climate change problems later in this century are overstated. However, these estimates could also possibly be overly optimistic – as modeling systems are not foolproof. If a person truly values the idea of intergenerational equity, perhaps it does not really matter whether drastic changes would occur in this century or another to follow.

What we do know is that unless we make immediate changes now, there will likely be catastrophic events in the future. We must eliminate our use of fossil fuels for energy, appropriately manage our forested lands, and increase our energy efficiency.

Some people claim that the temperature of the Earth has always fluctuated, which is true; however, it is the extreme *rate* of change that is now so concerning. It is not just that the temperature is changing; it is that it is changing so very quickly.

Of note, positive feedback loops (with negative consequences) are currently at work in the climate change arena. These have the potential to be very dangerous. Warm weather causes melting of permafrost, allowing tundra to release methane gas, which subsequently causes even more warming at a global level – this then leads to even more exposed tundra and methane gas; creating an upwardly spiraling acceleration of the process. Also, white ice reflects sunlight. As the ice melts, exposed brown soil absorbs more sunlight, which causes even more warming and more melting of ice at a local level.

Although it is very unlikely, it is certainly possible that thousands of scientists and their computer models could be wrong about climate change. But we must employ precautionary measures, because if these scientists are correct – and they most probably are – the deleterious consequences to our Earth and its inhabitants are so very devastating.

If fossil fuels continue to be utilized at the current level, they will soon be essentially depleted, probably before the end of this century. It is therefore a foregone conclusion that at some point humanity will need clean and sustainable energy, as it will be our only option.

Even the novice visionary can then deduce that it makes more sense to abandon fossil fuels now, and transition immediately to the use of readily available renewables – before we cause additional unnecessary and possibly irreparable damage to our oceans and the rest of our planet.

Fish for Dinner

It has been widely encouraged for humans to consume fish and other seafood, due to the health benefits associated with eating a high-protein food that also contains large amounts of vitamins and Omega-3 fatty acids.

In some locations, particularly in developing countries, the consumption of seafood is a necessary adjunct to a healthy diet. Due to geographic and economic constraints, inhabitants of some of these regions are dependent on fish and other seafood for adequate nutrition.

This is in contradistinction to many developed countries, where citizens can often obtain protein and vitamins from sources other than fish; such as beans, grains, nuts, leafy greens – and small amounts of meat, eggs, and dairy products if desired.

Concerning the heart-health benefits of Omega-3 fatty acids, there is certainly validity to this claim. One or two servings of fatty fish per week may substantially reduce the risk of heart disease.

People want to eat more fish; but the stocks of wild fish are dwindling – and there are presently too many people who want to eat them. As the world population wishes to consume more food than our oceans can provide, we have turned to farming fish and shellfish (aquaculture) to augment the wild supply of this commodity.

Performed correctly, aquaculture can take pressure off of fragile ecosystems, and may ultimately save our oceans from overfishing. On the other hand, irresponsibly managed aquaculture can be quite damaging to our oceans.

The benefits of aquaculture must be weighed against the environmental costs associated with this type of food production. In Asia, native mangrove forests are often cut down to provide habitat for shrimp farms. A large proportion of this shrimp crop ends up on restaurant tables and in supermarkets in the U.S. and other affluent countries. Not only important to local ecosystems, mangrove forests also help to prevent typhoon-related flooding. The unseen cost of cheap seafood includes damage to the environment as well as to man-made structures.

Currently, some varieties of farmed fish, including salmon, require a diet of food pellets derived from ground up smaller forage fish. It takes two to three pounds of wild forage fish to make one pound of farmed fish – a net loss for the oceans. The farmed fish is also less muscled than its native counterpart, containing a higher amount of fat and a smaller amount of Omega-3 fatty acids. Also, pink dye is added to the otherwise greyish-colored farmed salmon. In addition, some studies have noted higher levels of PCB's in farmed vs. wild fish.

To increase profits, farmed fish are grown in great numbers in close proximity to each other. This increases the rate of disease in many species; therefore, many of these fish are given antibiotics in with their feed. This can cause the familiar problems of drug resistance, emerging diseases, and contamination of watersheds.

Another problem with some aquaculture systems is the use of open water pens to contain the fish. Open water fish pens allow the spread of disease to native fish populations, and escaped fish have bred with native populations of wild fish.

Aquaculture now includes raising genetically modified (GM) fish, and Canada has recently allowed a GM salmon to enter its markets. This is the first GM animal approved for food consumption. This new fish species grows much faster than its wild cousin, and therefore could be quite profitable for a fish farmer to raise and sell.

Called AquAdvantage, this genetically engineered Atlantic salmon has also been approved by the FDA for sale in the United States since

2017 (labeling issues prevented it from coming to market until 2019). Although it is now legal to sell, many US grocery chains refuse to offer AquAdvantage salmon in their stores.

Here is the basic process for creating a genetically engineered salmon: A growth hormone-regulating gene from a Pacific Chinook salmon is first spliced into the DNA of an Atlantic salmon. Then, a section of DNA from a different species, the eel-like ocean pout, is also inserted into the DNA of the Atlantic salmon. This is called a promoter gene, which allows the expression of another gene. In the eel, this promoter gene is always active.

The final result is a fish that has a growth hormone-regulating gene that is constantly turned on; and it therefore grows throughout the year, unlike a wild salmon. Another manipulation is performed to render female fish sterile (males are not sold, and are used only for breeding); however, this technique is not foolproof, and interbreeding of a "sterile" fish with a wild fish is a possibility.

Many environmental groups are adamantly opposed to allowing the farming of genetically modified fish. Although there is no proof that consuming a genetically modified animal is detrimental to an individual person's health, there is also no proof that later health problems will not arise. The burden of proof must rest on industry to assure that a new product is safe, not on the consumer to prove that it is not.

In science as in life, there is usually no free lunch. When a drastic intervention in a natural process takes place, there are quite often unforeseen consequences – an occurrence that most scientists have noted many times throughout their professional careers. Laboratory created fish will likely enter wild populations, no matter how many safeguards a corporation is willing to adopt – and a genetically modified fish may possibly outcompete its wild cousins.

There are some important questions to ask: For what purpose do we wish to take these risks, even if these risks could be relatively small? Does the world population truly need a genetically modified fish to meet nutritional requirements, especially a predator-type fish that is dependent on the use of forage fish meal, causing a net loss to the oceans? Is this venture in line with humanity's overarching goal of lasting global happiness?

There are several companies interested in producing other genetically modified animals for food consumption. Once the door is cracked just a little bit, it is difficult to keep it from being flung wide open. This could be a dubious precedent to set, with corporate industry eager and ready to run through the entrance. Big business usually finds a way to the money.

Some aquaculture companies appear to be doing it right. Many have chosen to farm tilapia or tra (a type of catfish), two species that eat a vegetarian diet. These fish are fed pellets made of soy or corn and do not utilize any fishmeal; therefore, raising them is ocean-friendly. These fish can also often live in close quarters without requiring the use of antibiotics, and are also grown in ponds that are sequestered away from native waterways.

Some businesses are finding novel ways to deal with the waste produced by fish farms, rather than discharging the waste into watersheds. Although not yet economically feasible on a large scale, there are companies that are researching integrated aquaculture systems, where seaweed and shellfish are grown in conjunction with farmed fish, thereby reducing the amount of waste in the water.

Although aquaculture may not be needed to meet nutrition needs in many locales, it is definitely here to stay. There is no other way to satisfy consumer demand. As this is the route we have taken, it is imperative that due caution is employed. Varieties that are best suited to farming should be selected. This does not include varieties that are fed forage fish, raised in open ocean water pens, or are created in a laboratory. To protect adjacent watershed regions, waste management processes of fish farms must be closely monitored.

As noted, the Monterey Bay Aquarium Seafood Watch offers expert advice regarding seafood consumption. This organization provides a guide to help consumers decide on the best choices of seafood to purchase, including both wild and farmed varieties. Check their website for the most up to date information.

Especially in affluent countries, eating seafood should be considered a luxury. To maintain this luxury, wild stocks must be conserved, and farmed seafood must be harvested in an ecologically responsible manner. Individuals and corporations will need to change current patterns of polluting our atmosphere and water, and fishing fleets will need to stop over-harvesting threatened species.

Ideas to Help Protect Our Oceans

1. Choose fish varieties listed as Best Choices (Green list) on the Monterey Bay Aquarium Sustainable Seafood Guide; only occasionally purchase those listed as Good Alternatives (Yellow list); and forgo any species listed as Avoid (Red list).

Omega-3 EPA/DHA fatty acid related health benefits are presently countered by risks of chemical toxicity from mercury and persistent organic pollutants. Many nutrition experts believe that the benefits of eating seafood outweigh the risks, and suggest eating a serving 1 to 2 times/week. It could be argued that this recommendation is a bit imprecise; and that the frequency and amount consumed should depend on the seafood species and where it was caught. Stay tuned for new information, as recommendations could change.

It is possible that researchers might someday recommend eating seafood only sparingly (due to toxicity risk); and that we obtain our heart-health benefits by eating ALA-type Omega-3 fatty acids (from organic plant sources such as walnuts, flaxseed, and leafy greens) and making other lifestyle changes. Hopefully we will take better care of our planet, and future generations will be able to consume unlimited amounts of any species of fish without concern of toxicity.

2. Forage fish populations must be protected. Not only important in their own right, they are also an essential food source that is necessary to support predatory fish higher up in the marine ecosystem. Bays and estuaries that forage fish depend upon for spawning must be protected. Worldwide, approximately one-half of coastal wetlands have been destroyed by humans and used for development. If the spawning habitat of forage fish is ruined, the whole food chain above is imperiled. As most of the harvested forage fish are used for animal consumption (associated with poor feed conversion ratios), it may be reasonable to outlaw the practice of feeding forage fish to other animals. The Lenfest Forage Fish Task Force, a multidisciplinary group of thirteen preeminent scientists, has cautioned that forage fish harvests must be cut in half, if an ecologically sound and sustainable harvest is to be maintained.[71]

Consumers can also choose to eat less farmed fish (such as salmon), and less factory raised pork or chicken, each of which are often fed forage fishmeal. One can also avoid purchasing cat food that contains fish products.

We are accustomed to hearing pleas to save the whales......... now add to that and shout "Save the sardines, menhaden, herring, and anchovies!"

3.   A worldwide policy for wild fish harvesting and aquaculture production should be instituted. This should include universal laws requiring certain fishing grounds to lay fallow, and that outlaw commercial fishing of some endangered species such as the Bluefin tuna. There is currently no effective global policy. The third and last U.N. Convention on the Law of the Sea came in to force in 1994. This treaty outlines international regulations relating to mineral rights and fishing stocks, however, the United States has yet to ratify the agreement.   The convention mandated the formation of the International Tribunal for the Law of the Seas, which has the power to settle disputes between member nations.

After a more than two-decade hiatus, it is imperative that another U.N. conference is soon convened, and that all member nations modify the treaty to better regulate fishing catch limits. The United Nations Fisheries and Aquaculture department and many non-governmental organization (NGO) representatives could provide valuable input. It would be very beneficial to declare certain fishing grounds as off limits to commercial fishing vessels. It would also be useful to impose fines on individual countries whose pollutants, such as mercury, foul the water and poison an international food supply.

Also, disallowing subsidies to fishing fleets would be quite helpful. A sliding tax could be imposed on large non-niche fleets when certain catch limits are reached. This would more likely lead to a long-term sustainable harvest.

It is of critical importance that the United States government agrees to sign, ratify, and follow the proposed recommendations; demonstrating responsible leadership to the rest of the world. It is also imperative that all treaty regulations be strictly enforced. With input from members of the International Tribunal for the Law of the Seas, perhaps the United Nations Security Council could impose targeted sanctions against non-signatory or non-compliant nations. If no governing body steps up to take charge, the path is clear to a free-for-all in the open seas.

Choose leaders who demonstrate a concern for our oceans, and for those who do not wish to diminish the authority of the United Nations.

4.   We can decrease our personal energy consumption, including the amount of gasoline we burn and the amount of electricity we use. We can vote against politicians who continue to endorse burning coal for energy – removing a major cause of ocean warming and acidification, and mercury poisoning of our fish. It is also of great importance that we markedly reduce the amount of plastic we use. We can quickly suffocate ourselves by placing a grocery bag over our head, or accomplish it more slowly by allowing it to degrade in the ocean. 80 percent of all ocean debris comes from land sources, and most of that debris is plastic.[72]

Avoid buying convenience groceries packaged in plastic; use reusable shopping bags; limit the use of plastic garbage bags (compost fruit and vegetable debris; put dry garbage directly into the trash can); do not buy soda or water in plastic bottles; choose glass over plastic when possible; decline plastic lids, straws, and utensils when possible; re-use plastic lunch baggies; and recycle any plastic that you can.

Seal Lullaby

Oh! Hush thee, my baby, the night is behind us,

And black are the waters that sparkle so green

The moon, o'er the combers, looks downward to find us

At rest in the hollows that rustle between.

When billow meets billow, there soft be thy pillow;

Ah, weary wee flipperling, curl at thy ease!

The storm shall not wake thee, nor sharks overtake thee,

Asleep in the arms of the slow-swinging seas.

-Rudyard Kipling

Our Earth has remarkable powers of resilience and regeneration. Given enough time, deep scars can often heal. Although some species are forever gone, and serious injuries to the oceans and watersheds have been sustained, it is not too late for a great comeback. However, time is running very short. We must immediately listen to the advice of some really smart scientists, and change irresponsible patterns that mankind has only recently adopted.

Without the help of concerned citizens, the magnificent wild ocean could reach a point of no return. When we tell our great grandchildren about the pristine and bountiful ocean of our youth, they will either curse us for our selfishness and apathy, or praise us for maintaining its beauty.........and for preserving the wild creatures that lay "asleep in the arms of the slow-swinging seas."

It is our poem to write.

TWENTY

The Green, Green Grass of Home

"We shall require a substantially new manner of thinking if mankind is to survive."

-Albert Einstein

WHEN WE SEARCH for ways to personally improve the environment, one obvious place to look is literally in our own backyards. In the seventeenth century, British noblemen surrounded their estates with green lawns, kept closely shorn by herds of grazing sheep. Viewed as a sign of wealth and status, this custom eventually crossed the pond and has since become a revered American tradition – although we now typically use power mowers instead of sheep to clip the grass on our lawns.

It was at an early age that I developed a profound appreciation for the beauty of rolling expanses of lush, green grass. Indeed, owning a plot of grass was a part of my own American dream, evoking pleasant childhood memories of playing ball with my brothers and our friends; and of stretching out on a green lawn, gazing upward to watch a few clouds drift lazily across a summer sky.

But, if we are not careful, this pleasant dream can begin to morph into something more foreboding. For many adults, a perfectly manicured expanse of weed-free deep green turf has become a badge of honor and, somewhat curiously, is often equated with neighborliness and good citizenship. We have forgotten that our yard should be considered a refuge – a safe and comfortable place for playing games with our children or entertaining friends, while also serving as a haven for many living creatures. We have slowly changed our perceptions, conditioning ourselves to define a completely unnatural ecosystem as necessary and beautiful; often choosing to value the appearance of our yard over its usefulness as a playground for humans, and as a home to many diverse life forms.

We do so at a significant cost. Better adapted to the climate and terrain of the British Isles, a closely cut monoculture grass lawn is not suitable for many regions of America. In an attempt to maintain our unrealistic vision of what constitutes beauty, we fight the natural order of our environment, spend countless hours of time, and apply millions of pounds of toxic chemicals to our yards and gardens. It would of course be much more prudent to simply adjust our way of thinking, choosing to change our perceptions rather than to perpetuate this impractical dream.

In an effort to maintain an artificial beauty, we place the safety of our children and others at significant risk. Many lawn chemicals are very dangerous to our health, with some of them linked to increased rates of leukemia, lymphoma, and asthma. Children are more susceptible to the effects of these toxins, and they are of course the very ones who often play and roll around on our lawns. Our pets also run across chemical-laden yards, exposing themselves to high doses of toxins, inadvertently carrying them into our homes, further increasing our dose exposure as well as their own.

Attempting to create a flawless outdoor carpet of deep green grass and a weed-free garden, we often kill beneficial pollinators and countless other necessary organisms as collateral damage. Many of these applied lawn chemicals will also eventually leach into our aquifers and poison our drinking water supplies, ultimately ending up in our rivers, lakes, and oceans. The synthetic nitrogen fertilizers that we add to help the grass grow – and the gasoline burning mowers that we use to cut it back down – also emit greenhouse gases that accelerate climate change.

If you plan to someday build a new home, consider designing a yard with little or no grass. If you already live in a home with a grass yard, attempt to manage it responsibly, and maybe try to look at it from a new perspective. Adjust your mower blades to the highest setting and leave the clippings on the lawn, which is much healthier for the grass. Pull weeds in your lawn and garden by hand. If you choose to fertilize, do so sparingly, and consider using compost or an organic fertilizer without pesticides.

Accept a few dandelions, and encourage the growth of clover in your yard. I have learned to love clover. Clover adds valuable nitrogen to the soil, and is really quite beautiful when flowering. Deeming clover to be a weed is based purely on perception, and a misguided one at that.

Dandelions provide food for bees and birds. If you are not quite ready to make friends with dandelions – I am still working at this – you can simply dig them up rather than spraying them with chemicals. Dandelions may also be (at least partially) outcompeted by a mixture of clover and grass grown together in non-compacted well-aerated soil.

We can challenge current notions born of social conditioning, and change our perception as to what constitutes a beautiful yard. We can think of our parcel of property as an integral part of a broader ecosystem, remembering that what we put on our lawn can eventually end up in an ocean a thousand miles away – or perhaps remain very close by, in the bodies of our children or other loved ones.

A perfectly green yard without weeds and pests may indeed look quite beautiful when viewed in isolation. But if we choose to stand back, and widen our field of view, we will get an entirely different perspective. We will see that the chemicals that bring perceived beauty to our yards may also result in dead fish, sickened birds, collapsing bee colonies, and malignant tumors – none of which are the least bit beautiful.

Randy A. Siltanen

TWENTY-ONE

A Hungry Planet

"Concern for man and his fate must always form the chief interest of all technical endeavors. Never forget this in the midst of your diagrams and equations."

-Albert Einstein

GOVERNMENTS AND LARGE corporations often tend to use very short time frames when making policy decisions. However, when evaluating sustainability issues, it is imperative to look beyond current horizons. We cannot afford to merely focus on the next quarterly report, the next election cycle, or even the next several decades. We must look forward in to the next century, and the one following, ad infinitum.

We must acknowledge that, even without an increase in our population numbers, humanity is on an unsustainable course. We cannot simply ignore the plight of future citizens, or submit to the unhelpful attitude that it is too late to change our situation. We are faced with an immense but winnable challenge: To regenerate and maintain a beautiful and bountiful Earth; one whose ecosystems can forever sustain all present and future inhabitants.

The Green Revolution

The Green Revolution of the 1960's has been credited with saving approximately one billion lives. It also saved millions of acres of forests from being converted to farmland. That was a great accomplishment. Although this strategy triumphantly succeeded in preventing mass starvation, it was a temporizing measure that treated the universal symptom (hunger) of a few different diseases, rather than address the causes.

If a patient has malaria, one must indeed administer medications – even though these drugs are not without serious side effects. It is of course much better to try to avoid the problem in the first place, such as by providing bed netting to protect against mosquitos.

The root causes of widespread hunger are overpopulation, weather vagaries, soil degradation/erosion, and unequal and inefficient distribution of resources. These problems can also be exacerbated by poor societal choices regarding the use of farmland for biofuel and animal feed. This is where attention must be focused.

Although the Green Revolution was initially a tremendous success, it was a treatment that was accompanied by unwanted side effects. It could be argued that humanity is now essentially on artificial life support. We are feeding billions of people, but we are doing so with the use of synthetic pesticides and fertilizers, while also often diverting tenuous water supplies to previously non-arable land. Similar to an athlete using steroids, we are attempting to cheat the system; willing to risk a healthy tomorrow to win the match today.

High yield crops are depleting our soil nutrients. Many types of vegetables now contain lower levels of vitamins and minerals than before the Green Revolution. Fertilizers change the pH and composition of our soil, and nitrogen-rich runoff into rivers and estuaries results in enormous oceanic dead zones. Pesticides alter the root zone biome, while also killing beneficial insects and other creatures. They also put at risk the health of consumers, as well as field workers and their families. Irrigation has resulted in markedly lower water tables and increased soil salinity, making some farmland no longer productive.

Fence-to-fence monoculture crops take away cover from birds that may eat destructive insects. Deep tilling methods increase the rate of topsoil erosion, washing away our future and clogging our waterways.

Some areas in Iowa have reportedly lost approximately one-half of their topsoil. Humanity must safeguard its topsoil – it takes healthy soil to make healthy humans.

We are losing the safety of biodiversity in our food sources. Rust, a parasitic fungus that feeds on phytonutrients in wheat, oats, and barley, has plagued farmers for years. It is certainly possible that resistant strains of this and other pests could devastate a monoculture crop, particularly if it is a widely planted new species that has not yet stood the test of time. Seed banks may not be sufficient to feed the world in the event of a massive crop disaster.

Genetic Engineering: For Better or Worse

We have also intervened in a natural system by creating genetically modified plants. These have not yet brought inherently increased yields, and similar or better results can often be obtained by using less drastic breeding techniques.

Contrary to the proclamations of agribusiness, genetic plant modification is not necessary to keep people from starving. Indeed, it could possibly be a cause of future episodes of starvation. Relying on monoculture crops that may one day be vulnerable to disease is a risky proposition.

Genetic engineering has indeed proven to be quite useful in many circumstances – such as when used to identify plant breeding genes of interest, to study human disease, and to make medications and vaccines. There are also many clinical trials in progress that hope to cure diseases via somatic gene therapy (e.g. sickle cell disease). There is great promise in these **contained use** strategies, those in which there is no deliberate release into the environment of a GMO that can reproduce and spread.

This is in contradistinction to the current **non-contained use** of genetic engineering in agriculture, one where a new organism is intentionally introduced into an environment where it can reproduce and mutate, and cannot be controlled. This is a very important difference – a distinction often blurred by GMO food proponents who wish to paint with broad strokes, attempting to place all forms of genetic engineering into the same basket; inferring that those who urge caution are "anti-science" or "anti-technology." In truth, it is "anti-science" behavior to cheerily accept overly reductionist ways of thinking. Details matter. The use of genetic engineering in agriculture is an entirely different scenario than its use in health and medicine.

New scientific advances have certainly brought remarkable improvements to humanity. But one should be wary of claiming that all new innovations are universally wonderful – perhaps subconsciously doing so to avoid be labeled as old-fashioned or a Luddite. Not every new idea or technological advance is beneficial to society (chemical weapons come to mind). It is vitally important that humankind carefully chooses the most appropriate technologies to utilize. Decision trees must include very low probability events, particularly if such events could have extremely negative or irreversible consequences. Precautionary principles must be followed.

If there is substantial risk involved, new technologies should only be pursued for just cause, i.e. concern for the fate of mankind and the pursuit of Sustainable Global Happiness. The motives for producing currently available genetically modified foods – convenience, increased profits/lower costs, and control over markets – certainly do not qualify.

Genetically modified foods may indeed hold some promise for the future, particularly if world population numbers are not kept in check. But GMO crops that offer drought tolerance or intrinsically increased yields are still not commercially available. After twenty-five years since their introduction to the marketplace, what GMO's have mostly delivered is some plants that can make their own insecticide; and others that can withstand being sprayed with glyphosate and 2,4D – which has created an environmental nightmare. It is no wonder that the public is wary of genetic modification of the global food supply.

At this point in time, GMO's in agriculture are generating more problems than they are solving. As the saying goes, the proof is in the pudding – and, at least so far, the GMO pudding doesn't taste very good.

There are some people who may consider the act of synthesizing non-contained new life forms in a laboratory as tantamount to defiling a great masterpiece; particularly if these organisms are released into the environment without good reason. With each new stroke of the brush, a magnificent creation is slightly altered, every detail of which may be there for a reason, each possibly a purposeful interconnected component of a majestic design fashioned over billions of years.

Others may simply appreciate the immense grandeur of our cosmos and all of its related parts, even if it has arisen merely by chance; intellectually questioning the wisdom of needlessly intervening in a system that works so magnificently well when simply left alone.

The Future of Food

At current rates of population growth, experts predict that the world will need to increase food supplies by over 25% in the next thirty years – and most of this increased yield will need to come from already existing farmland. That is expecting a lot from new scientific breakthroughs; and from worn-out soils growing crops heavily dependent on fertilizer, and reliant on irrigation from shrinking and polluted aquifers.

Also, the predicted overall net effect of climate change is a reduction in global crop yield. In addition, critical insect pollinator species are already imperiled. Adding increased world population numbers to these present challenges may portend a troublesome future.

The most appropriate food production model is to utilize presently available non-dangerous technologies, while continuing tightly controlled research on genetic modification – looking to find plants that may truly have higher inherent yields or are more tolerant to weather related vagaries. At least presently, widespread implementation of GMO's should perhaps be considered as a method of last resort. Scientists may someday discover plant varieties with true increased yields, requiring few inputs, and resistant to climate events and insects. If they are able to do so, the issue of potential GMO implementation could be revisited – but only if less risky methods of food production are unable to feed the global populace.

The safest and most sustainable food production method *today* is to return to an organic-based agricultural model, avoiding the use of synthetic pesticides and fertilizers, as well as genetically engineered crops. However, it is unlikely that employing strict organic farming methods would be immediately tenable in certain regions, such as Sub-Saharan Africa, where large populations have become dependent on the addition of synthetic fertilizer to nutrient-depleted soils.

Advances in the field of **Biomimetics** suggest that nature often figures things out far better than can the human mind. Utilizing mimicry, Biomimetics involves studying the structure and function of biological systems, and then using these models to design materials and machines. For example, some engineers study the feathers of raptors to inspire new airplane wing design efficiencies, and others evaluate the structure of spider silk, a substance that is much more ductile and five times stronger by weight than steel.

Agroecology utilizes Biomimetic principles, essentially designing food systems to imitate the natural world – relying upon beneficial trees, plants, animals, and insects to help increase yields. One very successful Agroecology method employed in Kenya is the "push-pull" method of agriculture. In this system, the "push" comes from intercropping plants that repel pests in the rows between crops of maize or sorghum. The "pull" comes from planting companion crops around and among the cereal crops. These "pull" plants emit chemicals that attract pests, and some of these plants serve as a haven for natural enemies of some of these pests. One of these plants, Napier grass, even secretes a sticky substance that physically traps a borer larva pest.

The global populace has been conditioned to believe that genetically modified foods and synthetic pesticides are necessary to provide food for a hungry world. However, the field of Agroecology has documented superior methods for sustainably increasing yields, while also improving the environment. Unfortunately, incumbent leaders in agribusiness see no corporate profit in adopting these practices.

Olivier De Schutter, writing as the United Nations Special Rapporteur on the Right to Food, authored a UN news release that discussed the results of studies utilizing Agroecology methods.[73] The report is startling, not only because the results are so significant, but also because it received such little attention from the press. Here are some excerpts:

"To feed 9 billion people in 2050, we urgently need to adopt the most efficient farming techniques available. Today's scientific evidence demonstrates that **agroecological methods outperform the use of chemical fertilizers** (emphasis mine) in boosting food production where the hungry live – especially in unfavorable environments......To date, agroecological projects have shown an

average crop yield increase of 80% in 57 developing countries.......
Conventional farming relies on expensive inputs, fuels climate change
and is not resilient to climatic shocks. It simply is not the best choice
anymore today."

The report also points out that projects in Southeast Asia recorded
up to a 92% reduction in insecticide use for rice, with many resultant
benefits including important savings for poor farmers.

De Schutter goes on to say: "Agroecology is a knowledge-intensive
approach. It requires public policies supporting agricultural research
and participative extension services. States and donors have a key role
to play here. **Private companies will not invest time and money in
practices that cannot be rewarded by patents and which don't
open markets for chemical products or improved seeds...**
(emphasis mine.) We won't solve hunger and stop climate change with
industrial farming on large plantations. The solution lies in supporting
small-scale farmers' knowledge and experimentation, and in raising
incomes of smallholders so as to contribute to rural
development......If key stakeholders support the measures identified
in the report, we can see a doubling of food production within 5 to 10
years in some regions where the hungry live."

Using relatively simple Agroecological principles, higher yields can
be achieved than with conventional farming techniques that rely on
large amounts of chemical inputs. Implementing these practices will
take significant dissemination of knowledge.

Also utilizing new advances in technology is the practice of
Precision Agriculture, a farm management method that measures
and responds to inter- and intra-field variability in crops. Precision
Agriculture often utilizes satellite imagery, computer assisted irrigation,
crop yield monitors on GPS equipped combines, and sensors that
monitor such things as moisture levels, organic matter content,
temperature, and fertilizer use. These methods markedly reduce crop
inputs (like water), while also substantially boosting yields.

The problem of attaining sustainable food security can best be
addressed by markedly curbing population growth, using information
and technology in an appropriate fashion (Agroecology and Precision
Agriculture instead of excessive chemical inputs and genetic
modification), judiciously returning back to organic small farming
methods, and limiting the amount of land used to grow food for
biofuel or consumption by livestock. These changes will obviously

take time and tremendous political will to accomplish.

Climate Changes Everything

There are many problems of great concern, yet there is even one more; the wild card discussed previously, which is climate change. It is difficult for scientists to predict exactly how this will impact food supplies, but a few of years of drought would likely be devastating to the food production of many regions of the world.

Also, rising CO_2 levels decrease the nutrient value of many crops. Plants use increased levels of CO_2 to make more sugars, essentially diluting out protein and other nutrients. A plant may perhaps grow faster and taller due to the infusion of CO_2, but it is less nutritionally dense.

If CO_2 levels continue to rise as projected, the populations of 18 countries may lose more than 5 percent of their dietary protein by 2050, due to a decline in the nutritional value of rice, wheat, and other crops.[74] There are also recent studies that found CO_2 related reductions in iron content in staple food crops, which is likely to exacerbate present problems of iron deficiency in South Asia and North Africa.[75] Elevated CO_2 emissions could also drive 200 million people into zinc deficiency.[76] Zinc is a key nutrient for maternal and child health.

Throughout history, a lack of food has been accompanied not only by localized pockets of hunger and death, but also by enormous global social unrest and armed conflict. Even nations that can feed their own population will not be spared discomfort. Local food shortages often have global consequences.

Individual Action Ideas

Consume organic food. Again, this means eating mostly food that is grown without synthetic pesticides or synthetic fertilizers, and that is not genetically modified. As some areas are presently dependent on the use of synthetic nitrogen fertilizers, this action may not currently be feasible in all regions, particularly with our current population of

7.7 billion people.

Organic food production is likely to be the only agricultural method that is sustainable for the long term, offering the lowest risk to our planet and its inhabitants. Nearly everyone living in wealthy countries could eat organic food. Of the 7.7 billion inhabitants on Earth, approximately 1 billion eat too much, and approximately 1 billion do not get enough to eat. Consider trying to help level the playing field, and donate to one of the many fine non-government organizations (NGO's) that provide aid to global citizens residing in poorer countries.

Eat more like a vegan. Approximately one-third of the grain produced in the world is used for animal feed; and it takes approximately ten pounds of grain to produce one pound of beef. It also takes greater than ten times the amount of fossil fuels and water to produce one calorie of animal protein than it does to produce one calorie of plant protein.

It is estimated that nearly one-half of the water used in the U.S. is involved in the raising of animals for food, and factory farm runoff is one of the major polluters of U.S. waterways. Also, countless square miles of Amazon rainforest are being cleared to create farmland to grow crops to feed livestock. Eating fewer animal products allows much more food to be grown for human consumption, and may also keep grain prices lower for citizens in poorer countries. Eating a more vegan-like diet may also significantly diminish global greenhouse gas emissions.

Attempt to follow a more vegan-like diet if you can. Consider limiting your consumption of food from animal sources by eating smaller servings, or perhaps follow a vegan or vegetarian diet a few days per week. If you do eat animal products, try to predominantly consume products obtained from organically fed, free range, locally-raised animals. A little more vegan-like diet is healthy for the Earth; and usually healthy for the individual as well.

Use less energy and vote for clean energy. This will help to avert climate change and possible future weather-related food crises. Consider buying a smaller car, perhaps a hybrid or an electric vehicle. If you need a larger vehicle, you may wish to look for one with optimal gas mileage. Also consider driving less than the average person. A small hybrid car may get double the gas mileage of an SUV – but an SUV owner may drive less than half the miles than a hybrid owner, thereby producing fewer total emissions.

Inflate your car tires fully, and consider driving more slowly than the average person. Until laws change, consider driving about five or ten mph less than the posted speed limit (*too* slow is not safe on busy roads). Remember that each 5 mph of speed over 55 mph burns approximately 7% more fuel. If enforced speed limits were lowered to 55 mph the U.S. could save billions of gallons of gasoline (and dollars) per year. Lowering speed limits would decrease pollution and slow the rate of global warming, while also substantially reducing the number of traffic fatalities.

Use air travel less frequently. One long overseas airplane trip uses about the same amount of fuel per person as driving a car for a year.

Turn your thermostat at home down to 65 degrees F. in the winter. Wearing one layer of good long underwear allows a person to maintain a comfort level at a room temperature that is about 7 degrees lower than typical, resulting in up to a 30-40% decrease in space-heating energy use (the precise amount depends on the outside temperature).[77] This is a really easy way to save energy and money. Keep the thermostat at 75 degrees or higher in the summer and wear shorts.

Encourage the development of wind and solar energy technologies when you vote. Discourage the construction of new coal or natural gas burning plants and nuclear power producing plants. Vote strongly against the production of currently utilized biofuels, particularly corn ethanol, the use of which is tantamount to filling our gas tanks with food which could feed some of the billion hungry people in the world.

Embrace the idea of smaller family sizes. This point is critical. This is important for all countries, but it is particularly important in countries that cannot support the food needs of their population without imports. These imports will become increasingly more expensive due to market considerations and increased costs of transportation.

Have your voice be heard. Discuss sustainability issues with your friends and family. Consider checking out the website of the International Federation of the Organic Agriculture Movement (IFOAM - Organics International).

TWENTY-TWO

Jewel of the Galaxy

"There are two ways to live: you can live as if nothing is a miracle; or you can live as if everything is a miracle."

\- Albert Einstein

A RECURRING THEME of this book has been to highlight the elegant interconnectedness of many systems in our world. The inherent possible danger of intervening in these systems has been emphasized, particularly when intervention is done without just cause.

You may remember from science courses that an atom is a unit of matter, consisting of a nucleus surrounded by a cloud of negatively charged electrons. The nucleus of an atom is composed of various numbers of protons and neutrons, which are each made up of the even smaller elementary particles described in Chapter Two. These particles are held together by an immensely strong force, aptly – if not creatively – named strong force or nuclear force. This force is trillions of times stronger than the effect of gravity, and also holds together the neutrons and protons of the nucleus.

A surrounding cloud of electrons are bound to the nucleus by a much weaker attraction called electromagnetic force. Electrons located further from the nucleus are less influenced by this force and may be transferred to nearby atoms, or shared between atoms. This allows atoms to interact with each other, binding together to form molecules and chemical compounds, and ultimately the various substances and organisms that are part of our daily lives. Many of these molecules are very complex, such as DNA molecules, which contain approximately twenty thousand protein-coding genes.

For unknown reasons, many molecules eventually came together to form various types of cells. Over an immense amount of time, these cells ultimately coalesced to form complex living organisms – some that could even defy gravity and walk upright upon the Earth. Cells learned how to communicate with each other via chemical cues or direct links; as in the human brain where there are literally trillions of connections between various neuron cells.

Our daily functions also require numerous biological pathways, each composed of myriad intricate steps. Each of these various pathways also functions in an extraordinarily complex concert with the others, resulting in a dizzying unfathomable number of continuous interactions occurring every second within our bodies.

Each human is also a complex walking ecosystem; an organism made up of many different organisms. Composed not only of trillions of "human" cells, our bodies also contain about ten times as many cells of other organisms – including bacteria, viruses, and fungi – which add an estimated combined additional weight of approximately 3 pounds or so per person. Scientists are learning that the vast majority of these organisms of our microbiome are likely helpful to us, as we are to them; as part of a symbiotic relationship known as mutualism, an association that is valuable to both parties.

Beneficial bacteria on our skin feed on the secretions of our skin cells; in turn producing a moisturizing film that forms a protective barrier to keep out pathogenic species. In our gut, useful bacteria synthesize vitamins (folic acid, Vitamin K, and biotin), aid in digestion of complex carbohydrates, and even tutor our immune system. Although some bacteria and viruses are certainly pathogens (some viruses are even cancer causing), our immune system does a good job differentiating the helpful from the dangerous varieties, recognizing that the great preponderance of these organisms are either beneficial or harmless to us.

The Human Genome Project demonstrated that many viruses are also present in the cells of healthy human volunteers. As with bacteria, it is possible that there are unknown advantageous effects of some viruses in our bodies. Viruses are an important means of transferring genetic information between species, which increases diversity and drives evolution. In the oceans, viruses are the most numerous of all organisms, playing an essential role in photosynthesis and carbon cycling.

Our actions affect the organisms around us and, of course, they in turn have an impact upon us. We may toss a piece of plastic on the ground, observe it as it falls down a storm drain into a river and then out into an ocean harbor, settling at the bottom to smother essential life systems of the sea floor. Our actions return back to us, diminishing and polluting a source of nourishment that we may need to sustain ourselves.

We also interact with other higher organisms, as part of a human network that is much more interwoven and connected than some may realize. We tether ourselves, one to the other, through written words, sights, sounds, and touch. Sometimes these bonds are willfully broken. We may turn away from imperfect friends and family members, or they from us. Some of us may even choose to prematurely end our own lives, forgetting that our actions and lives are deeply entwined with those of others on this Earth. Left behind are bewildered children or other loved ones who must now navigate alone a novel maze.

Thankfully, there are those, too, who augment humankind's existence. These are the gifted individuals who connect to us with wondrous cords of beauty and strength; sharing their gifts of art, athleticism, compassion, humor, and intellect. This makes each of us stronger, wiser, and happier; improving on the whole intricate network that is humanity.

Multitudes of tiny organisms of the soil, each with a purpose, interact with the remains of plants and animals to provide a substrate for new plant life, and ultimately for all life on Earth. These organisms are also often dependent upon each other for survival. Filaments of fungi help to bring nutrients to the roots of other plants, receiving sugar in return. Vast networks of these filaments – emanating from a single organism – can cover many acres, and provide a medium for other plants to connect with each other.

For about 100 days each year, windstorms over Africa's Sahara Desert blow dust from the surface of the Bodele Depression, a vast dry area that was once an enormous lake. This dust storm travels westward across the continent, carrying with it the phosphorous, nitrogen, and iron laden remains of ancient fresh water plankton that once lived in the lake, and eventually drifted down to the lake bottom.

Prevailing air currents transport this mineral rich dust across the Atlantic Ocean to South America, where it mixes with raindrops and falls to the Amazon forest floor, providing essential nutrients for plant life. Heavy rainstorms eventually cause erosion of the forest floor, resulting in runoff of large amounts of plankton derived minerals into streams and rivers, which join together and flow into the Amazon delta and Atlantic Ocean, where the nutrient rich silt is then deposited.

In a majestic display of intercontinental natural mineral recycling, the remains of plankton, once living a thousand years ago and half a world away, now provide nutrients for the proliferation of massive amounts of new plankton in the sea, which in turn will produce life sustaining oxygen for the planet.

Phytoplankton and other plant life are of course dependent on the Sun to produce energy and oxygen through photosynthesis, just as humans are dependent on the Sun for the production of vitamin D; thereby extending the interconnectedness of all matter out beyond the limits of our Earth.

Our Sun, an average star in a galaxy of over 100 billion stars, pulses to the many incredibly complex rhythms it has been assigned; some of these recurring at intervals of a century or more. Produced by the fusion of protons at 27 million degrees Fahrenheit in the core, and influenced by an array of magnetic fields, high energy photons emerge 100,000 years later from the Sun's surface; and about 8 minutes after that reach the Earth as life-giving sunlight.

Our Sun also acts as the director of its own entourage of planets. Each planet performs its own dance; some in step with one or more moons, all in concert with others in the group, never crashing one in to the other. Ours is but one tiny solar system in a much larger galaxy that holds billions of such systems. In turn, our Milky Way galaxy is also an unpretentious yet integral part of an array of over 100 billion galaxies in the universe; extending forever into the darkness, and beyond the realm of human comprehension.

From the interactions of minute subatomic particles to the expansile properties of enormous galaxies into limitless space, the immense scale of our universe is extraordinary. Between these margins of the cosmos reside incredibly large and impossibly intricate systems of interrelated complexity, governed by physical laws and equations that even our brightest scientists can only vaguely begin to understand. And it all works flawlessly.

The oft-proven quantum physics theory of non-locality posits that an action of an entity in one part of the universe can simultaneously affect an entity in another part of the universe, acting faster than the speed of light. This suggests that in addition to the above examples of causally related interconnectedness, there may indeed be a more ethereal connection between all matter in the cosmos.

If we dare interrupt this magnificent concert, we may do so at our peril. The Green Revolution has shown that on occasion we may temporarily improve on individual aspects of nature, particularly when these are viewed in isolation. However, currently utilized agricultural methods have come at a great environmental cost. Similar to Newton's third law of motion, in Nature for each action there is often an opposing action, and there is simply no free lunch. Following celestial-born geologic rhythms, the Earth naturally offers up only such yield as can be sustained within a network of finely balanced interactive ecosystems.

Many people fail to see the interconnectedness of the systems of the cosmos. Some have even suggested that we dispose of our planet's nuclear waste by rocketing it far out into space. At some place and time this would have an effect. Our entire universe is interconnected and no action is without consequence.

I am not so naïve as to think that humans can walk along a trail without leaving a footprint. With a population of 7.7 billion humans there will always be some negative impact on our Earth. There is no way around this. All of us must eat, care for our infirmities, and clothe ourselves. We must shelter ourselves from the elements, and transport essential goods to each other. But it is imperative that we minimize our interventions in the workings of our planet and its interwoven intricacies; a masterpiece that has been nearly 14 billion years in the making.

We must be content to play our small part in a tremendously vast and complicated production, harmonizing with each member, no matter how minute or seemingly insignificant. If we choose to intervene, we must proceed very cautiously, and only with just cause.

Perhaps we should view ourselves as guests on this Earth. We must be very respectful of our dwelling place, and thankful for the opportunity to share in its abundance. We must take off our shoes and tread gently. We must not throw our refuse upon the floor. We must eat from the cupboard only that which is offered to us. Our presence cannot be invisible; however, we must try diligently to minimize our intervention in the flow of a household that already functions beautifully. To behave differently would show a great lack of respect, as well as very poor judgment. If we recklessly ruin this splendid home, there will be no replacement, and there will be no place else to go.

Every bit of matter in this universe is interconnected, through grand mathematical equations and unseen forces. Every atom, every organism, every human being, and every star in the universe are all part of a majestic living masterpiece, existing in a marvelously integrated system where no single event can occur in complete isolation.

Touched by a spark of life, our bodies are each living extensions of our planet; built of particles from its surface, destined to feel nearly a century of pain and pleasure before disassembling into dust, returning once again to our Earth.

Influenced by willful effort, even our minds are but projections derived from a brain comprised of atoms formed billions of years ago; once a part of numerous rocks, streams, and creatures of a previous time. Our happiness, our sorrows, our love and relationships, and even our dreams are all born of this mantle of life; all are a physical part of this world.

On our Earth, this beautiful blue jewel of the galaxy, everything and everyone are inseparably connected. When we impact but one part of our Earth, or any of its inhabitants, we impact the whole of our Earth. Our personal fate, the fate of other world citizens, and the fate of our planet are all dependent upon each other.

If we take great care of our mind and body, we will increase our individual level of happiness, and we will optimize our giving potential. And if we then strive to protect our planet and its creatures, and to increase the happiness of other world citizens by treating their concerns with respect and dignity, our efforts come back to us, further increasing our own level of joy. This is Sustainable Global Happiness. This is a life well-lived.

Epilogue

I propose that the meaning and purpose of life are to find and create Happiness – for ourselves, and for all present and future inhabitants of a safe and beautiful planet.

Details are very important, but they are easier to make sense of when viewed in the context of a well-constructed framework. First get the Christmas tree; then put on the ornaments.

Be grateful for the efforts of our soldiers – brave souls who do not turn from battle, offering their lives in valiant service to others. We must love our soldiers as our own children, assuring ourselves that the cause we ask them to fight for is worth the blood of our sons and daughters, in addition to the spilt blood of unknown innocents caught in the crossfire.

Intervening in natural pathways should not typically be considered an appropriate initial solution to a problem. To do so is to be lured into a seductive trap – what initially looks inviting may be harmful in the long run. Altering a natural pathway may occasionally be a reasonable consideration, but it should generally be viewed as an option of last resort. Use caution.

The Earth is our primary source of wealth. Without it, there is no wealth at all. This is the First Precept for human prosperity. All other economic constructs are secondary considerations. Wise orchardists will tend their trees with great care, ensuring a bountiful harvest of fruit for many seasons. We must fiercely protect our primary source of wealth.

When considering mankind's impact on our Earth, extend your time frame to plan for generations a thousand years from now. The futurist who is only concerned with the next several decades is a very myopic visionary.

Remember that our oceans and watersheds are like a giant bathtub where you cannot ever change the water. Dilution will only work for so long.

Consider eating fewer animal products; and consider avoiding eating processed and factory-raised meat altogether. This will decrease greenhouse gas emissions – which will help mitigate climate change, and help protect coral reefs and ocean fish populations. For many people in industrialized countries, this may also be better for personal health.

The use of synthetic pesticides and fertilizers is dangerous to you personally, and may be even more dangerous to your children. Genetically modified food introduces the possibility of perilous consequences, presently without good reason to take these chances. That may change.

The discovery of oil has allowed the world population to increase to an unsustainable level. Unfortunately, we must all begin to embrace the idea of smaller family sizes. 7.7 billion people are already too many for our Earth to sustain indefinitely. If population size continues to increase, all other measures to protect our Earth could be rendered relatively meaningless. This point cannot be overemphasized.

A swarm of locusts will lay a field bare and then soon perish; victims of the mass of their own great numbers and lack of new crops to devour. Any system with finite resource supplies cannot support continuous growth. This should be remembered when planning current economic and social policy. Infinite growth in a population or resource-based economy is not possible.

We have a very small window of opportunity to transition to an economy driven by clean and renewable energy technologies. That time is now.

With great power comes great responsibility. Our nation must demonstrate fiscal, social and environmental leadership; attempting to minimize any untoward global ramifications of our actions. We must lead by example. We must no longer delay the day of reckoning. We must face our economic and environmental concerns head on today.

There are many ways for a nation to pay for something that it wants or needs. It can pay by incurring a national debt, transferring this debt to future generations; in exchange for honor. It can use cost-cutting shortcuts that are paid for by environmental destruction; exacting an insidious toll on each global citizen. It can even pay with the lives of soldiers. Or, it can simply use the least expensive option – which is to pay with money. If you can pay for it with money, it's cheap.

Great achievements are realized through collaborative effort. Learn from others. Listen. Read.

Value your efforts over your results. Do your best, and then let the chips fall where they may.

Money cannot buy you lasting happiness – unless you share some of it with someone else in need. The more you give in life, the more you receive. Making someone else happy will make you happy.

You have the ability to control your mind. With concentrated mental effort you can truly change the physical structure of your brain. You can literally create new brain circuits, including one for optimism. Choose to be happy! It takes work.

Do not underestimate the invisible power that goodwill holds over public opinion. Win over the hearts of your detractors and enemies through acts of kindness and generosity.

Realize that your life will always be similar to a sculpture in progress – made of clay, not granite. Do not be afraid to challenge your belief system and make changes when appropriate. Life is a moving target. Evolve!

Remember the words of Albert Einstein: "Unthinking respect for authority is the greatest enemy of truth."

Young people: Be aware of the power of momentum, goodwill, and the sheer size of your numbers. Unite together to reach a just and worthy goal – and you will be unstoppable. Organize, collaborate, and vote!

Consider starting your day with this mantra: "Every day I will become stronger, wiser, and happier." I will be become more physically resilient through daily exercise, more knowledgeable and imaginative through continuous learning, and more joyful by choosing to frame life events in a positive fashion.

Here is a simple recipe for a great life: Live with joy and share your toys.

One last quote from Albert Einstein: "You can never solve a problem on the level at which it was created." Solutions to problems born of selfishness or unawareness must arise from higher levels of Transcendent thought.

Challenge yourself to think differently. Do not look with just your eyes. Unfetter yourself from tired dogma. Approach a challenge from a new angle.

Follow Nature's lead. Our Earth has been perfecting its ecosystems for over 4 billion years.

Submit to Providence – even if you are not exactly sure how to comprehend this universal Presence. Give of yourself to something greater than yourself. Love broadly, love deeply.

Sustainable Global Happiness is the crown jewel of a Creative

Universe. It is the coming together of person, people, and planet to achieve the full potential of each.

We live in the midst of paradise. You see what you look for.

I guess that is pretty much it. I have presented some fairly straightforward ideas for you to consider; although they are not always easy to follow. I know that I have certainly failed to observe many of my own suggestions on several occasions.

I do not always eat healthfully, and I will at times miss a day or two of exercise. I have delivered unkind words and actions; yet I am sometimes slow to forgive others. I have consumed more of the Earth's resources than necessary, and I have looked past those in need many times in my life.

This does not mean that I do not believe in the ideas that I offer, or that the words are unimportant. Rather it is that life's journey is quite difficult, and all who walk will sometimes stumble and fall.

But we can get back up, shake off the dust, and continue to move forward – attempting to become a little better version of ourselves, hoping to improve the health and happiness of the Earth and its inhabitants, present and future.

I hope that you have found some benefit from the lines on these pages. My wish for you is to discover great happiness through a life well-lived. The world is better, because of you.

Meditations and Daily Intentions

I am grateful for my family and friends, who add such joy to life.

I am grateful for the five senses bequeathed by Providence:

> I give thanks for the sight of aspen leaves, fluttering in a Summer breeze against a bright Wallowa sky.

> I give thanks for the feel of Tamarack needles, cushioning my steps on a late Autumn walk.

> I give thanks for the scent of the forests and the rangelands; the pitch of an alpine coniferous tree, and the leaves of sagebrush at lower elevation.

> I give thanks for the sound of the meadowlark, calling out across a grassy expanse.

> I give thanks for the sweet taste of the fruits of the Grande Ronde Valley, this place that is my home.

I ask Providence for the strength to weather the vicissitudes of life on our Earth; knowing that fairness was never promised. I ask for courage.

I ask for wisdom and skill, poise and dignity, equanimity and grace, compassion and patience, love and understanding, confidence and humility — so that my existence may in some small way help bring increased health and happiness to our Earth and all its inhabitants.

Randy A. Siltanen

Appendix

A Roadmap to the Future

WHEN PLANNING HUMANITY'S future, it is certainly important to look at the short term – making plans for the days, weeks, months, and coming year ahead. However, it is also imperative to look further; creating goals for this decade and the next, and the rest of this century as well. And we should not stop there.

Honoring the idea of intergenerational equity, humanity can extent its vision further yet, to include at least the entirety of this *millennium*. In geologic time, one thousand years is merely a blink of an eye.

Below, I will introduce three studies produced by different consortiums of experts from around the globe, each offering ideas to help ensure a sustainable future for humanity over the next few decades. I will then present a plan that includes the more distant future – a roadmap for the millennium entitled PEACEFOOD 3000.

Plans for the future will always need to be continuously revised as new circumstances arise. Black Swan events are inevitable, and the future can never be accurately predicted. It is precisely for this reason that the Precautionary Principle must be followed – plans and predictions for the future must include the possibility of very low probability events, particularly if such events could have catastrophic consequences.

Humanity must be prepared for any eventuality, knowing that even though many helpful new technologies and ideas will undoubtedly come forth, their appearance or relevance cannot be factored in with exact certainty. Technological advances may not be enough to stave off the effects of all future global challenges or disasters.

Later generations will almost assuredly value many of the same things that we do today: clean air, fresh water, verdant soils, social justice, and peace – our guiding stars to a desirable future for humankind. It is not possible to plot out an exact course to where we are going, but it is imperative to never lose sight of these bright lights, each of which will help point the way to the ultimate destination of lasting global happiness.

Although we cannot accurately predict the future, experts can model potential worst-case scenarios; putting plans in place should such situations arise. Contingency plans are indeed important; however, it is of course far better if problems can be avoided in the first place. As Albert Einstein said, "Intellectuals solve problems, geniuses prevent them."

Let's begin by looking at the United Nations Sustainable Development Goals (SDG's).

The Sustainable Development Goals

In 2015, the United Nations General Assembly came up with 17 global goals to be achieved by the year 2030. Known as the Sustainable Development Goals (SDG's), these are the successors to the Millennial Development Goals created in the year 2000. The idea of this plan is to help achieve a better and more sustainable future for all.

With a total of 169 target points to accomplish, the SDG's represent an ambitious roadmap; one that addresses poverty, hunger, climate change, environmental degradation, clean energy, health, education, economic growth, peace and justice.

The SDG's are a very well thought out and comprehensive assembly of interrelated goals and specific targets. However, there are oversights regarding two P's that have a critical impact on sustainability – *Population* and *Pesticides*.

Regarding *Population:* Sustainable Development Goal 8 (*Decent Work and Economic Growth*) aims for a target of 7% GDP (Gross Domestic Product) growth per annum in developing countries. That may prove troublesome. The General Assembly has recognized the need to decouple economic growth from environmental destruction and resource consumption; however, at this point that ideal has yet to be realized. Economic growth continues to march in lockstep with resource use and environmental degradation.

The SDG's do not mention the problems that overpopulation will bring. The population growth often required for continuous growth in GDP is not sustainable. In some of its other publications, the United Nations describes several population scenarios based on various fertility rates. However, the SDG's work under the assumption that there will likely be over 9 million people on the planet by 2050 – and that assumption appears to go unchallenged as a foregone conclusion. This is problematic; because overpopulation makes the realization of each of the 17 Sustainable Development Goals much more difficult to attain.

Unlimited population growth is not humanity's destiny, rather it is an avoidable outcome. It is imperative that humankind begins to rapidly decrease global average fertility rates toward 2.1 children per couple or less, starting now. Globally, reduced fertility rates have been achieved in several regions, simply by providing education and access to family planning. This has happened without the need for coercion or draconian top-down policies, which are neither desirable or necessary.

Regarding *Pesticides:* Sustainable Development Goal 2 (*End Hunger, Achieve Food Security and Improved Nutrition and Promote Sustainable Agriculture*) offers commendable general ideas, however makes no specific recommendation to decrease the use of highly hazardous pesticides. And Sustainable Development Goal 12 (*Responsible Consumption and Production*) emphasizes the importance of supporting small farm holders, noting that agriculture provides the livelihood of 40% of today's global population. But no specific mention is made of Agroecology methods of farming (although other UN publications tout it benefits), or the need to curtail the use of pesticides.

Abundant, nutritious, and pesticide-free food is a prerequisite for a healthy and peaceful global populace. The next study, the EAT Lancet study, focuses on Sustainable Nutrition; describing in detail the steps needed to feed our planet in 2050 – while also preserving the environment.

The EAT Lancet study: Food in the Anthropocene

This remarkable endeavor brought together 37 leading scientists from 16 countries, whose task it was to come up with a model for feeding an expected global population of 10 billion people by 2050. They did so, in fact quite admirably, creating a nutritious eating plan that is healthy for the individual *and* the planet. The EAT Lancet study is a virtual treasure trove of well-researched information and recommendations. Presented in a very organized style, the authors lay out a detailed roadmap to achieve the dual goals of optimizing both human and planetary health. However, their proposed ideas will not be welcomed by all.

If this ambitious plan is to succeed, it will not be without tremendous international cooperation and some very substantial personal lifestyle changes. One of the major points this study makes is that, by necessity, there will be a marked decrease in the amount of meat consumption – especially red meat (approximately one-half ounce eaten/person/day as a global average).

The authors state that much of humanity's daily protein requirement will need to come from tree nuts and legumes. Many confined animal feeding operations (CAFO's), especially beef feedlots and factory farmed pork operations, will be a thing of the past. The massive amounts of fertile US Midwest farmland presently used to grow soy and corn for animals will instead be used to grow a variety of food for direct human consumption, as this is a much more efficient way to provide calories. Grazing of less fertile native grasslands would continue. Deforestation for agriculture or grazing (or for any other reason) would be halted.

The EAT Lancet study offers extremely useful information, and should be recommended reading for every global citizen. There is some room for improvement in this study, however. As with the UN Sustainable Development Goals, this study also does not discuss in depth the two major P's that threaten sustainability – *Population* and *Pesticides*.

Regarding *Population*, this study accomplishes its useful goal, and that is to predict the changes needed to support an anticipated additional 2 billion mouths to feed by 2050; in total numbering nearly 10 billion global citizens. This is vital information, as all possible situations must be considered, and appropriate plans must be made.

However, it would be of great benefit if the authors could present a general range of what they consider to be an ideal global population number; one that does not threaten the sustainability of the planet and its inhabitants. Some experts believe that number to be between 2 billion and 5 billion global citizens.

The EAT Lancet study also gives short shrift to the discussion of *Pesticides,* and how they are affecting biodiversity and changing the biome – the *micro* biome (the multitude of tiny organisms living in air, water, and soil; and in and on the bodies of humans and all living creatures) and the *macro* biome (the remaining flora and fauna living in concert with Earth ecosystems).

The use of pesticides cannot continue at current rates – neither person, people, nor planet can weather the assault. Pesticides are already everywhere; they are present in our soil, water, and food – including children's breakfast cereal. Of note, in a recent study, 19 of 20 different beers and wines tested (including organic options) demonstrated measurable levels of glyphosate.[78]

Can humanity pull away from its dangerous addiction to pesticides? If so, is it even truly feasible, at a global level, to transform Agriculture to a completely organic system and still feed 9 or 10 billion people in 2050?

For that answer, we can look to the next study.

"Strategies for Feeding the World More Sustainably with Organic Food Production."

Published in *Nature Communications* in 2017, this study was also written by a consortium of global experts. It *does* consider the pesticide problem – as well as problems related to the use of synthetic fertilizers.

The authors of this comprehensive study wanted to evaluate if it is indeed possible to change to a completely organic system of global food production; growing food without the use of synthetic fertilizer or synthetic pesticides. This group determined that this would be a herculean task – *but it is possible.*

A conversion to 100% organic agriculture would involve considerable lifestyle alterations, as well as massive changes in farming methods (e.g. extensive use of leguminous cover crops to add nitrogen to the soil, etc.). This study evaluated effects of organic vs. conventional agriculture on land use, deforestation, greenhouse gas (GHG) production, Nitrogen and Phosphorus cycles, erosion, energy, water, and pesticide use.

For a 100% adoption of organic agriculture to be viable, it would entail: 1) Using existing farmland to only grow crops for humans, not pigs and cattle (called food-competing feed or FCF), and 2) Cutting food waste in half. The authors did not believe that conversion to a 100% organic food production model would be possible without co-implementing these two strategies as well – unless additional forest lands are used for crop production.

This study took into account the effects of climate change,

presenting models for different scenarios, noting that worsening climate change will negatively affect yields. It also factored in yield gaps, using an estimate of 25% production loss from organic vs. conventional agriculture (this uses the lowest organic yield estimates; the actual yield gap is much less). This study also presents detailed illustrations and tables comparing parameters based on *partial* adoption, i.e. outlining scenarios of various percentage degrees of implementation of models that abandon FCF systems, decrease food wastage, and convert to organic agriculture.

As with the EAT-Lancet study and UN Sustainable Development Goals, this study did not challenge the assumption of global population growth to a level of 9 or 10 billion by 2050.

If a perfect set of conditions were met, these experts proposed that the Earth could provide just enough food to feed the expected global populace in 2050, using purely organic methods of agriculture. The authors therefore answered a very important question.

However, the degree of international cooperation and individual behavioral change necessary to so radically transform the global agricultural system requires idealistic scenarios that may be unlikely to happen. In addition, this plan assumes that there are no massive crop failures or geopolitical events that threaten food security. Everything must go perfectly according to plan – and do so very quickly.

The important agricultural production and dietary changes that the authors propose are indeed worthy. **However, these methods must also be employed in tandem with a decrease or stabilization of global population numbers.**

A hybrid approach to agriculture will also likely be needed – an *almost* organic compromise, to serve as a bridging strategy until the global population no longer exceeds the estimated carrying capacity of a sustainable Earth.

"Organic" is a broad umbrella term, and it will need to be further subdivided into various categories. As an example, a future "almost organic" compromise for 2030 could possibly be: Zero herbicides, 25% synthetic insecticide use, 25% synthetic fertilizer use, and 25% GMO use (all relative to year 2020 levels).

In a hybrid approach, synthetic fertilizer use would generally be markedly curtailed; however, measured applications would be allowable in at-risk global locales (e.g. Sub-Saharan Africa). Synthetic pesticide usage would be greatly reduced, perhaps with an eventual outright ban on synthetic *herbicides*. Emergency-only application of synthetic *insecticides* to food (not fiber) crops could be applied selectively to limited acreage; however, ideally not in consecutive years, and only upon approval by both the EPA *and* a bipartisan state commission.

Of note, in 2018, 16 million acres of cotton and sorghum crops were approved by the EPA to be sprayed with sulfoxaflor insecticide as an "emergency" measure – for the *fourth consecutive year* in 12 of the 18 states granted approval. Sulfoxaflor is known to be very highly toxic to bees; and cotton and sorghum are known to highly attract bees. In the U.S., sorghum is used primarily for livestock feed and ethanol production, not for direct human consumption.

Yes, *it is possible*, at a global level, to transition to organic food production in most regions.

But can humanity *afford* the extra expense of organic food production? Many people believe that it is advisable to move in this direction; however, they are hesitant to do so – because they suspect that organic food will cost much more than food grown using current agricultural methods.

Here is some good news: People who are unsure of the economics of organic food consumption are in for a pleasant surprise. As it turns out, with economy of scale, the extra financial costs of transitioning to organic agriculture are really quite small.

Consider the following: 90 percent of global calories consumed come from grains (and potatoes), and most grains are processed into other items; such as corn into cereal, or wheat into bread and pasta. A corn farmer receives somewhere around 5 cents for the corn that goes into a $4 box of cornflakes, and a wheat farmer gets about 12 cents for the wheat in a $3 loaf of bread.[79] A rice farmer makes about 2 cents out of the 7 cents it costs for a bowl of rice.

So, for the sake of argument, let's assume that it cost farmers *triple* to grow crops organically (this is a huge overestimate – labor costs are higher with organic production, but input costs are less; and overall costs are only slightly more. One study showed a 10 to 25% increase in production costs for organic apples, another showed no significant cost difference to produce organic vs. conventionally grown potatoes).[80] If the growers then passed this *tripled* cost of production on to the consumer, the corn farmers would now receive an extra 10 cents for their corn, and the cornflake cereal price would bump from $4 to $4.10. The wheat farmers would get an extra 24 cents for their wheat, and a loaf of bread would increase from $3 to $3.24. The rice farmers would charge an extra 4 cents, and a bowl of rice would now cost 11 cents instead of 7 cents. Pocket change, really. And these examples wildly overestimate the production costs of organic food production.

In the US, we spend only 6.4% of our income on food, which is the lowest percentage in the world.[81] According to the USDA, about 8% of every food dollar spent in the United States goes to farm production costs.[82] The rest goes to processors, packaging, advertising, wholesalers, agribusiness, the transportation sector, restaurants, retailers, etc.

So, for every $100 of income we make, we spend $6.40 on food – of which about 50 cents (8%) goes to farm production costs.

Using the previous example, if we generously *tripled* what we gave the farmer to cover costs, asking that they grow their crops organically, he/she would receive $1.50 of every $100 dollars we make, instead of 50 cents. This would raise the cost of our food just one dollar higher, to $7.40 out of every $100 we make. 7.4% of our income spent on food would still be the second lowest in the world (Singapore is 6.7%) – and we would remain nearly a percentage point ahead of the United Kingdom (in 3rd place at 8.2%).

Can humanity afford organic food? Yes! We can *very easily* afford it, especially if consumers demand it, and economy of scale forces kick in. In addition, when considering the secondary *ecologic* costs (which also translate into future *financial* costs) of maintaining the agricultural status quo, organic farming is by far the better bargain.

A Roadmap to the Year 3000

The excellent studies above outline several great ideas to maintain the health and happiness of the Earth and its citizens *for the next few decades.* They are each a very good start – but they need a booster shot. Their success is predicated on a series of events that must all work perfectly, and even then, they do not extend beyond the timeline of 2050.

Short term goals are indeed essential, but if we do not also look beyond that point, are we not myopic visionaries, at best? Do we wish to plan only for a tolerable existence of humankind 30 years from now, essentially kicking the can down the road, leaving our children to deal with the next 30 years after that, and so on? The problems of each generation will become more difficult than those of the previous.

A comprehensive plan for the future must concede that the indefinite sustainable carrying capacity of Earth may be substantially less than 7.7 billion people. Presently, 820 million Earth inhabitants are undernourished – about 1 in 9 global citizens. An effective plan must note that most studies predict a net negative effect on world food production with rising global temperatures. It must realize that essential pollinator species are imperiled, soil health is diminishing, and aquifers are drying up. It must acknowledge the enormous task of changing global behavior patterns of consumption – which are getting worse instead of better. This plan must insist on massive changes to our present models of food production.

This wide-ranging strategy must prepare for the *possibility* of 10 billion people by 2050, and 11 billion by 2100, certainly – but these should not be default numbers. The EAT Lancet study notes that even if their recommendations are followed perfectly, our Earth cannot indefinitely sustain a population of over 10 billion people. Every major problem that the Earth and future generations face is made worse by an increase in population.

We are presently on a trajectory that will test the absolute limits of our planet's resiliency. That is comparable to driving a racecar around a curve, increasing its speed until finding the point at which it careens out of control. Humanity is not in a race, and there is no need to challenge our Earth's absolute boundaries.

A ballpark population estimate of 5 billion healthy and happy global citizens is perhaps a reasonable and sustainable planetary target; one that is preferable to a target population of 10 billion people who are just barely hanging on.

Population study luminaries Paul Ehrlich and Thomas Malthus were partly right, it is just that their timing was off. A finite planet cannot sustain infinite population growth.

The United Nations predicts that by the end of this century, global fertility rates will decrease to replacement levels of 2.1, and that the world population will then stabilize at 11 billion.

A couple of thoughts come to mind. One, predictions for the future are often wildly inaccurate. Two, if humanity is indeed heading toward a fertility rate of 2.1, it is more logical to aggressively increase global education and access to contraceptive measures quickly – to reduce birth rates *now*, rather than wait until we have 11 billion people on the planet before doing so.

A Path Forward

We can integrate the ideas of the above three studies – while adding a few necessary recommendations – into a summary of nine items, using the mnemonic PEACEFOOD. The timeline is stretched far beyond the 2030 and 2050 dates of the three studies, extending to the year 3000.

The idea of reducing global population numbers is at the forefront. This plan also assumes an agricultural model that includes only very limited use of synthetic insecticides, an eventual ban on synthetic herbicides, much smaller amounts of synthetic fertilizer, and very limited acreage of GM crops (however possible use in the future is not excluded).

The foundation of this plan for sustainable global health and happiness is a planet of abundance. PEACEFOOD 3000 represents strategies to sustainably provide healthy food and water to the populace of a safe and beautiful planet. This plan focuses on the base layers of Maslow's pyramid, emphasizing meeting basic safety and physiologic needs – Peace and Food – in a sustainable fashion. The universal availability of healthy food, clean air, and fresh water engenders a peaceful planet.

The first target of PEACEFOOD 3000 is to reduce population numbers; by lowering fertility rates via improved education and access to contraceptive measures. If the foundation of humanity's happiness is an abundant Earth, the cornerstone is a sustainable population. Overpopulation intensifies nearly every challenge that faces our planet and its people.

PEACEFOOD 3000
Population- Energy- Agriculture- Climate- Eating
Forests- Oceans- Open spaces-
Democracy/Diplomacy/Demilitarization

1. **Population**: Rapidly decrease global fertility rates to less than 2.1, with an initial target goal of a steady-state Earth population of approximately 5 billion (down from 7.7 billion presently). Future ideal global population numbers can be adjusted up or down, depending on technological advances.

2. **Energy**: Carbon and Nuclear free by 2030. Wind/Water/Solar technologies replace coal, natural gas, and nuclear energy. Vehicle fuel efficiency standards increased by 5%/year, starting 2021. Producing or importing new internal combustion engine (ICE) cars/trucks is banned by 2025. All ICE vehicles will be retired from roadways by 2040. Federal gas/diesel tax is immediately raised to $1/gal (18.4 cents presently), $2/gal by 2025, and $3/gal by 2030. Tighten energy efficiency standards for commercial buildings and homes.

3. **Agriculture**: Goals for 2030: Regenerate and sustain land, water, and air for future generations.

   A). "Almost Organic" agriculture model. Synthetic insecticides rarely allowed (emergency use only). Synthetic herbicides are banned. Weeds are cultivated by hand, machines, and robotics. Global synthetic fertilizer use is halved by 2035, utilizing Precision Agriculture and Agroecology techniques. Goal of further halving synthetic fertilizer use again by 2050.

   B). Fertile farmland is not *primarily* dedicated to raising food for animals. Beef, sheep, and goats will be grass-fed and grass-finished, closely simulating wild herbivore feeding and movement patterns. Grazing of cover crops and post-harvest material by livestock (including pigs and chickens) as a *secondary* project is encouraged. All farm animals will have daily access to outdoor living space and are treated humanely. No farm crops are used for biofuel.

   C). Biodiverse green space on all farms is encouraged, encompassing approximately 5% of property. No ground is left uncovered by plant life. Cover crops in all fields (mowed or roller-crimped and then over-seeded). No-till.

D). Recycling of Nitrogen and Phosphorus from human urine, using "no mix" toilets, and filters in sewage plants.

4. **Climate**: Reduce greenhouse gas (GHG) emissions 50% by 2030 – especially CO_2, methane, and nitrous oxide; with net zero emissions by 2050. Address the *CO_2 problem* by changing to sustainable energy and electric vehicles; the *methane problem* by eliminating feedlot cattle operations and fracking for natural gas; and the *nitrous oxide* problem by markedly decreasing synthetic nitrogen use. Phase out hydrofluorocarbons use. Eliminate cap and trade schemes. Penalty taxes (e.g. a carbon tax) are incurred for high GHG emitters (applied progressively, where increasing levels of emissions over the cap incur an increasingly higher percentage of revenues in penalties). Consider conservation payment strategies for sustainable land conversion and restoration efforts.

5. **Eating** Habits: Global campaign to reduce food waste 25% by 2025, and 50% by 2030. Decrease consumption of meat and animal products. Meat protein is in part replaced by protein from tree nuts and legumes. Individual meat consumption quantity will be influenced by global population numbers, climate change factors, and market forces.

6. **Forests**: No deforestation, beginning immediately. No new trees planted for biofuel. Sustainable, non-clear-cut production from existing managed forests is allowed, with a diverse polyculture replanting after harvest.

7. **Oceans**: Sustainable harvest management. Moratorium on fishing for threatened species. Fishing subsidies are phased out by 2025.

8. **Open** spaces: *Half Earth* strategy begins immediately, with full implementation by 2070.[83,84]

9. **Democracy, Diplomacy, and Demilitarization**: Champion equality for all Earth citizens, regardless of gender, color, race, religion, age, or sexual orientation. Encourage the ideal of a strong United States helping to lead a strong United Nations. Foster ongoing global discussions that consider the ideas of a universal living wage and health care for all. Acknowledge the existential threat that nuclear weapons and warfare present to a global populace. Promote peace.

As humankind fully embraces the ideas of international and intergenerational equity – the notion that the lives of all present and future global citizens are as important as our own – many world challenges begin to take care of themselves.

What You Can Do – Today

:

Consider choosing a small family size.

Avoid using synthetic pesticides in your yard. No "Weed and Feed." Talk to park, school, and golf course superintendents about decreasing and eventually discontinuing the use of pesticides. Encourage natural methods of weed control.

Travel less. Spend some vacations taking in regional attractions. Take long-distance and overseas trips only occasionally. Encourage tele-conferencing instead of traveling to meetings.

Consume a little less. At least 3 planet Earths would be needed if every global citizen lived like an American. Reduce, reuse, and recycle. *Reduce* is the most important.

Embrace Sustainable Nutrition – It is good for you and good for the planet. Eat locally grown organic food. Try to not waste any of it. Plant a garden, flowers, and fruit trees. Compost fruit and vegetable debris. Eat a little less meat. If you eat beef, buy grass-fed/grass-finished meat from a local producer. If you eat pork, favor pasture-raised options. If you eat chicken, look for free-range selections.

Go electric. Encourage the development of wind and solar energy technologies, to assure that your electricity comes from clean and renewable sources. Consider trading in an internal combustion engine vehicle for a new or used electric vehicle (EV). The vast majority of our frequent travel destinations are within the battery range of even older model EV's. Consider buying an electric bike or scooter.

Regional commercial travel in airplanes powered by batteries and/or hydrogen (obtained by electrolysis of water) will soon become a reality. This may someday extend to longer flights. This technology will come sooner rather than later, if research and development costs are shared by the public sector.

Conserve water and energy by washing clothes and linens less often, line-drying items when possible, and showering more quickly. Purchase fewer new clothes. Consider shopping at consignment clothing stores. Make your garments last. Consider spot-cleaning some items of clothing instead of washing after each use. Avoid buying microfiber garments (polyester, acrylic, nylon), as washing releases plastic microfibers into waterways and the ocean, and also into farmers' fields.

Realize the strength in your numbers. Vote for those who wish to balance the federal budget. Vote for those who believe in scientific analysis and rigor; pushing for funding in Science, Technology, Engineering, and Mathematics (STEM). Vote for leaders who believe in Clean and Renewable Energy. Vote for those who support a strong Environmental Protection Agency (EPA). Vote for leaders who want America to help lead a strong United Nations.

It is truly beneficial for our Earth and its inhabitants if a few people make major lifestyle changes. But it is far more impactful if billions of people make even small lifestyle changes. Sustainable Global Happiness depends on visionary leaders with the courage to enact laws to make this happen. Choose your leaders wisely – and then please vote!

Notes and References

1. A University of California Davis study from 2014 also showed that pregnant women who lived in close proximity to fields and farms where chemical pesticides were applied experienced a significantly increased risk of having a child with autism spectrum disorder or other developmental delay. Shelton J, Geraghty E, et al. "Neurodevelopmental Disorders and Prenatal Residential Proximity to Agricultural Pesticides: The CHARGE Study." *Environmental Health Perspectives* 122 (2014).

2. Harvard T.H. Chan School of Public Health
    https://www.hsph.harvard.edu/nutritionsource/anti-nutrients/

3. Sellmeyer DE, Stone Km et al. "A high ratio of dietary animal to vegetable protein increases the rate of bone loss and the risk of fracture in postmenopausal women." *Am. J. Clin. Nutr.* 73 (2001) 118-122.

4. FAO Newsroom. Food and Agriculture Organization of the United Nations. "Livestock a major threat to environment." 29 November 2006.

5. Union of Concerned Scientists. "Solutions for Deforestation-Free Meat." June 2012.

6. Foley, J. "It's Time to Rethink America's Corn System." *Scientific American* 5 March, 2013.

7. Nationalgeographic.com. "Thirsty Food."

8. Tomley F, Shirley M. "Livestock Infectious Diseases and Zoonoses." Philos Trans R Soc Lond B Biol Sci. 2009, Sep 27.

9. Nationalgeographic.com. "Water Conservation Tips."

10. Harari, Y. *Sapiens, A Brief History of Humankind* (2011), 88

11. Harvard T.H. Chan School of Public Health. www.hsph.harvard.edu. The Nutrition Source. "Healthy Eating Plate vs. USDA's MyPlate."

12. Consumer Reports. www.consumerreports.org *"How Much Arsenic Is in Your Rice?"* Nov 18, 2014.

13. Longo, Valter. *The Longevity Diet* (2018), 37,59.

14. Fulgoni, V. "Current protein intake in America; analysis of the National Health and Nutrition Examination Survey, 2003-2004. "*American Journal of Clinical Nutrition* (2008); 87.

15. Young V, Pellet P. "Plant proteins in relation to human protein and amino acid nutrition." *American Journal of Clinical Nutrition* (1994) 59Pan A, Qi S, et al.

16. "Red Meat Consumption and Mortality: Results from Two Prospective Cohort Studies." *Archives of Internal Medicine,* 2012 Apr 9; 172(7): 555-563.

17. Harvard T.H. Chan School of Public Health. www.hsph.harvard.edu. The Nutrition Source. "Omega-3 Fatty Acids: An Essential Contribution."

18. Markham B. *MiniFarming, Self-Sufficiency on ¼ Acre.* (2010).

19. Scientificamerican.com. EarthTalk "How Dangerous is Pesticide Drift?"

20. Bee Informed Partnership, Eleventh annual national survey of honey bee colony losses. http://beeinformed.org. In collaboration with the Apiary Inspectors of America, with funding by the USDA.

21. Intergovernmental Science-Policy Platform on Biodiversity and Ecosystem Services (IPBES) On Pollinators, Pollination and Food Production (2016).

22. Ibid.

23. Kopec K and Burd L. "Pollinators in Peril." *Center for Biological Diversity.* February 2017.

24. Intergovernmental Science-Policy Platform on Biodiversity and Ecosystem Services (IPBES) On Pollinators, Pollination and Food Production (2016).

25. Smith M, Singh G, et al. "Effect of decreases of animal pollinators on human nutrition and global health: a modelling analysis." *The Lancet,* online July 16, 2015.

26. Virginia Institute of Marine Science. www.vims.edu Dead Zones, Lack of oxygen a key stressor on marine ecosystems.

27. Broderick N, Robinson C, et al. "Contributions of jut bacteria to *Bacillus thuringiensis*-induced mortality varies across a range of Lepidoptera." *BMC Biology* December (2009)7: 11

28. Aris A, Leblanc S. "Maternal and fetal exposure to pesticides associated to genetically modified foods in Eastern Townships of Quebec, Canada." *Reproductive Toxicology* Feb 2011.

29. Vendomois J, Roullier F. "A Comparison of the Effects of Three GM Corn Varieties on Mammalian Health." *International Journal of Biological Sciences* Dec 2009; 5(7): 706-726.

30. Environmental Working Group. "Body Burden: The Pollution in Newborns. A benchmark investigation of industrial chemicals, pollutants and pesticides in umbilical cord blood." July 14, 2005.

31. Schwartz J, Begley S. The Mind and the Brain, Neuroplasticity and the Power of Mental Force (2002).

32. Diamond J. Collapse: How Societies Choose to Fail or Succeed (2005).

33. Harari Y. Sapiens. A Brief History of Humankind. (2011).

34. Ceballos G, Ehrlich P, et al. "Accelerated modern human-induced species losses: Entering the sixth mass extinction." Sci. Adv. 1, e1400253 92015.

35. Pew Research Center "The Changing Global Religious Landscape." (2015). www.pewforum.org

36. "Chinese Traditional Religion." Religionfacts.com. 21 Nov. 2016.

37. "MEPS vote to ban the use of palm oil in biofuels." *The Guardian* theguardian.com April 4, 2017.

38. World Wildlife Fund. www.worldwildlife.org/threats/deforestation-aand--forest-degradation.

39. "Costs of War." *Brown University Watson Institute of International and Public Affairs*. watson.brown.edu April 2017.

40. Desilver, D. "What does the federal government spend your tax dollars on? Social insurance programs, mostly." *Pew Research Center.* pewresearch.org.

41. "263 million children and youth are out of school from primary to upper secondary." www.unesco.org United Nations Educational, Scientific and Cultural Organization.

42. Quote from Leo Tolstoy's book *The Kingdom of God is Within You*. Wilder Publications 2008, page 108.

43. "Development aid in 2015 continues to grow despite costs for in-donor refugees." The Development Assistance Committee: Enabling Effective Development." *Organization for Economic Development*. Table 1 OECD.org.

44. Zinn H. "A Just Cause, Not a Just War." *The Progressive.* July 16, 2007.

45. Martenson, C. *The Crash Course: The Unstainable Future of Our Economy, Energy, and Environment* (2011).

46. Hawkins, P. *Drawdown: The Most Comprehensive Plan Ever Proposed to Reverse Global Warming.* (2017)

47. Rickard, J. *Currency Wars: The Making of the Next Global Crisis.* (2011) p. 38.

48. www.usdebtclock.org.

49. Tse, P, 2011, China's rare-earth industry: U.S. Geological Survey Open-File Report 2011-1042, 11p.

50. BP Energy Outlook 2017 edition.

51. Machol B, Rizk S. "Economic value of U.S> fossil fuel electricity health impacts." *Environ Int* 2013 Feb; 75-80.

52. Union of Concerned Scientists (UCS). *Catalyst* Volume 14, Summer 2014 issue.

53. https://www.scientificamerican.com/article/can-corn-ethanol-be-made-sustainable/

54. Jacobson M, Delucchi M. "A Path to Sustainable Energy by 2030." *Scientific American* Nov 2009.

55. www.fueleconomy.gov.

56. Freidman T. *Hot, Flat, and Crowded. Why We Need a Green Revolution – and How it can Renew America.* (2008).

57. Singer, P. *The Life You Can Save. How to Do Your Part to End World Poverty*. (2010)
58. Pfund N, Healey B. "What Would Jefferson Do?" Chart of Historical Average of Annual Energy Subsidies: A Century of Federal Support. Sept 2011 DBL Investors.
59. Vidal, J. "Cut world population and redistribute resources, expert urges." *The Guardian* 26 April 2012.
60. World Footprint. *Global Footprint Network* www.footprintnetwork.org.
61. Striessnig E, Wolfgang L. "How does education change the relationship between fertility and age-dependency under environmental constraints?" *Demographic Research* Vol 30, Article 16, P. 465-492.
62. "Global per capita fish consumption rises above 20 kilograms a year." *Food and Agriculture Organization of the United Nations* (2016) www.fao.org.
63. "The State of World Fisheries and Aquaculture 2016." *Food and Agriculture Organization of the United Nations* www.fao.org.
64. Lenfest Forage Fish Task Force. *Lenfest Ocean Program*. oceanconservationscience.org.
65. De Silva S, Turchini G. "Towards Understanding the Impacts of the Pet Food Industry on World Fish and Seafood Supplies." *Journal of Agricultural and Environmental Ethics*. (2008) 21:459).
66. Westmeyer M. "Shrimp Fisheries Improving in Gulf of Mexico, Thanks in Part to Seafood Suppliers." *Ocean View*. NationalGeographic.org. Feb 9, 2015.
67. Pearce F. "The Nitrogen Fix: Breaking a Costly Addiction." *YaleEnvironment360* e360.yale.edu. Nov 5, 2009.
68. "New Government Study Shows Many Toxic Chemicals Polluting the Columbia River." *Columbia Riverkeeper*. columbiariverkeeper.org. May 8, 2012.
69. "Conserving Our Treasures Under the Sea." *NOAA Habitat conservation*. www.habitat.noaa.gov.
70. Wilkinson C. "Status of Coral Reefs of the World." (2008). *Global Coral Reef Monitoring Network and Reef and Rainforest Research Centre*, Townsville, Australia.
71. Pikitch E, Boersma P, et al. "Little Fish Big Impact: Managing a crucial link in ocean food webs." *Lenfest Ocean Program*. (2012).
72. "Toxicological Threats of Plastic." Trash-Free Waters. epa.gov.
73. "UN expert makes case for ecological farming practices to boost food production." *UN News Centre* www.un.org 8 March 2011.
74. Medek D, Schwartz J, et al. "Estimated Effects of Future Atmospheric CO2 Concentrations on Protein Intake and the Risk of Protein Deficiency by Country and Region." *Environmental Health Perspectives*. August 2017 Volume 125, Issue 8.
75. Smith MR, Golden DD, et al. "Potential rise in iron deficiency due to future anthropogenic carbon dioxide emissions." *GeoHealth* Volume 1, Issue 6, 2 August 2017.
76. Myers S, Wessells K, et al. "Effect of increased concentrations of atmospheric carbon dioxide on the global threat of zinc deficiency: a modelling study." *Lancet Global Health*. Online July 16, 2015.
77. De Decker K, "Insulation: first the body, then the home." *Low Tech Magazine*. www.lowtechmagazine.com Feb 27, 2011.
78. CALPIRG: https://calpirg.org/feature/cap/glyphosate-pesticide-beer-and-wine EcoWatch. https://www.ecowatch.com/glyphosate-wine-beer-testing-2553632957.html

79. National Farmers Union. https://1yd7z7koz052nb8r33cfxyw5-wpengine.netdna-ssl.com/wp-content/uploads/2018/04/032818-FarmerShare.pdf
80. Sustainable Agriculture Research and Education (SARE). https://www.sare.org/Learning-Center/Bulletins/Transitioning-to-Organic-Production/Text-Version/Economics-of-Organic-Production
81. World Economic Forum. https://www.weforum.org/agenda/2016/12/this-map-shows-how-much-each-country-spends-on-food/
82. USDA Economic Research Service. Year 2017. https://www.ers.usda.gov/data-products/food-dollar-series/documentation.aspx

83. World Economic Forum. https://www.weforum.org/agenda/2016/12/this-map-shows-how-much-each-country-spends-on-food/
84. Half-Earth Project. https://www.half-earthproject.org/. The Half-Earth project is working to save half of the land and sea to safeguard the bulk of biodiversity, including ourselves. This is an ambitious project that likely requires stable human population numbers (and perhaps a decrease). The plan must be adjusted/ tailored in certain areas to ensure adequate food production in at-risk locales. See study below.
85. Mehrabi, Z, et al. "The challenge of feeding the world while conserving half the planet." Nature Sustainability, August 2018
86. Harvard T.H. Chan School of Public Health. www.hsph.harvard.edu. The Nutrition Source. "Fish: Friend or Foe?"

Index

"Tell me, what is it you plan to do with your one wild and precious life?"

-Mary Oliver, The Summer Day

Randy A. Siltanen

Randy A. Siltanen is a physician who lives with his wife Diana (above left) in the mountainous region of Northeast Oregon. Dr. Siltanen has worked in Primary Care medicine and Diagnostic Imaging.

Elias (above center) is now off to college at the University of Oregon. Older sister Laura lives in Washington state, and older brother Christian resides in Colorado.